TALES OF AN EXTRA LONG AWKWARD PHASE

GAWKY

Margot Leitman

SEAL PRESS

GAWKY
Tales of an Extra Long Awkward Phase

Published by
Seal Press
A Member of the Perseus Books Group
1700 Fourth Street
Berkeley, California

www.sealpress.com
www.margotleitman.com

Library of Congress Cataloging-in-Publication Data

Leitman, Margot,
Gawky : tales of an extra long awkward phase / by Margot Leitman.
pages cm
ISBN 978-1-58005-478-2
1. Leitman, Margot. 2. Comedians—United States—Biography. 3. Tall people—Humor. I. Title.
PN2287.L358A3 2013
792.702'8092—dc23
[B]
2012041687

10 9 8 7 6 5 4 3 2 1

Cover and interior design by Domini Dragoone
Printed in the United States of America
Distributed by Publishers Group West

For Dan

Thanks for loving me

Contents

AUTHOR'S NOTE

Hi, and thanks for buying/borrowing/downloading my book. Seriously. I appreciate it. Now, the stories you are about to read in this book are mostly true comedic portrayals of my youth to the best of my memory. They are written for entertainment purposes and with the kindest of intentions. I've tried to keep things as accurate as possible *as I remember them*. I must point out that I have indulged in a few too many dirty martinis as an adult, which may have affected the way I remember things. Maybe I went to school with you and you remember something differently. That's fine by me. However, most likely if I went to school with you, you won't remember any of this stuff anyway because you've moved on with your life and are not concerned in the least with my petty tales of growing up too tall.

While I have condensed or rearranged some timelines for clarity, and created a few composite characters so the reader's head doesn't explode keeping track of all the faces from my youth, I've done my absolute best to keep things real. I've changed names and identifying characteristics of almost everyone in these tales. (Unless, of course, the person asked for his or her real name to be used because they, like me, seek attention wherever they can get it. I understand.) So if you're reading this book and you think a character is actually you, congrats! You really made an impression! (Or not, maybe it isn't you. What, do you think the world revolves around you? Come on!)

Lastly, I wasn't one of those spazzy kids walking around with a recording device at all times (though I did keep extensive cat journals detailing the hardships of being a tall teen in the hopes that I'd one day be discovered for the genius diarist I was). Some dialogue is simulated as to what was *probably* said in the moment. Also, I'm a comedian. So although these stories are true and this all happened, I have gone for the laugh here and there. Forgive me. It's my job . . . really, it is. When I fill out forms at the doctor's office, under "Occupation" I put "Comedian," so you know I mean business. My hope is that you will laugh at my horrendous teen years and feel better about yours. Okay, I think that's it. Enjoy the book. I loved writing it a lot more than I loved going through all these changes. And I hope after you read this, whatever rough memories you have of adolescence will be a little funnier in hindsight.

Introduction

I had a regrettable physical condition when I was a child. It was not a debilitating illness or missing limb or anything particularly life threatening, but it was life affecting, sure. I was tall. And I mean, really tall: five foot six midway through fourth grade. Picture a giant, gawky child, a kid in every sense of the word, inhabiting an adult's body, but unlike in the movie *Big*, I couldn't blend in to save my life. There are some tall girls who glide through rooms with elegance, every article of clothing hanging just so on their perfectly proportioned bodies. These are the girls who have thin wrists with dainty bracelets, perfect posture, and a stylish selection of scarves. Then there are the athletic tall girls, the ones whose big feet seem to accent their toned and tan legs. These are the tall girls who look hot while running cross-country and whose naturally pin-straight hair always looks impeccable even after a three-hour volleyball match.

Then, there are the rest of us. Olive Oyl, Mackenzie Phillips, and "Big" Ethel Muggs (Jughead's tall and ugly stalker from the *Archie* comic books) all fall into this category. And me. We're the tall girls who are always tripping over our own feet, who never look normal in any size clothing, and who are constantly screaming "Wo-oah!" as we grab the tablecloth in a desperate attempt to break our fall and take the entire dining room table down with us. Chances are you know one of us, or are one of us, or sympathize with us. We're a delightful bunch, and have all had our fair share of teasing.

And now, on top of being gigantic in the height category (I eventually capped at five-foot-ten after a half inch more growth *after* I started college), I am about to have a baby. Because weight-gain-wise I haven't turned completely into a sweaty hippopotamus, I wishfully and unrealistically assumed that meant the baby was going to be a dainty little six or seven-pounder wearing tiny, clean, white newborn onesies and gliding out into the world in a virtually painless forty-five-minute labor. That was until I went to the doctor the other day. The second the sonogram began, he exclaimed in his former-beach-bum California accent, "Woah . . . this baby's got a huge head!" Before I could declare my concern that something was wrong, he guided the machine down my belly farther and continued, "Which is directly in proportion to its *huuuge* body! This is gonna be a big one."

Of course it's gonna be a "big one." How could I have possibly thought, even for just one day, that anything associated with me could be petite? I was in the seven-pound range when I was born, making me "average." This was the first and last time my size was average. Average is all I have ever wanted to be. By the time I was eighteen months old I was in the ninetieth percentile for height. By age two I was in the ninety-ninth percentile . . . and I stayed there for the next sixteen years.

Look, I'm well aware that there are much worse physical attributes than being tall. And if you're good at volleyball or basketball, or pretty enough to model, then being a tall girl at a young age is actually an asset! But if you're like me, uncoordinated and incapable of taking a decent photo, let alone looking anything but gawky while walking, then being tall is just a waste. It's a gift left unopened on Christmas morning, sitting there collecting dust, only to be shoved in a closet and opened years later by an unappreciative adult who just doesn't get what is so cool about a hot-pink Tamagotchi.

I compiled this larger story of how I came to grips with my size and all the bumps along the way mostly onstage. A few years ago, my hilarious, accomplished, and articulate friend Jim O'Grady emailed me a few hours before we were both on a storytelling show together. He wrote, "I'm switching to stories about growing up sensitive and artistic in the suburbs of New Jersey. Because *that's* never been done before." He was right. I was telling the same story in different ways over and over again. I couldn't believe how many separate stories I had about being this gawky teenage girl. But when I compiled them together, it made sense as to how I ended up here. Here: about to give birth to a giant baby, albeit now in Los Angeles instead of the Garden State.

To avoid becoming the size of a full-fledged hippopotamus, I've been doing a lot of walking (insert your very own "who walks in L.A.?" joke here). With too-small feet (only a size 8½) to hold up my too-tall body, and now a pregnant belly, I have wiped out publicly countless times. In fact, I wipe out *only* when I'm in public. The worst is when I get up, exaggeratedly going through all the motions of finding out just what it was that offset my balance. Was it a crack in the sidewalk? A large rock? A fallen branch from a nearby palm tree? No . . . it was *nothing*. It's always nothing at all that has made me fall, splattered on the sidewalk with shopkeepers and local customers all gazing out store windows to make sure I haven't killed my unborn child with my sheer lack of basic balance. The worst that has happened is permanent scarring on my knees from falling in exactly the same way repeatedly. And by the way, I thought I was supposed to get boobs out of this. Isn't that the exchange? You carry a child for over nine months, feel like crap, gain a bunch of weight, but have huge knockers? Why am I still packing a rack the size of Shelley Duvall's? Pregnancy is starting to feel a lot like middle school . . . always waiting for boobs.

I'm hoping that if this baby is a boy, he will be thought of as strong and mighty and will be picked first in gym class and will be fought over by admiring girls who want to be his prom date. But if it's a girl, I fear that she too will have an "extra-long awkward phase" and be forced to be funny to overcompensate for her garish size. We shall soon see.

But for now, let's get started on some stories of "growing up sensitive and artistic (and may I add *tall*) in the suburbs of New Jersey." Away we go.

CHAPTER 1:

The Jersey Girls

At a time when other kids were obsessing over Sweet Valley High books and Lisa Frank Trapper Keepers, and the teen idols were Debbie Gibson and Tiffany, two pop stars who performed in shopping malls, I had a couple of distinct role models of my own: Penny Marshall and Carol Burnett. I too was tall, gawky, and hunched over due to my early-onset scoliosis. When compared with my BFF and business partner, Amanda, I too was the "funny one" (a nice way of saying the "not pretty one"). I'd watched every single *Laverne & Shirley* and *Carol Burnett Show* rerun by the time I was eight, sitting on the peach living room carpet I was (and still am) allergic to. I even asked my mom to buy me an *M* brooch, in the same style of the *L* that Laverne had sewn onto all her sweaters. I wore it to school every day in hopes of starting a brooch trend, which sadly never caught on. My favorite *Laverne & Shirley* episode was season 6, episode 113, when Laverne and Shirley finally escape their impending doom of living in Milwaukee and working in Shotz

Brewery forever. In this pinnacle turn of events titled "Not Quite New York," the girls pack up everything they have and move across the country to Hollywood to become movie stars. When the twenty-five minutes were up, my mom was weeping at the end of an era. I however felt invigorated, ready to get cracking on my quest to avoid a boring fate. I was going on to bigger and better things than suburban New Jersey had to offer. You wouldn't find me working at the local Fotomat on weekdays, bowling with divorced softball coaches on Friday and Saturday nights. I, too, was going to amount to something. I had a hard-core addiction to tall, funny ladies with bad posture and continued to watch these shows religiously in hopes that some of their confidence would rub off on me.

Even though Laverne was hunched over and funny-looking with a wardrobe resembling an old spinster's, Lenny of Lenny & Squiggy was still so madly in love with her he had to gnaw on his own palm to calm himself down. And Carol Burnett got to kiss all sorts of hot guys, like Harvey Korman and Lyle Waggoner, because she was funny and on TV. Laverne and Carol Burnett were comfortable in their own skins. I was not. There was no way I could rock those pocketed '70s Bob Mackie pantsuits in the same powerful way that Carol did. Whenever I tried Carol's trademark tugging-at-the-ear send-off in the mirror, I looked as if I were removing wax buildup. Carol Burnett looked cool . . . I did not.

I grew six inches in fourth grade, ending the year at five-foot-six. Which means I *started* the year already five feet tall. I was essentially a giant child. In our class picture that year, while all the other kids stood on a riser, I had to stand on the floor in order to be the same height as everyone else, including my teacher.

Towards the beginning of fourth grade I brought in a photo of my family vacation to the Southwest. It was a photo of a huge mountain with my very tall older brother and me looking miniscule standing below it. My father, Bob, a Bronx-born academic, told me it symbolized how small we were in comparison to the hugeness of Earth. I liked it because it was the only photo in which I actually looked tiny. I stood before my class in my first-day-of-school outfit, a hot-pink patterned button-down paired with hot-pink wooden button earrings on my newly pierced ears, and proudly displayed the photograph in its painted gold frame. Pretending I came up with them on my own, I used my father's words to explain to the class, "So as you can see, me and my brother are, like, really small in comparison to the hugeness that is Earth. Any questions?"

Carl, a newcomer to the class, raised his hand. "Um, this is more of a comment, but it's impossible for you to look small. I mean even next to a mountain, you're still the tallest girl in the class. In the whole school, I think, as far as I can see." Humiliated, I looked at my mousy teacher for support. She smiled back at me in a way that I could tell was insincere because her eyes were frowning. She was probably exhausted from mal-nourishment. If I had to hear one more time about how she had recently lost sixty pounds, I was going to fake a "family emergency" and leave school early that day. All I ever saw her eat was sugar-free cookies hidden in her desk drawer. She didn't care that someone was embarrassing me. She was dreaming of Boston creams. She looked at me as if to say, *You're huge, Margot, what do you want me to do about it? Those are the facts. Have I told you I recently lost sixty pounds?*

That pretty much set the tone for the rest of the year. I realized I would have to accept forever being the type of girl on the lower half of a chicken fight. I certainly wasn't ever going to get a piggyback ride from any of my friends' dads; that option expired around age five. I would have loved to have been petite and cute like Paula Abdul, spending my time tap-dancing beside a cartoon cat or telling the world I was "Forever Your Girl." But that wasn't the path my family's genetics had mapped out for me. I was on my way to being a woman, albeit about eight years too early. So knowing that I was certainly not "Forever Your Girl," or even forever *a* girl, I decided to make the best of it.

Before my growth spurt I really excelled at gymnastics. Not in an uneven-bars, backbend-on-a-balance-beam kind of way, but in a double-jointed, can-put-my-legs-behind-my-head-easily-to-make-a-human-pretzel-and-impress-kids-before-class kind of way. My extra-bendy body made me a real force to be reckoned with on the extra-bouncy gymnasium floor. After I reached the size of an above-average grown woman by age eleven, my future as a gymnast was clearly about as realistic as my future as a horse jockey. Then I became useless in P.E. class, picked last every time even though one would think I was the strongest. Somehow my long legs that bent backward like a flamingo's made me run more slowly than the short, chubby kids always chosen before me. Plus the lack of left-handed equipment—you'd think the school could invest in just one left-handed baseball glove—made me a real train wreck out on the field.

No matter where I was, some grown-up would always make me feel as if I were doing something wrong just by existing in this body. I was once removed from the monkey bars by a middle-aged recess monitor with a big butt who told me that my shirt rode up too much and boys would get the wrong idea. It wasn't my fault my extremely long and rapidly growing torso made it impossible for my shirts to fit me properly for longer than a month. And believe me, the boys weren't getting the wrong idea; they were all a foot shorter than I and terrified of my Lee Relaxed Fit Extra-Long Riders. At this point I wasn't quite sure what "the wrong idea" even meant. To me, the "wrong idea" was to accuse a little kid of trying to seduce a playground of prepubescent boys just by existing in her body. It seemed that many adults were uncomfortable with a girl my size playing with all the other kids who still could be described as "cute." Just because I was growing at a faster rate did not mean that I was now a sex-crazed teenager. I was still a kid, but the adults projected early sexualization on me, as they couldn't wrap their heads around how else to treat this girl/lady they were encountering.

My band teacher, Mr. Fervor, was one of the worst. He treated me differently than my BFF Amanda, who was allowed to share a chair with him when assigned the coveted job of sheet-music-page-turner. When it was my turn, I squeezed myself down next to Mr. Fervor and he quickly got up. "Uhh, hey, Margot, hey, uhh, I think you should pull up your own chair. I don't want any of the kids here to think the wrong thing." Again with the *wrong thing*? I was humiliated. Did Mr. Fervor actually think my fourth-grade classmates would suspect us of having an affair? Don't flatter yourself, Mr. Fervor. At that age, Fred Savage was more my type.

Meanwhile I was taller than my teacher and was held to a more mature standard than my smaller classmates. If they cried in class over teasing or a grade, they were just kids being kids, and were sympathized with accordingly. If I cried, I looked like a blubbering grown woman in a homemade skirt set.

My parents tried their best to be compassionate, reminding their friends not to make weird comments about how huge I was every single time they saw me. I didn't want to be reminded how gigantic I was by aging hippies, so I appreciated that my folks often created a diversion. What I did want was teenage boys to pick me up the way slutty girls were in Mötley Crüe videos. But I was ignored by teenage boys, who were much more interested in fully developed teenage girls, who were in their prime in late-'80s hair-metal Jersey.

Pretty quickly I began to detest school, where I always felt like a giant loser. My grades were fine, but even in academia my body rebelled against me. I'm left-handed, and despite the lot of genius lefties—Ben Franklin, Julius Caesar, Carol Burnett—I was frequently accosted about my messy handwriting. The fact that my left hand smeared every letter as soon as I wrote it was compounded by the fact that I took an artistic license with the alphabet. To me the alphabet was boring and I wanted to spice it up a bit by adding my own spin on certain letters.

I'm sure no one would have questioned famous lefty Henry Ford if his
g's flared out a little too much. Instead, I was tested for dyslexia about
once a year.

*   *   *   In my free time I fantasized about being a glamorous,
exciting, older woman like my British grandmother, a five-foot-eleven
grand old dame who lived in an apartment on the Upper East Side,
sold Cartier silver, and drank gin martinis with dinner every night. I
even hoarded candy cigarettes in my bedroom and practiced smoking
them in my grandmother's hand-me-down 1970s pink marabou negligee whenever I couldn't sleep. Sure, I was well beyond the age when
playing dress-up was appropriate. But childhood had seemingly come to
a screeching halt for me when I shot up past all my classmates and most
of my teachers, so I occasionally caught up on kids' stuff when no one
was looking. "Look, dahling," I'd say, a white powdered sugar cigarette
dangling from my red-stained lip, "I'd love to stop by tonight, but I've
already had eight gin and vodka martinis, and I'm ready to call it a
night. I already have on my *negligee*."

Perhaps a leaning toward fantasy ran in the family. I had caught
my older brother, Greg, and his friends digging through my dress-up
drawers on more than one occasion. He would have elaborate wrestling matches with his buddies in full costume and wigs. Wrestling was
huge at the time, so huge that GLOW (Gorgeous Ladies of Wrestling)
was created to keep up with the demand. Perhaps my brother and his
friends were loosely inspired by some of these "gorgeous ladies." My
brother's wrestling matches were a perfect combination of drag show
meets Ultimate Fighting Championship and I loved when he would
stage them. I admired how much they all committed to their characters.
One of the most memorable matches was Surfer Dude (my brother) versus Russian Babushka Lady (his friend). In the midst of the match, his

friend's mom called to tell him he was late for dinner. Scared of getting in trouble, but still in full costume, the friend ran out the door in a floor-length gown and Russian fur hat, borrowed my brother's banana-seat bike, and pedaled off into the distance. Although I was concerned about getting two of my best dress-up items back, I did enjoy imagining the friend showing up for dinner looking like a sweaty, overdressed Russian madam in a *schmata*. Just the thought of him eating his Hamburger Helper in full drag made me proud of my brother's choices in friends.

My mother, Pam, was obsessed with British culture, and seemed to observe as many British traditions as the Queen herself. By the time I was seven, I had learned to fake an allergy to Yorkshire pudding, believing, like most kids, that pudding should be made of chocolate or banana—certainly not beef. My mother served me tea in a bone china teacup every morning before school, along with a marmalade-drenched biscuit that seemed to be made entirely of sesame seeds. Even though she was born in Pittsburgh, her mother was born in England, so I understood the allegiance. Still, the constant bragging about how her mother won the "Cutest Baby" award on the boat from England to America, despite my grandmother being almost five years old at the time, needed to stop.

My mom oozed with confidence. Being tall ran in her family, and because she had also had an early growth spurt, she had perspective on my situation. She knew this time would pass and someday I would be proud of my size. She was convinced that being tall eventually would be an enviable quality and that my "girl, you'll be a woman (a little too) soon" stage was simply temporary and that good times lay ahead. Mom was five-foot-nine and proud of it, constantly having "height contests" when friends or family came over, just so she could win. Everyone would groan as she would line us all up in descending order and then say, "Oh, looks like I'm at the top again!" She was ever eager to place her cousins back to back, whipping out her tape measure to settle a dispute. In these instances I watched from the sidelines, knowing that given the direction I was headed, I would be the undisputed winner in no time at all. With a five-foot-eleven grandmother, a six-foot-tall father, and a five-foot-ten great-aunt, my mom was always excited to hold the height contests when those particular family members were not in attendance. She wasn't a competitive person, unless it came to things that really didn't matter. It did bother me that my mother seemed to have blocked out her awkward stage or perhaps had never really had one despite her early-onset uberheight. A cheerleader in high school because "there were just no other sports offered to girls during that time," my mother counterbalanced her extreme height with athleticism, making it an asset rather than a curse.

★ ★ ★ When I was eleven years old, I was diagnosed with scoliosis during a routine test at school (which was much less embarrassing than the time both Amanda and I were diagnosed with lice—Amanda had the good idea to tell everyone we had "fevers" to explain why we were being forcefully removed from class). I really wasn't surprised. It seemed impossible that I could grow this fast and not have some sort of medical problem along with it. I was glad it was a seemingly minor case, and I didn't have to wear one of those embarrassing back braces in addition to my mother's homemade blouses.

I found my monthly visits to the scoliosis specialists to be a complete waste of time, but Mom almost seemed to enjoy them. While the nurses would measure me, comment on how unusually tall I was, then run their hands along my *S*-shaped spine, my mother loved to tell them proudly that height ran in the family. Then, some young doctor right out of *General Hospital* would guide my mother's hands over my spine, asking her, "There, do you feel it? That's where it curves. That's what we have to look out for." I don't think she actually felt the curve, but she sure felt that hunky doctor holding her hands.

Every time we left, the receptionist would say, "We don't need to see Margot for another few months."

My mother would respond, "How about two weeks?"

Years later I understood that my unnecessarily frequent visits to the scoliosis doctors were simply my mom's version of *Playgirl* magazines. She could glance from afar at the accomplished, unattainable beauties and then innocently walk away as if nothing had happened. I finally figured it out when a hot dark-haired doctor finally looked her right in the eye and said, "Really, Mrs. Leitman, she's fine. The *S* in her spine has not increased at all over the years. There is absolutely no reason at all to come back here."

As we got in the car my mom smirked to me, "Well, I wouldn't say 'no reason at all.'"

Considering I spent most evenings rereading *Bop* magazines in bed and fantasizing about various stars from the rotating T.G.I.F. sitcom lineup on ABC, it was nice to know I wasn't alone.

My brother was also tall, but in a good way. Unlike me he was coordinated and good at sports. Also, being tall at a young age looked good on a boy and went especially well with his wiry hair and fully formed teeth that would require no braces. As he was four grades ahead of me, we were never in the same school at the same time. His friends liked to taunt me by pronouncing my name backward—"Tog-ram"—and were all eccentric, studious types like him. Greg always had perfect grades, which infuriated me, as he seemed to spend the majority of his time re-creating iconic films and books on a borrowed camcorder. My parents never invested in a family video camera because they claimed they wanted to "live in the moment." I believe it's because they wanted minimal evidence that their daughter ever looked like a towering young Scandinavian villain with mosquito-bite boobs. Or they figured they could save some money by pretending they didn't realize that Greg had not returned that camcorder to his wealthier friend. The one time I asked my mom about it, after Greg had the camcorder in his possession for over a year and had used it incessantly, she said, "If Greg's friend wants it back, all he has to do is ask."

Meanwhile Greg was very busy with his moviemaking career. By the time I was nine I had played "Connie" in Greg's re-creation of *The Godfather* (Parts 1 and 2; I was not cast in Part 3, much to my dismay) and was "hired" as production assistant on his video re-creation of the epic poem *Beowulf*. Being demoted from actress to PA proved my point that no one wanted this unfortunate stage of my looks on record. Even my own brother would rather use a marionette than me, a *live* person, to play the female roles in *Beowulf*.

Instead of clamoring to fit in with my brother's staff of film-loving friends, I turned to my longtime best friend, Amanda. Amanda had a much younger brother we could boss around, and I liked that dynamic a lot better. She was the other half of my amateur pop duo, "the Jersey Girls"—so named because we lived in New Jersey and we were girls. This wasn't Short Hills/Cherry Hill type of Jersey— this was Central Jersey, bordering on the Jersey Shore. Ours was a town where an old drunk pimp named Squirrel strolled up and down Main Street every day, overly tan Italian Americans snapped gum and flexed their muscles on the boardwalk, and cool teenage girls used zinc oxide as a lipstick. Denim cutoffs were the epitome of style for men, usually accented by a ponytail and a stained white T-shirt. Many people commuted to New York City for work, including my father, as the majority of local opportunities were limited to teaching in the public schools, landscaping, or bartending at one of the bars in this small town. We all lived in the shadow of the great and powerful Jon Bon Jovi, who used the local water tower in the cover art of his latest album, aptly titled *New Jersey*. It seemed a lot of Bon Jovi's songs were written about the everyday people in our area. The first verse of "Livin' on a Prayer" seemed as if it were about our local

"Tommy and Gina." With some minor changes. In our town it would go something like this:

> *Lisa used to work as a stripper*
> *Now she's a waitress where she serves pork ribs to truckers*
> *To truckers*
> *Kevin mows lawns all day*
> *He cries 'cause he's sunburned*
> *Lisa whispers, Baby it's okay . . .*
> *I've got aloe.*
> *She says you've gotta save up to get that next tattoo*
> *It doesn't make a difference if it's black and white or color*
> *We've got each other and we don't need no others*
> *To get through the day*

Inspired by the local legends, Amanda and I spent most of our afternoons locking ourselves in her room and rerecording our demo on her Fisher-Price tape recorder. Amanda was very pretty, normal-size, and terribly naughty. She was tan even in the depths of winter, while I sported a pale, gaunt look even in the throes of summer. I was capable only of burning or freckling, never achieving a golden tan like Amanda's beautiful skin could. Her hair was naturally straight, whereas mine was big, and not in a fun Jersey-in-the-'80s kind of way, but more of an old-spinster-gussied-up-for-the-widowers-at-temple kind of way. At times my mother had ironed it like they did in the '60s, but I never let her finish the job, as I would panic mid-iron. Being eleven years old and having a steaming hot iron directly next to one's skull can be a terrifying experience. Even my mother's utterances of "Beauty must suffer pain" did not make it any easier. My hair was much more cut out for crimping.

I really needed Amanda by my side to get a record deal; she'd be the face, but I'd be the talent—there was a reason Laverne needed Shirley after all. And if our demo sold, there was still time to cash in on the Debbie Gibson phase and begin touring the world wearing funky hats.

Among our roster of original songs so far were "In Love with a Star" (written about *Growing Pains* heartthrob Kirk Cameron). It had a great hook:

Chances are . . . I'm in love with a star

We also wrote "I Don't Even Know What Love Means," which counteracted the main message of "In Love with a Star." With the less brilliant lyrics:

You want me to tell you I love you
But I don't even know what love means

After *Laverne & Shirley* season 6, episode 113 "Not Quite New York," I was inspired by the girls' tenacity and realized I needed to kick my songwriting up a notch. One afternoon, alone in my bedroom, suddenly the lyrics just began flowing out of me.

And I'd be thinking of you
Oh I just can't bear it but I know it's true
And you'd be thinking of me
Oh I know it I know it I can see
And we'd be singing this same song
Oh I know it I know it but I wish I wasn't wrong
Listen boy and listen well
I don't want them to know so don't tell
Because I am thinking of you
Oh I just can't bear it but I know it's true.

This was good. Much better than *Chances are . . . I'm in love with a star.* I was on to something with these incredible lyrics. They were vague yet specific. I could imagine a girl listening to this soon-to-be-hit on her Walkman and substituting either a cute boy from class or teen heart-throb Michael J. Fox for whom she was "thinking of." This song had no limits. But I was more of a writer than a musician, and I wasn't sure how to go about setting it to a tune.

The pressure was too much to bear. I had to impress Amanda, and I had to be a star. So I did the unthinkable: I stole the melody from Wham!'s "Wake Me Up Before You Go-Go." I loved George Michael so much. I loved his album *Faith,* even if it was inappropriately sexual for a girl my age. I loved his butt, and I loved that he wrote a song called "I Want Your Sex," which caused my mom to blush and then change the channel every time it came on the radio even though I knew she loved it, too. A few years had passed since "Wake Me Up Before You Go-Go" set the world on fire, inspiring thousands of pale teens to don knock-off "Choose Life" T-shirts. I figured everyone in my hometown had moved on to Bon Jovi, and no one would remember poor old Wham!

It worked like a charm. A few days later, when I premiered the song in Amanda's bedroom, she thought it was pure genius.

"Margs, we should totally take this to Mr. Fervor, he's super connected in the music industry."

Perfect. This was a great opportunity to prove to our band teacher that I wasn't just some oversize fourth-grade deadbeat who had switched from flute, to clarinet, to sitting in the audience taking notes during band class. He'd be amazed by my songwriting talent. He might call me a prodigy. And then he'd put me in touch with some of his Hollywood connections.

Amanda and I stayed after in band class the next day and showed Mr. Fervor our brilliant opus, handwritten on Mead loose-leaf paper.

"You girls wrote this all by yourselves?" asked Mr. Fervor.

We both nodded. I fought the urge to call Amanda out for taking co-credit for a song I had both slaved over *and* stolen.

"Well, do you want to sing it for me, then?" he asked.

Amanda and I enthusiastically nodded. I counted off, "One, two, three, four," the way I'd heard Bruce Springsteen do on the many, many live concert albums my parents owned.

Amanda and I proudly sang "Thinking of You" to the tune of "Wake Me Up Before You Go-Go" a capella. I twirled the hot-pink jelly bracelets on my wrists to distract myself from the fear of being found out. We finished the song, took a pregnant pause, and waited for Mr. Fervor's response. Then we hit the jackpot.

"Well, girls, I'd love to work with you. How'd you like to perform this song in the school and community assemblies? I'd be happy to play the accompaniment. Sound good? Sound cool, girls?" Mr. Fervor always spoke as if he were at a beat poetry slam. Amanda and I nodded furiously. "Oh and, girls, or 'Jersey Girls,' should I say, a song this good is sure to get stolen. Believe me, I'd look into copyrighting this puppy." Mr. Fervor had clearly been through some ups and downs in his music career, leading him to err on the side of caution.

Amanda and I left Mr. Fervor and began to jump up and down, screaming as soon as we were out of the room. A record deal was a mere assembly away! That afternoon, I followed Mr. Fervor's advice, and with my mom's help, sent the song off to the Copyright Office to claim my legal ownership of a song stolen from Wham! My mom seemed super knowledgeable in the art of copyrighting something, most likely because, as she had told me countless times, it was her father who had come up with the original formula for sugarless gum at the candy factory he had worked in. But because he didn't properly take ownership of the formula, it went to the company and we never saw a dime of the Trident/Extra/Carefree empire. She also told me repeatedly that he came up with the formula for chlorophyll gum, what Clorets were made from. My mom was the last remaining chewer of Clorets gum and was solely responsible for keeping them in business. That being said, she was extra supportive in making sure I got what was rightfully mine from this song . . . that Wham! actually wrote.

I was officially on my way to massive success as a pop star. I couldn't wait for that assembly, and I hoped a big agent in the crowd would see beyond my awkwardness to the musical prodigy lying within. Then my life would really begin. Maybe in my tear-out photos in *Bop* magazine I wouldn't look so tall. As long as I wasn't always standing right next to Amanda, I was sure they could fudge it so I looked normal size.

I also had a secret backup plan on the off chance there were no big-time Hollywood agents in the audience of the Lloyd Road Elementary School. I had learned from watching Madonna interviews that getting no attention is worse than negative attention. So, the next best thing to getting discovered as a musical prodigy would be to get caught publicly for stealing the song. A part of me secretly hoped my teacher would stand up and say, "Everyone hold your furious applause. The Jersey Girls have clearly ripped this song off from Wham! Call the police! And thank you, yes, I have lost weight. Sixty pounds to be exact." Then I would be whisked off stage in handcuffs screaming "Get me a lawyer!" The options—record deal or arrest—seemed equally appealing to me. I'd end up forever labeled a bad girl or a genius. Either way, I'd come out on top.

The day of the assembly arrived. While Amanda and I waited in the wings of the auditorium, I peeked out to see who was in the audience. All I could see were my schoolmates and teachers, no recognizable showbiz types. No men in top hats or guys with big mustaches. No ladies in mink stoles holding clipboards to take notes on the talent of Central Jersey. I didn't have much time to get nervous or think about the ramifications of getting caught stealing from Wham! There was barely any time before Mr. Fervor proudly said, "Please welcome the Jersey Girls!" and Amanda and I took the stage to moderate applause. Mr. Fervor began playing the piano with all the enthusiasm of a coked-up Elton John performing "Bennie and the Jets." Amanda sang through her nose, and I faked that I could sing the best I could, wondering if any of these pimple-faced squirts would have the guts to point out that I was a fraud.

We finished the song and everyone clapped politely. No one seemed all that impressed. No one stopped in the hall to tell us we were child prodigies. No one offered us a recording career. No one even accused us of stealing the song from Wham! All we received was the same polite applause that the little boy who had done the recorder solo had gotten.

The school assembly was kid stuff, I reassured myself. We'd get our real shot at the parent/town assembly that night.

I warmed up all afternoon, doing vocal exercises in my bedroom I had learned from Miss Piggy. I stuck out my flat chest and squealed, "mee mee mee," just as I had seen her do in the latest Muppet movie. Miss Piggy was also an exciting and glamorous woman like my grandmother, even though she was a pig and a puppet. And she tamed that big blonde mane of hers in a way I longed to master.

That night at the town assembly, once again Amanda and I waited in the wings. I knew this was a huge risk—it was highly likely someone out there would recognize the song. What had started as a simple few words on loose-leaf paper had now turned into a live concert event in front of every single person I had ever met. What's worse, I had now copyrighted a Wham! song as my own and was taking innocent Mr. Fervor and my best friend Amanda down with me.

With the fear of the devil in me, Amanda and I hit the stage and rocked the night away. We did all the moves I carefully choreographed—*step, touch, sway, repeat*—with a precision unmatched in any of our tedious rehearsals. Amanda again sang through her nose while I tried to sing on key. I was extra careful not to let the *step, touch, sway, repeat* mess me up while I tried to remember the lyrics I had penned privately in my bedroom. The refrain was the easiest, as it was the most blatant rip-off of "Wake Me Up Before You Go-Go." Thankfully, we made it through disaster-free, and that stupid kid with the recorder didn't steal too much of the spotlight. Amanda and I lingered a little too long bowing to the crowd, savoring the high of nailing it.

Then we looked out into the adoring crowd. Not so adoring. Once again no one seemed all that impressed. No one seemed to notice that the melody was stolen. I looked out at my mother, expecting to find her weeping with joy over the discovery of her daughter's innate musical talent. There she was, head towering several inches over the other big-haired women, clapping politely, her eyes dryer than I had *ever* seen them in my life. Apparently Laverne's sojourn to L.A. in season 6, episode 113 "Not Quite New York" was more moving than her daughter's big solo in front of the whole town. I stared at her extra long to see if she was bragging to others, saying, "That's my daughter, the tall gifted one." Not a word. Meanwhile my father hadn't gotten out of work in time to make it, and my brother hadn't come. No one seemed to care about my big moment.

Amanda and I lingered a little longer on stage till the clapping faded into silence. Finally, we untriumphantly departed.

After the concert, we all went to Friendly's, where I got my usual, the clown sundae with the cone on top made to look like a clown hat. I pushed my spoon into it thinking, *This isn't a clown, it's just an upside-down ice-cream cone. The thrill is gone.* Amanda and I ate our sundaes and didn't speak of the George Michael–size elephant in the room—but I knew she knew I stole the song. That night, lying in bed smoking one of my Stallion brand candy cigarettes, I wondered if our usual Friendly's waitress had ever wanted something more; she looked even more tired than usual.

A few days later I mailed a cassette copy of this potential #1 hit to the Kirk Cameron mailing address I had ripped out of *Bop* magazine. I'm still waiting for his reply.

CHAPTER 2

A Very Tiny Grown-up

After the assembly turned into a nonstarter, Amanda and I spent the next year practicing our dance routine to Chaka Khan's "I Feel for You," which consisted mostly of homoerotic grinding mixed with a few kick ball changes. By sixth grade, all our activities seemed to have developed a new undertone of sexuality. I believe one of our songs at that stage actually had the lyrics *I want you inside of me.* One day, when Chaka Khan was boring us, we caught a commercial for a phone-dating service and Amanda sweet-talked me into placing an ad. I pretty much did everything Amanda said, because her mom had the good snacks like Devil Dogs and Fruit Roll-Ups, and I didn't want to be banished back to the land of cheese and raisins where I came from. But I instantly saw a second reason to get excited about our ad: Maybe I would meet an older man who would understand me and my giant-child predicament, the way Amanda never could, and possibly be able to look into my eyes without the assistance of a stepstool.

For this particular dating service, you had to first call and leave a voicemail version of your "profile" for potential suitors. Then you could listen to other people's profiles and leave messages for them. After a while, if you *really* liked the person, you could leave your home phone number, and the potential mate would call, and then you'd go on a date and do dirty things that I had thus far practiced only on my Fred Savage poster.

I was pretty calm about the whole thing; it was only a voicemail, and I had about a dozen or so opportunities to get out if I wanted, considering all the steps until an actual date. So, first, we created my profile.

I used my interpretation of a "sexy" voice (based entirely on women I saw during an awkward viewing of the James Bond film *Octopussy* with my parents). I didn't fully understand the plot of *Octopussy*—there was a lot of hullabaloo over a Fabergé egg. This seemed ridiculous, as my grandmother had fancy eggs like that lying all around her New York City high-rise and no one seemed to want to kill her over them. But Octopussy's voice was sexy in a Kathleen Turner kind of way, and so I used her as inspiration and recorded this audio profile:

Hello. My name is Margot. I like to have fun. I'm five-foot-six, weigh about 115 pounds, and have blue eyes, blonde hair, and freckles. I'm an aspiring singer currently recording my demo with my writing partner. I love to dance, and right now my favorite song is Chaka Khan's "I Feel for You." So if you feel for me, leave me a message.

It was sheer brilliance, and completely true. I didn't lie about being twelve years old; I just left it out. Amanda was really impressed. She insisted we move right on to hearing the guys' profiles and leaving messages for them. We probably gave the equivalent of a Match.com "wink" to about sixteen men, ranging from twenty-five to thirty-one.

A few called back and left replies. One guy's message stood out above the rest. He had a nerdy, nasal voice, but he sounded friendly:

Hi, my name is Paul; I'm a thirty-year-old bank teller who lives by the shore. I enjoy surfing or just lying on the beach. I'm five feet tall, so if you think good things come in small packages, leave me a message.

I felt an instant connection to him. Paul was a tiny grown-up and I was a giant child. I felt that we could meet in the middle somewhere, and for just one second I could feel normal. Perhaps if Paul and I got married, our children would have a good shot at being average height and avoid the bizarre woman/child phase I was going through. Paul would understand me the way only a thirty-year-old undersize man could. Plus he was really good at puns, which I appreciated.

Amanda related to my quest for fun—for her, this was a perfect diversion from watching her mother sprinkle glitter on Styrofoam for the Bat Mitzvah centerpiece business she ran out of their garage. But she couldn't really understand how meaningful this could be for me—to meet a man of my own kind, weirdly heighted and treated differently for it.

In just two days, I went through all the appropriate steps with "good things come in small packages" Paul. I left him my profile; he liked it and then left me a personal message in my box. Apparently, Paul also had an affinity for Chaka Khan. I left him a message in my Octopussy voice and he left one in return. This went on for about a week (all charged to Amanda's mom's phone bill). Then Paul left me this message:

Hi, Margot, it's Paul. I'd love to talk to you one-on-one this week. I was wondering if I could get your phone number so we could talk beyond these voicemails. Hope to hear from you soon.

Amanda was psyched. "Margot, he's totally rich. I mean, he's a bank teller! Like, how many more opportunities are you going to get to go out with a rich guy? No one is rich here. Paul is rich. Rich, Margot! Just do it! Give him your phone number!"

Amanda was right; no one had big money in our town. My mom was a schoolteacher, my dad got home at 9:00 PM every night from a New York City commute just to make ends meet. A lot of locals ran landscaping businesses on the weekends, sold Avon or Amway or Mary Kay as a side business, and ran daycares out of their living rooms. I had seen how the other half lived on my weekend visits to my grandmother in New York City and wanted a piece of that taxi-riding, takeout-ordering, Duane Reade–shopping lifestyle. Linking up with Paul the tiny bank teller could be my ticket out. Maybe I wouldn't end up working as a Friendly's waitress (my hometown's version of Shotz Brewery). Maybe this was my season 6 very special episode of *Laverne & Shirley*, or should I say *Margot & Amanda* episode 113 "Not Quite New Jersey." And so, I wrote yet another script and proceeded to leave Paul this message:

Hi, Paul. It's Margot. I'd love to chat with you directly, so if you could give me a call tomorrow AFTER THREE, that would be great. Make sure it's AFTER THREE; I will be at . . . uh . . . work. Until three. Recording my demo from eight to three. Anytime after that. But before nine. Actually before eight is good, because ALF is on tomorrow and I just love that show, and really would prefer not to miss an episode. Okay, give me a call. My number is—

And then I proceeded to give a thirty-year-old man my parents' phone number so he could unknowingly call and try to date me, a gargantuan, gawky girl who hadn't even gotten her braces *on* yet.

Amanda told me I did a great job on the message. I humbly agreed. I thought the *ALF* part really personalized it.

"Look, Margot, if it's true love, he'll wait. Paul will wait. Don't tell him your real age," Amanda warned.

The following day during school, however, I started to get nervous. I was in too deep—how quickly I had become a gold-digging hussy! I barely got through the day; every time I glanced over at Amanda, she nodded her head and gave me a generic hand signal, which I knew meant *go for it*. At lunch that afternoon Amada had all the good stuff—Lay's potato chips, that fluorescent orange spreadable cheese with the red plastic spreader, and Ecto Cooler, the limited edition *Ghostbusters* Hi-C juice box. Only the coolest kids at Lloyd Road Elementary School had Ecto Cooler. I had a Thermos filled with skim milk or room-temperature tap water, depending on the day. Amanda even had a crazy straw. I couldn't let her down.

When I finally got home from school I was in a full-blown panic and wanted to tell my mom everything. But instead I did what I always did when I went to my own house, instead of Amanda's: I folded endless laundry, composed mostly of my father's hole-filled socks and underwear. Laundry was the chore I minded least, as it held little opportunity for me to break something due to my clumsiness and, in my mother's words, "lefty-Louie-ness." Dusting was a high-risk chore for me, especially with my grandmother's Cartier castaways all over. Washing dishes was also dangerous, as I lived in fear of ever nicking one of my mom's bone china teacups (again).

I took my mind off the never-ending underwear by watching reruns of *Moonlighting* on Lifetime, hoping Cybill Shepherd and Bruce Willis would just do it already. I had heard from Amanda that there was one episode where they finally had sex, and I watched reruns religiously, hoping to catch it. She told me it was really dirty and really gross, which only made me want to see it more. Then, around five o'clock, the kitchen phone rang. My body froze, my legs felt like lead. I could not move. My mom answered, and in a surprisingly calm voice said, "*Maaargot*, phone call. It's Paul!" No questions asked.

I grabbed the phone and pulled the cord as far away from my mother as I could get. Somehow I managed to get all the way into the laundry room and was even able to shut the door. I took a deep breath, a multitude of thoughts running through my head. I wanted to tell Paul I was having an identity crisis due to my unexpectedly large size. I wanted to tell Paul that Amanda made me do it and I just wanted her to think I was cool. I wanted to tell Paul that I fancied myself a "Laverne DeFazio" type, if only he could wait a few years. I wanted to tell Paul I, too, understood what it felt like to be weird. Instead I took the phone and in a shaky twelve-year-old voice said this:

"Hi, Paul. I'm twelve years old."

Silence. Silence that lasted longer than that awkward viewing of *Octopussy* with my parents. Finally, in that nerdy, nasal voice I first fell in love with, Paul spoke.

"You're twelve years old."

"I'm twelve years old."

Pause.

"You're twelve years old."

"I'm twelve years old."

This phone call was rapidly becoming an exercise in the Meisner technique.

"Well. Good-bye then," and Paul hung up on me.

I felt a hitch in my throat. There went my big chance. I blew it. Instead of running away with Paul to his jet-setting thirty-year-old bank-teller lifestyle a few towns away, I found myself dumped by an aging, undersize phone dater in my parents' laundry room at age twelve. I stood there in shock until the irritating phone-off-the-hook noise snapped me right out of it.

I hung up, half wishing my mom would ask who Paul was, but she never did. I went back to folding the laundry and hoped that I hadn't missed Bruce Willis and Cybill Shepherd doing the nasty. As Bruce and Cybill bickered on-camera, I wondered if Paul was okay. This was my first breakup, but being a thirty-year-old big-time bank teller, Paul had probably seen it all. Hopefully he wasn't too heartbroken. I imagined him at work the next day, counting piles of fresh money and thinking about what could have been. I had a lifetime of dating in front of me, but Paul was thirty! How much more time could he possibly have to find his true love? Maybe a nice, five-foot-tall, age-appropriate girl would come to his window at the bank the next day and they'd look into each other's eyes and just know it was meant to be. Maybe Paul would be able to get through this and come out a "bigger" person.

The next day at school I told Amanda he never even called. "That's what men are like, Margot. Take it from me," she said.

CHAPTER 3

Oven Door of Sin

As sixth grade continued, my breakup with Paul the tiny bank teller was easier to get over than I thought it would be. I learned from a brief period of sneaking episodes of *General Hospital* on Amanda's recommendation, before getting caught and grounded for it, that the best way to end your heartache over someone is to replace that special someone with another. Before my grounding I learned a lot about love through *GH* supercouple Felicia and Frisco's tumultuous relationship. After Frisco presumably died working undercover for the WSB (World Security Bureau), Felicia quickly moved on to Colton Shore, the very man who tried to kill her beloved Frisco. I figured I should follow Felicia's lead and move on from Paul the tiny bank teller, even though I had heard via Amanda after my grounding that Frisco had faked his own death and was back with Felicia after her brief bout with amnesia. I figured the odds of anything involving a faked death and amnesia happening to me and Paul were slim, so it was best to keep myself open for new options in love.

Before Paul, my interactions with boys had all been in my imagination. I wanted *Growing Pains* breakout star Kirk Cameron to be my boyfriend, so much so that I kept a diary of love letters to him. They were all addressed to "Pretend Kirk Cameron," because even as a kid, I knew that I needed to get real. There was no way this quick-witted wavy-haired dreamboat would ever go for me. My love for Kirk was so true that I had a torn-out photo of him from *Bop* magazine proudly displayed on the back side of my school locker door. Every time I opened my locker, I was greeted by this nonthreatening sex symbol with sandy blond hair and a clean record.

I also wanted to make out under a maple tree with Fred Savage, just as he had with Winnie Cooper in the flawless pilot to *The Wonder Years*. I wanted to be someone's Winnie Cooper. Instead, I was most people's Becky Slater, the freckle-faced obnoxious tween whom Kevin Arnold only dated to make his real love, Winnie, jealous. Pretty, big-eyed brunettes like Winnie always got the guy, it seemed. Samantha Micelli, played by Alyssa Milano on *Who's the Boss?*, was another pretty brunette who seemed to have skipped puberty and gone straight from cute kid to hot teen. Fair, pubescent girls like Becky Slater, Kimmy Gibbler, and me never seemed to get the guy. Kelly Kapowski got Zack Morris on *Saved by the Bell*, and even Uncle Jesse from *Full House* paired off with Becky (played by beautiful brunette Lori Loughlin). But the Becky Slaters of the world were limited to a four-episode story arc or at best were forced to wear horrible spandex camel-toed short sets like Kimmy Gibbler.

I briefly had an obsession with the British guy from *Grease 2*, daydreaming of him singing catchy musical theatre numbers to me in the same manner he had to Michelle Pfeiffer in the movie that seemed to be endlessly playing after *Teen Witch* on TBS. Then, one Saturday afternoon, bored with my favorite number from *Grease 2* ("Let's Bowl, Let's Bowl, Let's Rock 'n' Roll"), I changed the channel to MTV.

Music videos were responsible for many of my fashion choices, catchphrases, and dreams. After I saw Lita Ford slide across the floor in her ripped jeans in the "Kiss Me Deadly" video I took a pair of left-handed scissors to my Lee Relaxed Fit Extra-Long Riders and tore those bad boys up. After Michael Jackson made choreographed all-male jazz dancing look tough I longed to have an occasion to yell in someone's face "You ain't bad, you ain't nothin'!" After seeing Jon Bon Jovi pop out of a moving platform beneath the floor to uproarious applause in the "Lay Your Hands on Me" video I wanted to someday matter that much to a crowd of hair-sprayed fans.

Music videos were essential companions to hit songs and were imperative to stay abreast of if you wanted to avoid becoming a total loser (which I was well on my way to being). Often, at school, Amanda would talk about the latest Richard Marx video, while a gaggle of girls crowded around listening as if she had the key to life. I had no idea who Richard Marx was or what songs he sang. I pretended I did, though, nodding my head and agreeing that "Hold On to the Nights" was a far superior song to "Right Here Waiting" even though I had never heard either song. They sounded pretty lame to me, in comparison to sexy rock hits like "Kiss Me Deadly."

As a preteen trapped in a high schooler's body, my little-girl mind was continuously being sent confusing oversexed messages. For example, after I saw the music video for Warrant's "Cherry Pie," I thought sex involved baked goods being dropped in one's crotch. I knew I had to be wrong, but I was scared to ask anyone about it. And who could I ask? My brother was too involved in creating a detailed spreadsheet of our home movie collection, Dad was always working, and my mom would love that I was opening up to her so much she would try to have "that talk" with me every day over high tea. Amanda seemed to have all the answers, but admitting to her that I did not know anything would majorly take me down a few notches in her eyes. Amanda was already a bit out of my league friend-wise and I couldn't risk losing her. So instead I let all the stimuli around me run wild in my mind, turning to no one for answers and coming to my own deranged childish answers. For example, I believed oral sex was talking about sex on the phone. Oral hygiene meant a clean mouth, so why wouldn't oral sex mean talking dirty on the telephone? I'll never forget years later being humiliated while on the phone with an overly wise boy from class. "Do you even know what oral sex is?" he asked.

"Yeah," I said, "we're having it right now."

Then, one particular Saturday, as I was watching MTV and folding socks, a man came on the screen and changed my life. I certainly did *not* want him to be my boyfriend. I had no desire to go on a romantic date with him; I didn't want to make out with him under a maple tree. For the first time in my life I wanted to do dirty, dirty things with a man and not speak to him afterward. I wanted to do them with R&B singer Bobby Brown. This was when Bobby Brown was just a cute guy in Hammer pants singing R&B songs in an attempt to launch a solo career post–New Edition. This was a glorious time for Bobby.

Watching Bobby Brown's low-budget video for the post–"My Prerogative" sleeper hit "Roni" for the first time in my life, my pants got wet and it was *not* due to peeing. The video was entirely made up of blurry, live-concert, low-budget footage edited together and filled with Bobby's oversexed antics, including lambada-ing before that was a thing and a lot of pounding on his sweaty hairless chest as he sang this forgettable R&B song. Bobby stood onstage shirtless, wearing nothing but a pair of satin, royal-blue parachute pants. This was hot with a capital *H*, and the wet feeling down below was a shockingly titillating feeling that I would have paid more attention to had I not been completely mesmerized by this young man's pajama pants and huge swinging wiener. I almost cried when he crawled across the stage on all fours with his tongue hanging out like a rabid dog. He was just stinking of sex! When he stood on the giant speakers during the song's breakdown clapping his hands, I just knew I needed to one day lose my virginity to him. The man who once sang "Cool It Now" would now become my secret lover.

A few years before "Roni" debuted, Bruce Springsteen had brought Courtney Cox (another cute brunette) onstage in the "Dancing in the Dark" video, and every girl in my school fantasized about one day having the opportunity to *step touch repeat* with the Boss. But Bobby took the audience volunteer pas de deux to a whole new level. The chick Bobby chose to dance with was certainly not an actress who had been planted in the audience and would soon be cast in Must See TV shows like *Family Ties* and *Friends*. Bobby's choice of a lucky audience member to rub up against could best be described as *an attainable woman*, which I felt meant I had a chance with this filthy, gap-toothed boy. This woman was wearing little makeup and sported an unfortunate-looking pageboy. She was a little overweight and had virtually no rhythm. Bobby had to ask her to remove her jacket and then a cardigan to reveal an olive-green turtleneck.

She was my hero. My hero in a turtleneck. I wanted to be her.

Then again, my height was constantly making people think I was older than I was. The local movie theatre manager never wanted to let me in at the children's rate, even though he was also the assistant principal of my school. When I handed in my paperwork to quit gymnastics classes (for obvious height reasons) the girl behind the desk said, "Aren't you that girl always hanging out with girls so much younger than you?" So maybe I had a chance to be Bobby's next victim. Perhaps if I could get tickets to Bobby's next show at the Garden State Arts Center, I could achieve my dream of rubbing my pelvis against a man with a Gumby haircut. If only my mom would let me go!

In the meantime, I would sit in front of MTV for hours, suffering patiently through crappy Milli Vanilli videos, various Paula Abdul atrocities, and unsexy Roxette ballads just waiting for Bobby Brown and his swinging big dick to come back and create that unexplainable feeling in my slightly irregular underwear bought in bulk at the Hanes outlet.

I went through a brief religious phase around this time, wearing a green stone cross I had purchased at a local flea market. My mother told me it might put off my father, raised Jewish but now an atheist, but otherwise she thought it was "very pretty." I stroked my green $2 cross fervently while praying to God that "Roni" would come on. *Please, please, please make this next video Roni, God. I will do anything you ask of me; I'll even eat a few bites of the next batch of Yorkshire pudding. I'll even put my dad's tighty-whities away in his dresser after folding them. Just make the next video "Roni."* My prayers never worked. Unfortunately, "Roni" had not reached the same level of rotation as "Don't Worry, Be Happy," a song and video about as sexy as the "Top That" rap from *Teen Witch.*

My absolute favorite part of the "Roni" music video was when Bobby snapped open the waistband of his pants and swirled around in slow motion looking down at his crotch. I had no idea of the true implications of his choreography—that he was looking at his own erection as he did this. I had no clue he was snapping his pants to check that he was absolutely ready to sleep with whoever was closest the second he stepped offstage. And I somehow missed the enormous outline of his donkey dick showing through the sateen of his Hammer pants. I thought the snapping open of one's pants while twirling your pelvis was a new dance craze and I should practice it at home for the next school dance.

My body was developing at such a rapid pace I didn't completely understand these erotic desires Bobby Brown was expressing onstage. Although I was tall, I didn't have big boobs like the girls in Bobby's audience crying at his onstage magic. If I was growing body hair, it wasn't noticeable. My mom and dad's genes combined had given me ultrablonde body hair. I had even inherited what I referred to as "clear eyebrows," which were the exact opposite of the sexy Brooke Shields or Cindy Crawford dark, brooding brow. My eyebrows most closely resembled those of an albino's, which was true of the rest of my body hair, making it virtually invisible. I understood the value of not having to spend endless dollars on waxing and various other hair-removal treatments, but every time we had "health" class, I learned that growing body hair was a sign of puberty. Being very tall with no boobs and what appeared to be no body hair was very confusing.

None of my health teachers discussed what might happen down below when watching a Bobby Brown music video. From what I had learned so far, sex was about periods, AIDS, and poorly made birthing videos. No one had mentioned big schlongs in loose pants or damp undies while watching MTV. More than a little lost, I figured it would be best to just learn Bobby's erotic choreography myself and take it from there.

First I needed to find the right environment to practice the twirling penis dance move. We had mirrors in my house in private places like bathrooms and bedrooms, but I preferred the kitchen oven. In my house our oven was installed about halfway up in the wall. An average-size child could perhaps see a reflection of his or her face, but because I was so tall, I could see a perfect reflection of my midsection. Soon, the oven door became a secret mirror where I could dance dirty with myself while no one was looking. I would practice the "snap waistband/twirl pelvis/look at my dick" move over and over, carefully observing my reflection in the oven door. The isolation of just the pelvic area being visible in the oven door made the dance extra erotic, like a peep show where I was both the star and the audience. My unneutered dog, sensing the air of sex in the room, would join in on the action by humping my rejected Popple.

One afternoon, while staring at my midsection in the oven and practicing the "Roni" snap over and over again, judging if I had completely mastered the art of looking at my own "dick" or if I needed more work on the pelvis-swirl part, I looked up and saw my older brother standing in the doorway. He was watching me with horror. I had no idea how long he had been there, but I knew he had seen enough.

"Margot, what are you doing?" he asked, staring at me with disgust and a slight twinge of fear.

What was I doing? Well, I was thrusting my hips and staring at my denim-clad crotch in the oven door. I could say I was just dancing, but how would I explain why I was looking down my pants? My dancing certainly had progressed from juvenile grinding to Chaka Khan's "I Feel for You" to controlled eroticism for which I am still thankful for the oven door. But how could I explain this type of personal progress to my teenage brother? Lucky for me, he didn't have his "borrowed" camcorder out, capturing this disaster for all eternity. Still, surely he had seen the "Roni" video—maybe if I just laid it all out there, he would understand. I mean, everyone watched MTV all the time, right? Except I had never actually seen Greg watch MTV; he was always too busy reading, doing his schoolwork, or building his VHS collection of classic movies taped off the Turner Classic Movies channel.

Finally I just told him the truth. "I'm practicing my 'Roni' dance." And in lieu of asking further questions, my brother walked away, shaking his head but letting it go. Maybe he had never seen the video for "Roni" and didn't understand. Or maybe he *had* seen the video for "Roni" and needed no further explanation. I didn't care; I just prayed he wouldn't tell my parents or his friends. Maybe my little green stone cross had the power to make this prayer actually work.

Soon after, I bought Bobby's album *Don't Be Cruel* on cassette at Nickels so I could listen to "Roni" at my leisure, now doing the dance in the privacy of my bedroom, rewinding it over and over again, twisting and grinding to the best song ever. I didn't care that this was not a hit song for Bobby Brown. For me, it was #1.

To a twelve-year-old girl, everything about Bobby Brown embodied sex. His moves, his lips, his lyrics. He even performed that infamous, hungry Madonna "Express Yourself" crawl before Madonna herself did it. I was amazed by how a simple, one-camera, cheaply made live video of one young sexy man singing a so-so song could evoke such a strong chemical reaction. Judging by the quality of the video, I was sure it was taped on one of those camcorders you had to strap to your chest along with the VCR—you know, the original "portable" camcorders that the proudest dads invested in only to be outdated five minutes later by something that was *actually* portable? Amanda's family had one of those, and I was always jealous of their ability to record the happier moments of life and rewatch them later to revel in how amazingly well everything was going for them.

Bobby also had a good life in my mind. He was touring the country singing hot songs and filming it all. He was almost subtle in his seduction, not like those manufactured man-girls from Milli Vanilli, who I believed were an insult to my womanhood. I thought Bobby was about as sexy as it could get. There would never be a hotter man; there would never be a hotter song; never would I ever again feel the way Bobby Brown made me feel. After years of having trouble sleeping, I would now look forward to going to sleep so I could lie in bed and dream about dancing with Bobby myself, alone, while wearing a turtleneck. The idea that something so sexy was humanly possible made me feel alive and invigorated to start my next day.

Then, one afternoon, while I watched MTV and stroked my green stone cross, praying to God that "Roni" would come on, a new video for Bobby Brown's song "Every Little Step" premiered. Bobby and the dancers wore matching black-and-white costumes, not Hammer pants and Costco turtlenecks. The video looked professionally recorded and was precisely choreographed. Bobby no longer was allowed to run around onstage freestyling his own dance moves. Someone had started controlling his sexiness.

But I still knew what lay beneath. I decided that Bobby was probably dating the backup dancer on the right because I thought she was the prettiest. She was a thin, light-skinned black girl with long black hair and a killer strut. I thought she was the most beautiful woman in the world. Move over Laverne and Carol Burnett, there was a new tall woman to emulate and her name was Tanya. I didn't actually know her name was Tanya—there was no Google at the time—so I created a name for her and hoped that Bobby was with her. Perhaps in a few years when I grew into my frame, I could look like that too. Maybe I could have a career as a Bobby Brown backup dancer. After all, I had worked very hard at mastering the nuance of his choreography in my oven door.

Every time this video came on, which was much more frequently than "Roni," I found myself watching Tanya more than Bobby. Whereas with "Roni" I was mesmerized by Bobby's allure, in "Every Little Step," Tanya stole the show. Because I found Tanya to be so beautiful, I assumed that I must now be a lesbian. Why else would I be so enthralled with her? Tanya wore above-the-knee black boots and had long curly hair that looked like a darker version of Whitney Houston's desirable locks in the "I Wanna Dance with Somebody" video. She wore a skintight black Lycra dress that accentuated all the right parts of her body in a way that my unitards for modern dance class never did. There was no other possible scenario beyond sheer lesbianism to explain my attraction to Tanya. I would come out to my parents when the time was right and would hope for their blessing. My mother would be initially concerned about how I would be able to reproduce in a girl/girl relationship, but I would assure her that love between two women means twice the uteri and my lesbian partner and I would find a way to bear her grandchildren. Being a lesbian was fine with me; it seemed like a cool artsy thing to do. Even Madonna was sometimes gay, and she was on top of the world. Plus, my parents had forced me to watch a movie a few weekends before called *I Love You, Alice B. Toklas*, and Alice was lesbians with Gertrude Stein. Gertrude was a cool depressed author, which was another possible career option for me if dirty backup Bobby Brown dancer didn't pan out. Even though being a lesbian seemed very exciting to me, I was sad because I had to now break up with Bobby. Well, more like break up with the video for "Roni."

I began fantasizing about Tanya while lying in bed, sleeplessly wondering how I would phrase my coming out to my parents. I imagined Tanya teaching me her sexy strut, instructing me how to properly strap up my thigh-high boots, and helping me develop my repertoire of booty-shaking dance routines to Bobby's latest musical masterpiece. I was sure that what I had for Tanya was love and love only, but I needed to be sure I was truly full-force gay, or at least bisexual, a word I'd learned from my surrogate "big sis," Madonna. After all, just a month before I was certain I wanted to rub my crotch against Bobby's groin while he sang slow jams to me. Maybe I didn't truly love Tanya in that way.

So I decided to try out my "I'm probably a lesbian" theory on a friend of mine. I use the term *friend* loosely. She was more like the smartest girl in my class who was always placed in a higher small group than me. My teachers would always vaguely describe the groups under names like the leopards, the reindeer, and the turtles. I may have been just a reindeer but I was smart enough to know I didn't want to be a turtle. This girl was most certainly a leopard. She had always worn glasses and had braces and wore her hair in a bun. Then one day she got contacts, grew boobs, got her braces off, and let down her hair. It turned out she had beautiful long, silky hair that looked like the ladies on the covers of romance novels in the magazine aisle of ShopRite. I could imagine her swinging her mane in slow motion while romantic music played during a beachside love scene. She looked like the "after" pictures in the copies of *Cosmo* I would sneak off and read after my grandmother would fall asleep on her chaise lounge clutching her martini in one hand and dangling a lit cigarette in the other. Surely with that hair this girl had a better understanding of sex than I did and would be open to making out with a tall girl with clear eyebrows. Maybe she would think my invisible eyebrows were mysterious, like Mona Lisa's.

I invited her over one day under the ruse of coming over to "look at my books." I thought that would appeal to a leopard. After a disgusting snack of dry biscuits with marmalade and black tea prepared by my faux British mother, we headed upstairs. I apologized for my mom's terrible snack selection, explaining that I lived in a Fruit Roll-Ups- and Hi-C-free environment. "Maybe that's why you're growing to be so tall," said the Newly Hot Hair Girl. I wanted to tell her to shut up and kiss me. I knew I was tall; with my gene pool there was no other option. I certainly didn't need marmalade to aid my growth. Duh.

"Well, here are my books," I replied, barely gesturing to the shelf, in the same way the haggard older *The Price Is Right* models displayed a "lovely dinette set." I was desperate to change the subject away from my height, as I was sure that would be a turnoff for her.

"I like the color in here. Mint green. Nice."

"Thanks. My mom painted it. She said it was a cool, calming color." *Enough small talk. Let's get to it.* In the "Roni" video, Bobby drags the boring-looking girl across the stage by the hand and says, "What we about to do, baby, you don't need that coat, that sweater, or nothin'." Then he towels off the sweat from his brow as she removes her cardigan to reveal her olive-green turtleneck. "This ain't gonna hurt . . . not a bit," he says as he stares at her rack, which is so big it still reads loud and clear through a loose-fitting turtleneck. Bobby didn't talk about paint hues; he got down to business.

I needed to act fast. As the Newly Hot Hair Girl went to grab a book, I leaned in at the same time, knocking the book to the floor. Then, I used a move I had learned from Kirk Cameron on *Growing Pains* and leaned down slowly to help her pick it up. Inch by inch, we rose all the way up and then locked eyes and stared at each other. Then, I mustered up the strength, thought of Bobby and his turtleneck-wearing audience volunteer, and leaned in to kiss the Newly Hot Hair Girl moving slowly and methodically, imagining she was not the girl whose baking soda volcano erupted first during a class science experiment but instead was a sexy black backup dancer for my generation's Elvis Presley. When I reached about one inch from her braceless face, she snapped, "What are you doing?" It was the exact same tone my brother used when he caught me snapping my pants and looking at my non-dick's reflection in the oven. I pulled away. Silence.

Sitting in my knock-off Benetton sweatshirt in my mint-green bedroom in suburban New Jersey, I became suddenly aware that I was no Tanya, and I certainly was no Bobby. I was not even a lesbian, and I was certainly not a tender Roni. I was just a lonely, confused, oversize little girl. I was a way-too-physically-advanced-for-her-age weirdo, and I had just added one more person to the list of people who considered me a freak. I had to save what little dignity I had left.

"What? What are you talking about? I'm just getting my book. Relax."

Relax? What a douchey thing to say to a girl I had just failed at mouth raping. If she hadn't pulled away, this would have been my first live sexual experience ever. The Newly Hot Hair Girl went in the other room and called her mom from our tan clunky telephone, begging her to take her home early.

She waited outside on the front bench for her ride all alone. She refused the cup of tea my mother offered her and wouldn't take a dry biscuit either. I watched from the window to make sure she got picked up okay. I didn't want to go down and wait with her; that would make matters worse. Plus, I'd have to face my mom and explain what was going on. I didn't want to have to tell the Queen of England that my new friend was leaving because I thought I was a lesbian because no one monitored my television intake and now I was a bit oversexed from too much Bobby Brown and too little Richard Marx. I thought it would be best to use the traditional British way of dealing with certain shameful things: ignore the situation, pretend everything is just fine, and never speak of it again.

Luckily the Newly Hot Hair Girl told no one at school. Or if she did, she was smart enough to tell only the mean girls who would whisper behind my back but never to my face. No one ever called me gay, and although the Newly Hot Hair Girl never volunteered to partner with me on school projects, she didn't treat me as if I had the plague either. She was just scared of me enough to not want to push my buttons. It was kind of exhilarating actually, to have someone a little frightened of me.

Regarding Bobby and his crew, I had no choice . . . I immediately broke it off with Tanya. My imaginary fling with the sexiest backup dancer who ever lived had died, for real, unlike Frisco on *General Hospital*. MTV took the "Roni" video out of rotation and replaced it with Neneh Cherry's "Buffalo Stance," which was a little too overproduced for my taste. There were way too many graphics and costume changes, and the cameras used to make that video definitely were not purchased at a garage sale like Bobby's. With "Roni" no longer on the air, I was forced to break up with Bobby as well.

And considering the way things turned out for Bobby, a widower's life of drugs, divorce, and a terrible reality show, I'm very thankful I got out of that "relationship" when I did.

CHAPTER 4

Big Plans to Do Good

By this time, I started to wonder whether I was going about life all wrong. Middle school was only a few months away and I looked like a flat-chested seventeen-year-old missing a few teeth. My two inane attempts at a premature love life—phone-dating a bank teller and living vicariously through Bobby Brown—had both horribly backfired. If I kept this up, I'd end up a gold-digging harlot by age thirteen, or worse. I could get teen pregnant or infected with AIDS—as I had heard could happen if one went down the wrong path.

My school was very big on educating students about the wrong path. We were subjected to terrifying assemblies where we were "scared straight" by former convicts and drug addicts. I heard all about the dangers of pot, smoking cigarettes, alcohol, and sex. Once my school even hired a haggard-looking guy to come in and tell seventy-five impressionable sixth graders about the time "I was so jacked up on heroin that I took out my own eye!" I didn't want to become a bad girl and end up taking out my own eye. Even though the guy seemed to have somehow gotten it back in just fine.

During my sixth-grade year in particular, my school was really on a tear to curb any sort of undesirable behavior. *The Simpsons* had recently started airing, and it really took off, causing every other kid in my school to don a T-shirt featuring Bart Simpson riding a skateboard/Homer Simpson eating a donut/Marge Simpson looking fabulous with her blue beehive hairdo. I didn't wear a *Simpsons* T-shirt, or want one. That would be *soooo* mainstream. I wanted to live on the outskirts of the social norms. I sported a lot of homemade blouses, made by my mom, instead. My mom was a fabulous seamstress, and I liked telling people I had "designed my own clothes," though in reality I had just picked out the fabric at the fabric store—usually the loudest prints possible—while my mom did the rest of the work. My homemade blouses fit my extra-long torso unlike store-bought shirts, which, due to my growth spurt, abruptly became more like Jessica Hahn–esque crop tops after about one wearing.

Also, I had actually never seen *The Simpsons*. My brother was always using the television to tape classic movies so he could log them into his massive document that I often caught him staring at with pride. I wasn't sure how many of these movies he actually watched, but just knowing he had them on tape was enough for Greg. Someday he would be free from chores and homework and sports practice and be able to watch every movie ever made, an ambition similar to my father's dream of one day finally using all those tiny soaps and shampoos he'd collected from business trips over the years. So, without ever seeing an episode of *The Simpsons* or owning any *Simpsons* attire, I was unaware of how the *Simpsons* were influencing my school. Until one day our principal, Mr. Luskavitch, a man who was at the very least ninety years old, came to pay our class a visit.

Mr. Luskavitch was a Russian immigrant with thick glasses and an even thicker accent. He seemed remarkably out of touch with

America's youth and an odd choice to be principal of such a young bunch. He wasn't an intimidating man, except for his weird fingers. I had a major fear of old people with strange fingers ever since a way-too-young viewing of the movie *Cloak & Dagger,* in which a gloved elderly woman accompanied by Dabney Coleman chloroforms a young boy and then removes her glove to reveal she has only three fingers. Three gross fingers and two stumps, to be exact. This image haunted me so much as a child that it took me literally years to recover. It manifested as a fear that every time I used the toilet, her three-fingered wrinkly hand would rise up through the basin and pull me in. (I wasn't too frightened of Dabney Coleman because I had also seen *Nine to Five* on TBS and knew he had broad range as an actor.) My phobia of the three-fingered woman developed into a temporary obsessive-compulsive disorder in which I had to flush the toilet, wash my hands, run to my room, hide under the covers, and then count to thirty in order to know I was completely safe from three-fingered murder via toilet. I performed this ritual religiously until I saw the movie *Cocoon,* which replaced all my fears of gloved senior citizens with a new fear of people removing their skin in the shower to reveal that they were truly aliens. It's been explained to me dozens of times that the aliens in *Cocoon* were "nice aliens," but to a little girl with a very active imagination and a pension for irrational fears, "nice aliens" are just as horrific as "shitbag aliens."

But I digress, back to Mr. Luskavitch. His fingers were totally creepy. On par with the *Cloak & Dagger* villain, but not quite as creepy as unzipping one's skin. Upon his visit to our class, he stood in front of the room and began his presentation.

"There is a very popular show on television right now, and most of you have heard of it. It's called *The Simpsons.*"

The class grumbled with excitement, thinking that maybe Mr. Luskavitch had taped a few episodes on his VCR and we'd be spending our math period laughing over Maggie's uptight demeanor versus Bart's joie de vivre.

Mr. Luskavitch continued, "Now, there are two main characters on the show, Bart and Lisa." He paused. I was pretty sure, judging by my schoolmates' T-shirts, that there were more than two main characters on the show, but it wasn't my place to nitpick, having never seen an episode and all. I loved how Mr. Luskavitch's Russian accent really hit the *t* on *Bart* and I didn't want to throw off his game.

"Now, everyone," he went on, "who do you think you should try to model your behavior after? Bart or Lisa?"

Everyone in my class called out "Bart" in a failed attempt at hilarity. Mr. Luskavitch didn't seem amused.

"Actually," Mr. Luskavitch said, with a stern voice, reminding us of the seriousness of the situation, "you should all try to be like Lisa. Do your work, don't talk back, engage in extracurricular activities, and obey your parents. Don't steal. Don't act up. Don't copy homework. Do good deeds. Don't be Barts. Be Lisas!" Then Mr. Luskavitch shook his crooked finger at all of us and left the room. He'd really nailed the presentation. Mr. Luskavitch left us wanting more.

As we all opened up our math textbooks, I could hear Mr. Luskavitch walk into the classroom next door and repeat his speech word for word: "There is a very popular show on television right now, most of you have heard of it. It's called *The Simpsons*."

Inspired by Mr. Luskavitch to be a Lisa and not a Bart, to do good in the world and make my parents and teachers proud, my next scheme was to become appreciated in my town by doing something good and getting oodles of attention for it. Maybe if I actually accomplished a good deed, grown-ups would have something else to make small talk with me about besides my height. I signed up to volunteer for an Earth Day beach cleanup at the scummy beach on the wrong side of the tracks. Instead of the usual "Wow, you get bigger and bigger every time I see you" from every family friend I encountered, they would say "I heard you saved a beached whale from the dangers of litter . . . amazing!"

Here, if ever, was an opportunity to paint myself a hero, to change my own destiny. Accompanying me were two boys from my school: a practically-out-of-the-closet fifth grader who loved to dance with scarves as much as I did and a bucktoothed problem child headed for juvie, whom I hovered over by at least four inches. It seemed odd that we three were the ones who volunteered for this. I wondered if the problem child was already doing community service for a secret crime he had committed. Maybe I was associating with a convict. How exciting!

The effeminate boy's presence also confused me. Was he just trying to give back to his community? Or was he maybe, just maybe, trying to get closer to me? I had heard that a lot of cool girls had gay BFFs and maybe he was looking for an in with me. Maybe this boy thought I was a worthy candidate for fun friendship.

Or maybe these guys were also moved by Mr. Luskavitch's motivational speech, and now they wanted to make sure they became Lisas, not Barts, too.

*   *   *   The beach cleanup was run by a nice, aging hippie, about my height. In my experience, most skinny adult women with long frizzy hair and high-pitched voices end up being first-grade teachers or working in a nature center. I had been pleasantly surprised when Amanda and I watched *Airplane!* together and saw Julie Hagerty, a skinny adult woman with lonely frizz for hair and a high-pitched voice, cast as the sexy female lead. This actress delivered her hilarious lines with a straight face, adding more to the humor of it all. She played the main stewardess, the one who had the *Saturday Night Fever* parody dance scene. If parody dancing was an actual career option, I wanted in. A career based on silly dancing could be just the perfect path for my lanky frame. Also, I loved how *Airplane!* played up the sexual tension between her and the hot, tan leading man. Someone someone would love me so much they would board a plane full of wacky passengers in an attempt to win me back. To add to my excitement, one of my father's cool New York City friends actually started dating Julie Hagerty. Although I requested her presence at both Thanksgiving and New Year's Eve, they sadly broke up before I got a chance to meet her. The kids at school were not impressed.

Thus I had a respect for Beach Cleanup Lady because I could imagine her exchanging campy dialogue with Leslie Nielsen. She was in charge of us, and even though we were on the wrong side of the tracks, she was going to keep us safe. This was the part of town where I had heard teenagers went to do bad stuff. The tail end of the '80s, heading into the '90s, was the perfect time to be a rebellious teen in Central Jersey. This was the side of town I imagined teenage girls wearing low-cut tank tops and ripped jeans came to smoke cigarettes and funnel beer. I didn't quite know why anyone would go to the trouble of drinking beer through a funnel when the can or bottle is especially designed for drinking, but to each his own.

Beach Cleanup Lady told us in that screechy voice, "Children, please clean up the best you can. But if you find *anything,* and I mean *anything* that makes you feel unsafe, call for me immediately. Just yell 'STOP!'"

With her shrill voice ringing in my ears, I began picking up the trash on the beach with tremendous effort, blowing past the short, slow-poke boys. I weaved in and out of sandy pieces of Hubba Bubba and bottle caps, looking for something dangerous so everyone would thank me for taking the offending object off our beach. Most likely the *Asbury Park Press* would run a front-page story on me: HULKING HEROINE SHORE TO PLEASE. No longer would Jon Bon Jovi be the pride and joy of our area. I would take over as being the most famous person ever to come from here. I would be revered for all eternity in the same fashion

Dr. Heimlich was. I too would be a lifesaver, and my name would be synonymous with making the world a safer place.

Then, suddenly, the bucktoothed problem child started screaming for help. I dropped my trash bag and ran awkwardly with the Beach Cleanup Lady to his aid.

"What's that?" I asked, staring down at a long glass pipe. It had a little bit of black soot around one part of it, giving it the look of some of my grandmother's glass Cartier collectables that she had placed too closely to her Manhattan windowsill. I always wanted to pick them up and give them a once-over with the bottom of my shirt, but I lived in constant fear of breaking anything. I had a knack for breaking only extremely valuable things, so I always felt it was best to simply leave the soot as-is on the Cartier lion sculpture.

Beach Cleanup Lady took a long, deep breath as a crowd gathered around. "Kids, I'm sorry to say, and I really hope it isn't, but this looks like something people use to smoke drugs. This is a crack pipe. It's what crackheads use to inhale their crack."

I was terrified. I didn't know people were smoking crack in my town. I thought all the people at the scared-straight school assemblies had been outsourced. Since when did we have crackheads? Why hadn't any of them been hired to speak at our school assemblies? Why weren't we properly utilizing our local resources? This was Earth Day, for goodness' sake! Bon Jovi and Bruce Springsteen never sang about crack!

Then again . . . maybe my hometown wasn't so boring after all. Instead of remaining frozen in fear, I got excited. I approached the rest of the beach cleanup more like a drug bust/archaeological dig. If I found a crack pipe, maybe I could present it during the next school assembly in the same way those cops a few weeks ago had shown us evidence from their drug busts. I'd stand before all my classmates in the cafetorium with the crack pipe prominently displayed in an unbreakable Lucite container and also projected onto a large screen so everyone could see what I had found. "You see, kids," I'd say, "we can make a difference in our community. I am tired of taking a backseat to crime. Remember, if you're not part of the solution, you're part of the problem." There would be a pause before uproarious applause, then a standing ovation, then a Q and A that would go into overtime and cut into everyone's recess. But no one would care, because they had the ear of the local hero. The person that just couldn't turn her back on local crime. I was no longer just the tallest girl in school. I was now the person who had made a difference. I would save our noble community from the dangers of hard drugs and litter all at once.

I searched the beach. I looked for something—anything—that people could possibly smoke crack out of. I found empty snack-size bags of Doritos, most likely discarded by some lucky kid whose mom let him eat that kind of stuff. I found used straws, Popsicle sticks, pennies, and even a few nickels. Then, after about a half hour of boring G-rated beachside findings, finally I landed on it! A plastic tube, about four inches long, was buried in the sand under a pile of fly-covered seaweed. It was caked with sand and sun-bleached, but it looked as if it was once a light shade of pink. It had a weird claw-like end to it on one side, and on the other it had some pretty ridges, apparently for traction. Jackpot.

"Stop! Everyone stop! I have found another crack pipe!"

The cleanup crew all froze in terror, as I stood up taller than ever, ready to be congratulated for saving the day. I couldn't wait to give a presentation on the dangers of beachside drug use at my school's next assembly. As our fearless leader walked over, I knew the damage I had caused to Paul the tiny bank teller and the Newly Hot Hair Girl I had nearly kissed would be washed away when I saved my town from the dangers of crack cocaine.

Beach Cleanup Lady held the plastic tube in her latex-gloved hand. She twisted and turned the tube, tapped the sand out of it, then held it up to the sunlight. It seemed she was verifying exactly what it was. Then she got a look on her face as if to say, *Aha, I know exactly what this is!* She smirked a little to herself, and being that there were no other grown-ups there to share whatever grown-up conclusion she had just come to, she launched into a seemingly forced performance, faking her ignorance.

"Hmm . . . I'm not sure what this is," she said. "I don't think it's for drugs. But I'm not sure, so I'll take it for now. To be safe."

She inspected the tube one more time for safety. "This could be very dangerous, Margot. Thanks for bringing it to my attention."

She put the thing in her plastic bag and everyone went back to cleaning up the beach. I knew she knew what it was. Why wasn't she telling us? Why did she let the bucktoothed kid get all the glory and leave me to the boring pennies and Doritos bags? I was devastated. I had wanted to be a hero, like the bucktoothed kid. He'd get to tell the story over and over of how he'd found the pipe. Was it so wrong to want attention for something noble, instead of my size? I didn't mind all eyes on me if it was to congratulate me for saving schoolchildren from the dangers of the white rock. Instead I felt like the girl who cried crack pipe.

I spent the rest of the cleanup dragging my feet and hanging out with the practically-out-of-the-closet-musical-theatre-loving kid. I don't think he was truly all that interested in making me his #1 BFF after all, but at least he was polite. I found a few Rolling Rock bottles, but I had seen my parents drink those at their wild New Year's Eve parties each year; they were nothing to get excited about.

The rest of the afternoon was just as uneventful, and I went home disappointed.

The next few times I hung out with Amanda, I refused to watch *Airplane!* and insisted we work on our homoerotic dance routines instead. Amanda liked *Airplane!* because her mom had it on VHS and it had real boobs. But I couldn't handle it anymore; the horrible letdown of the beach cleanup had made watching *Airplane!* with its Beach Cleanup Lady-esque female lead nothing but misery.

✱ ✱ ✱   A few months went by. Then, one day in school, I felt an unusual pain in my stomach. It was almost the end of the day, and I didn't want to go to the nurse's office because she always took my height and weight even if I just needed a Band-Aid. With stomach cramps like this, the last thing I needed was to learn that I had grown even one-quarter of an inch more since I had been there last week for a much-needed ice pack after hitting my head on the classroom bookshelf. I toughed it out until the end of the day and slowly walked home. When my mom came home about an hour after I did, she quickly deduced that I had gotten my period for the first time.

"You're lucky you didn't bleed all over your peach pants," my mom said. "I know this is difficult for you, Margot. Probably none of the other girls in your class have their periods yet, but I think you're more mature. Aren't you lucky to be tall?"

My mother, at five foot nine, was always reminding me how lucky I was to be tall. All her reasons were equally sucky—*You'll always look older than you are. You can wear men's pants! Shop in Big N Tall stores! No need for a stepladder!* But none were as sucky as pretending that it was a gift to get your period before your classmates. I sat in the wicker chair unable to hide my pout. My mom looked at me and said with compassion, "Well, sweetie, what do you want me to say?"

I suddenly realized that my mother, who had spent a lifetime crying over nonsense like season 6, episode 113 of *Laverne & Shirley*, didn't quite have the perfect recipe to make me feel better when something upset me. While I could quell my mom's tears by telling her that Laverne and Shirley would always be best friends at heart even though their lives were going in a new direction, my mom did not have quite the same knack for succinct, calming words of wisdom. Instead she kept trying her best, saying, "It's fine. You'll be fine, sweetie." She put the kettle on, as she always did at 4:00 PM, her all-American New Jersey version of high tea. Contrary to what various Maggie Smith characters had told her throughout the years, tea did not solve everything. My father had now been reduced to an all-hot-chocolate hot-drink diet in a protest against my mother's tea addiction. He was a little old to fake being allergic to tea, but I could tell he wished he could. When my dad's mother passed away, I had never seen so many used tea bags lying around the kitchen sink. My mother downed the tea like an Irishman downing whiskey at a wake.

The teakettle whistled, as she slowly and methodically prepared the black tea in her sterling silver Cartier teapot engraved with someone else's initials, another of the free castoffs we got from my grandmother's job. She looked over at me, her too-tall daughter sulking in peach pants at the kitchen table. "Well, is there anything I can do for you?"

I looked up, trying to discern whether she was being genuine. She seemed desperate to make me happy and I knew it. This was my window. What did I want? Ice cream? A Kaboodle? New pants? Then it hit me: I had seen ads on TV for 1-900 numbers and desperately wanted to call. After what happened with Paul and the phone-dating hotline, I had grown fearful of getting in too deep on the telephone. What if I called the New Kids on the Block 1-900 number and inadvertently seduced one of them using my Octopussy voice? The prospect was both thrilling and terrifying.

At the time, 1-900 numbers were the latest invention, and definitely one of the most high-tech. For only $4.95 a minute, you could call anyone from He-Man to Grandpa Munster, from Paula Abdul to hunky hair metal band Warrant. I wasn't sure how exactly they worked. Was Grandpa Munster just sitting around waiting for the phone to ring in full stage makeup and costume at all times? Were all five members of Warrant constantly together in case of a call, or was there some sort of high-tech hookup that could conference them all in? And how did He-Man speak directly to anyone, considering he was a cartoon? Thinking too much made my head want to explode. Calling and talking to a drawing seemed like a total rip-off, but calling and talking to a live band of hot guys seemed like a good investment of my mother's side money from her jewelry-making business. I had never been allowed to call one of these numbers before because of the price. And I could never sneak and call one because the tan clunky telephone was in my parents' bedroom, where my mother was often rearranging her stringed pearl collection.

But this was my chance; very rarely did I have my mother in a position where she actually felt sorry for me. She thought because I was tall like her that I truly had it all. But right now, in this moment, I had her in the palm of my hand.

"Well," I began in a soft, purposefully childlike voice, "I have always wanted to call the NKOTB hotline."

I was a fan of New Kids on the Block but not a superfan. There were girls in my class that had NKOTB curtains up in their bedrooms. That was taking it too far. I had ugly curtains with dainty old-fashioned ladies on them that my mother had sewn herself. As much as I hated those curtains, I thought they tied the room together a lot more than cloth patterned with images of Donnie Wahlberg. But I had been to one New Kids concert, where I was positive Joey McIntyre waved directly at me from the stage (probably because he could see my towering head over the crowd of normal-size girls), and I had also slipped a copy of Amanda and my Jersey Girls demo to a security guard to pass along to the New Kids' manager. If anything, a chance to chat on the 1-900 number would be a good networking opportunity and a way to follow up regarding our big-time music career that was just waiting to get off its feet.

The New Kids were older than me but not as much older as Grandpa Munster, so I figured my mother would have to say yes. And she'd be glad that I wasn't asking to call who I really deep down wanted to call . . . those bad, long-haired, leather-pants-wearing boys from

Warrant. She hesitated for a moment, stirring her tea, clanking the spoon against the walls of her bone china rose teacup from England.

"Fine, Margot. Just call it. Anything to wipe that puss off your face."

Wincing at the word *puss*, I thanked her and ran upstairs to my parents' bedroom so I could seduce a New Kid in privacy (after all, I was a woman now). I shut the door and dialed the number with shaky hands on our clunky tan telephone. As I dialed I debated whether or not to use the same approach I had used with Paul the tiny bank teller on the phone-dating service. I could give them all my relevant stats, just leave out my age, lack of boobs, mouthful of baby teeth, and current gross status of being on the rag.

It rang once, and before I could even take a deep breath and ask to speak with Jordan, then Donnie, then Jonathan, a recorded message from all five New Kids, including gross Danny, began to play. They kept using their song titles in their sentences, "Thanks for calling, 'We'll Be Loving You Forever.' You're our 'Cover Girl.' What, do you have to go so soon? 'Please Don't Go Girl.'" I slammed down the phone, completely disappointed. I knew I should have called 1-900-909-JEFF for the DJ Jazzy Jeff and the Fresh Prince hotline instead.

I was about to storm down the stairs when I made the bold choice to call Amanda and tell her my big news. Of course I'd pretend everything was fabulous. Getting my period was the one thing I had over her, even though it was painful and messy.

"Hey, Amanda, guess what? I'm a woman now, *if* you know what I mean. And my mom felt so bad she let me call the New Kids on the Block number!"

"No way," Amanda said.

"Oh yes. I spoke with Donnie Wahlberg for a while. Jordan couldn't come to the phone. He was recording in the studio." I chose to play up my second-favorite New Kid; that way it was more believable.

"Wow! I wish I got my period. You. Are. So. Lucky. NKOTB? For real?"

For once I was cooler than Amanda, even if it took a painful shedding of my uterine lining to accomplish it! I wanted the moment to last, but Mom was calling me from downstairs, so I told Amanda I'd talk to her later, and walked back to the kitchen for my first lesson on maxi pads and tampons. I found the last remaining unripped wicker chair and sat in it, leaning into the wooden table. I hoped my Girl Supplies 101 lesson would be slightly less traumatizing than that nightmare-inducing birthing video from health class. It would be impossible for this to be worse.

"Okay, Margot, as you know, this is a maxi pad," my mother said, daintily sliding a maxi pad across the kitchen table as if she were a hand model in a Lee Press-On Nails commercial. She seemed to really be enjoying this. My grandmother always had perfectly manicured long red nails so she could elegantly showcase the items she was selling at Cartier. She used to say the secret to keeping your nails long was "How you use them." My mother seemed to be using her medium-length nails with chipped beige nail polish to the absolute best of her ability while displaying this maxi pad. My grandmother would be so proud!

"*Aaand* . . . this is a tampon." She delicately removed the tampon from the wrapper, careful not to damage her two-week-old home manicure any further. "And this is the tampon applicator." She separated the tampon into two pieces. The applicator looked very familiar to me. My mom continued, "Some girls, older girls, prefer this to the pad. We'll worry about that later."

I looked at the applicator. It looked familiar. It was a four-inch-long plastic tube with a claw-like top and some ridges around the bottom . . . Hey! I knew where I'd seen one of these before! The beach cleanup! The poor man's *Airplane!* lady had duped me—that bitch! Beach Cleanup Lady was in her forties; she knew exactly what a tampon applicator was. Why did she think it would be more appropriate to suggest a tampon applicator might be a device used to smoke crack? Why did she pretend not to recognize it? Why couldn't she just pretend it was a crack pipe and let me have my moment for once in my life?

"That's a tampon?" I seethed.

"Yes."

"And that's a tampon applicator?"

"Margot, I just said that, yes."

"So why did the woman at the beach cleanup tell me she had 'absolutely no idea' what it was?"

"Well, maybe she was trying to protect you," my mother said, fiddling with a Carefree pantiliner wrapper.

"Protect me from what? Menstruation?" I was disgusted. "Can I go now?" I asked, desperate to get out of there before my mother busted out a birthing video from her private stash in the same manner my health teacher had sneak-attacked us. I slithered up the stairs to my room and opened up a pack of candy cigarettes, channeling my grandmother. I was sure that in her Manhattan neighborhood everyone was discussing tampons with great vigor and honesty. The highlight of my decade so far was calling the NKOTB 1-900 number as a result of getting my period. I really needed a fresh start. And worst of all, that bucktoothed kid had stolen all my glory with his golden-ticket crack pipe, while I made the world safe only for squeamish Jersey teenagers and perhaps a seagull or two.

I was done with being a little kid in an oversize body. I just wanted to be a true teenager, not a giant child. I wanted my equivalent of coming to America on the boat from England like my grandmother had. She must have been so inspired and excited for her totally new life in a new place filled with new opportunities. Maybe middle school would be that place for me.

CHAPTER 5:

Sticking Your Neck Out

I couldn't wait for this stupid time in my life to end. I had heard that teenagers were allowed to pick out their own outfits, and the wild ones got sent away to boarding school. If only. Getting my period was the first sign that I was becoming a teenager—my age was slowly matching my size. I couldn't wait to kiss troubled boys and have artistic happenings à la John and Yoko with the new kids in public regional middle school. I couldn't wait to feel normal. Hopefully seventh grade would be everything new and different I was waiting for.

Middle school began, and there were, in fact, many changes. No longer did I have to walk home from elementary school alone while mean Sharika Jackson yelled "Margot Fargo farts a lot" out the window of the school bus at me. I didn't even fart a lot. I did trip and fall down a lot, but I guess "Margot Fargo is really klutzy" didn't have the same zing.

Sharika was a heavyset girl with a huge personality. Despite her being in special-ed classes she was confident and popular. I don't know why Sharika Jackson had it out for me. She seemed like such a fun girl except when she was screaming at me out her bus window. During elementary school recess she would stand on the sidelines listening to her Walkman while the rest of us played stupid sports that I was constantly getting injured during, like kickball. Kickball was always a perfect opportunity for a ball to fly directly at my head, as it was always the highest target on the field.

One day, during a kickball game, our old Russian principal Mr. Luskavitch, or as Sharika called him, Mr. Luck-a-vitch, came out to observe. Sharika was busy listening to her En Vogue cassette tape as usual when she saw him across the field. She called across the kickball game, "Hey, hey! Mr. Luck-a-vitch!" He looked over at Sharika and waved. She continued, "Man, I love this song!" And then she began to serenade Mr. Luskavitch with En Vogue's biggest hit, "Hold On."

Her plus-size body swayed along with every lyric that she sang perfectly on key across the kickball field.

Ooh!
My first mistake was
I wanted too much time
I had to have him morning noon and ni-i-ight.

Mr. Luskavitch shook his crooked fingers in the air, dancing the best he could at his age to the music, and then called across the field, "You sing it, Sharika!"

"Thanks, Mr. Luck-a-vitch!" she shouted back as the rest of us played our boring game of kicking a stupid red ball around a dirt field. "God, I love this song!"

Mr. Luskavitch smiled and went back to the game, unembarrassed by being serenaded by a big-mouthed twelve-year-old girl. I was almost envious of Sharika and Mr. Luskavitch's friendship. They seemed kind of close. Why was she so fun-spirited with an old Russian man and so taunting of me? And why did Mr. Luskavitch allow her to listen to her Walkman at recess while the rest of us were forced to play dangerous kicking games?

That was last year. Now I took a bus home, too, and Sharika wouldn't be able to taunt me out the bus window about the made-up flatulence problem she was so kind to endow me with. I took a tiny bus, known as a "tart cart," driven by a nice obese woman named Randi. Randi liked to discuss the details of her impending divorce with us, and as the child of happily married parents, I really got into the juicy details of it all. Her ex seemed like a real scumbag, and I told Randi every morning that today would be the day he'd finally sign those divorce papers. When that day finally came, I was over the moon for Randi. Our morning discussions then moved to how she would bridge her way back into the singles scene after all these years. I had no idea what kind of singles scene my town offered, but if anyone could make it happen, it was Randi.

I loved my bus, and not just because the majority of its passengers were picked up in front of a bar. What type of school system sets up one of their early-morning bus stops in front of a bar? As the drunkest of the drunk would stumble out in the morning, Randi would pull up the extra-small bus to pick up the kids from that neighborhood just in time so they wouldn't have to interact with the alcoholic locals. I often wondered if Randi's ex was passed out somewhere in that local dive bar. The way she talked about him, I wouldn't be surprised. My bus may have been small, but it surely had character.

I loved it because it was filled with dangerous teenagers, like Craig Sandowski, who wore a Megadeth PEACE IS SELLING BUT NO ONE'S BUYING T-shirt and a fresh hickey to school every day. A few months into the school year, Craig Sandowski got expelled for putting an explosive device in a school toilet. I stand by Craig and believe him that his intentions were nothing major. He wasn't intending to blow up the school; he just wanted to make the toilet explode, and to cause a spectacle, which he did achieve. But the school didn't see it as a successful science experiment; instead they viewed it more as a death threat to students, teachers, and faculty, so they expelled him. I never saw Craig Sandowski again after the incident, so I mostly socialized with Randi and encouraged her to get back in the saddle. The bus wasn't the same without him.

Over the course of our first six months in middle school, Amanda and I drifted apart. There was no fallout, but our middle school was much larger than our elementary school—kids from four different elementary schools were combined into it—and that simply gave her more options for friends. To my chagrin, Amanda drifted naturally toward the normal-size girls who brought Lunchables to school. There was no room for a towering friend whose mom packed cream cheese sandwiches on pumpernickel. It didn't help that I had just discovered my father's record collection over the summer and was now eschewing the fashion and musical trends of my own generation. While most kids donned Hypercolor T-shirts and Starter jackets, I wore fringed vests and flared jeans.

My father, however, was thrilled. As a man who bought his entire wardrobe at Costco, he was overjoyed I was not becoming a slave to fashion. And as the ultimate music buff, my dad was incredibly pleased that someone was finally getting some use out of his formerly dust-collecting record collection. The only thing that would have made him happier would be if I actually started using the tiny soaps and shampoos from his business hotel complimentary toiletries collection. When my father told me all about the controversial protest methods during the Vietnam era, I wondered how he could be so happy stuck in the suburbs after doing something so supercool as barely escaping the draft. I had never heard of anything so dangerous and I wanted nothing more than to be transported back to his glamorous heyday of the '60s and '70s and escape the impending lameness of the Jersey Shore in the '90s.

At the start of the decade, on New Year's Eve, when the clock struck midnight, I had been at a grown-up party with my parents watching their friends get drunk. Too young to have my own plans that night, as my older brother had, and too old to be in bed, I was forced to hang out with the aging Rolling Rock swiggers as they rang in the '90s with great hope.

My mother came over to me right after the ball dropped and said, "This is going to be your decade, sweetie. Your '60s. You're going to fall in love, figure out what you want to be when you grow up, find out what you really care about, and take a stand. This is your time!"

Then she ran off to drink Bahama Mamas with her college roommate.

The grown-ups at this party all seemed elated at the promise of a new decade. The lavish '80s had not sat well with my parents' baby boomer friends, and they were optimistic for this new time. They weren't so keen on Reagan or the past decade's extravagant spending and excessive lifestyle. From a distance, to an overdeveloped tween in central New Jersey, the sluttiness of the '80s seemed pretty rockin' to me. But as the year played out and Wilson Phillips, Bell Biv DeVoe, and Nelson topped the charts, I wondered if this was, in fact, "my time." It seemed like a pretty stupid time to me and didn't hold a candle to my mom and dad's. Where was the war? Where was the good music and fashion? Bart Simpson was voted "Entertainer of the Year" by *Entertainment Weekly*. Not Bob Dylan, not Joni Mitchell, but a small, yellow, cartoon boy voiced by a woman was the entertainer of the year! And everyone was still wearing those stupid *Simpsons* T-shirts everywhere I turned. I resented that Jesus Jones was telling me "Right Here, Right Now," when there were *many* other places I would rather be. This was not my '60s. This was not my time.

The horrific nature of current music made me desperately in need of an artistic outlet. Thankfully, after much cadging, my mom did agree to upgrade my modern dance classes to more advanced sessions in the arty town of Red Bank, ten minutes away. The girls there weren't my types—they had names like Penelope and Theodosia, and although they were also tall, they wore their hair in buns so tight they were painful to look at—but my teacher, Julie, was a cool free spirit who was more into *feeling* the dance than being technically good. I wasn't technically good at anything, but I did have feelings. And I loved dance apparel in and out of the studio. To me, nothing looked hotter than a ballet skirt over jeans. So between "feeling the dance" and wearing footless tights, modern dance became my favorite hobby. It was the only true passion I had.

Back at home, I started isolating myself upstairs and rebelled against the cool-girl uniform of the time: Umbros (fluorescent long plastic shorts), Skidz (basically pajama pants with a road sign patch on the butt), and Z Cavaricci pants, of which the only thing sexy was the designer label right down the crotch. After each treacherous day at school, where I dodged hallway fistfights and buffered a daily dose of teasing for my '70s-inspired outfits, I'd enter my mint-green sanctuary, pull on leg warmers, and put on a little "Ziggy Stardust." I made mix tapes of my favorite classic rock songs off my father's record collection on the hand-me-down record/double cassette player from my grandmother. I cut out pictures of rock stars from vintage *Rolling Stone* magazines and hung them up on my metal closet doors with magnets, because I wasn't allowed to put tape on the walls. I wrote lyrics from the Doors, Lou Reed, Allman Brothers, and David Bowie songs on my door and all my notebooks. I hung inspiring quotes from cinema ("So be it," from *Pump Up the Volume* starring Christian Slater) and literature ("I belong! I am important! I am somebody!" from *Go Ask Alice*—my favorite book and an anthem for all misunderstood teens) on the inside of my closet. Mostly I'd sit up in my room and brood, then write in my journal, secretly hoping that one day it would be read and I'd be touted as literary genius in the way that lucky suicidal teen from *Go Ask Alice* had been. Other than dance, my dream was to be as famous a journal writer as Anne Frank, without having to endure the Holocaust.

At school, I flip-flopped among social circles, but none seemed to fit. Most girls wore Champion sweatshirts in bright orange and deep purple, while I wore my deceased aunt's vintage black velvet blazer. I was teased for wearing velvet during the warm-weather months but I just ignored it. No one in my town had any taste and for whatever reason I'd decided it was against my moral code to sell out for them. I did things my own way. Who says black velvet can't be worn after Memorial Day?

Eventually, I hit it off with a girl at my bus stop, which was, just my luck, *not* situated directly in front of a local dive bar. My bus stop was a boring old safe-neighborhood corner. Her name was Alyssa, and she had really big boobs. She lived in my neighborhood and I was grateful that she took a liking to me, though this was probably only because she was new to this school district and desperately needed a friendly face . . . that, and there was barely anyone else at our bus stop.

Because of her C-cup breasts, Alyssa was immediately popular at school, but she didn't care. Like me, Alyssa received attention for a physical trait, and while hers garnered flirtation from cute boys and mine inspired taunting from cute boys, we still had an instant connection. A few weeks after I befriended her, she invited me one Sunday afternoon to true popular girl Jessica Rosenstein's bedroom. Jessica Rosenstein was popular for doing all things right, like knowing how to fold her notes in the most complicated folds that were impossible to ever fold back. There, in Jessica Rosenstein's domain, I was surrounded by gum-smacking, fake-nail-wearing teenage girls, and they didn't look pleased to see me. (The only gum I ever had was packs of my mom's Violet gum, a purple gum scented like floral perfume that tasted exactly like hand lotion. She'd moved on to that after our local drugstore discontinued her beloved Clorets.) As Jessica Rosenstein's four-foot-ten mom looked up at me, showed us to Jessica's room, and said, "Have fun, ladies!" I tried my best to hide behind Alyssa and her huge rack. But all eyes were on me, the oddly dressed, flat-chested tall girl, and it took everything I had not to take my five-foot-eight-inch lanky body and run gracelessly through the streets of Jersey. I knew immediately this wasn't going to be a fun afternoon. As I scanned the room, taking in Jessica Rosenstein's Bell Biv DeVoe cassette tapes and massive lip-gloss collection, I wished I had chosen to stay home and hang out with my parents' weird Trivial Pursuit league instead. I fiddled with my vintage brooch as Alyssa introduced me to eye rolls and confidently joined the group.

I didn't want to be at Jessica Rosenstein's house; I would much rather have been writing depressed musings about how alone I felt in my cat journal. Jessica Rosenstein, on the other hand, lived for awkward teenage activities like this, things like school dances, sleepovers, and Bar Mitzvahs. She loved having braces, she loved going through puberty, and she loved the ubiquitous cologne Drakkar (which I'd learned I was allergic to after sitting next to the football coach's son on a long bus ride. Thank God Drakkar didn't make a chewing gum, because my mom probably would have bought it in bulk at Costco).

After a few minutes of discussing Clearasil versus Noxzema, Jessica Rosenstein introduced to her rapt audience what may have been the cruelest game ever. I don't know who invented it, or what it's called, or if it was really even a game, though I imagine it's familiar to mean girls everywhere. The game went something like this. Jessica Rosenstein said in her Valley Girl/Jersey accent, "Okay, let's all sit in a circle and say what we *honestly* think of each other. I mean *honestly*, girls. Like, don't hold back. This is our opportunity to tell each other what we really think, you know, to help each other."

I knew this was a bad idea. I had nothing in common with these descendants of the White Lipstick Posse—a clique of teenage girls who hung out at the neighborhood swim club wearing zinc oxide as a lipstick. These girls were younger sisters of those teenagers; I was the younger sister of a wiry-haired, movie-loving bookworm of a brother. I shouldn't have even been at this get-together. I was just tagging along with Alyssa. I wasn't sure if Alyssa had ever played a game like this in her old school as she sat there stoically. My guess is she was trying to remain as invisible as she could despite her good looks, so they wouldn't choose her. Alyssa was so cool the smell of fear could not be detected through her just-tight-enough tank top. Her strategy worked.

Instead, of course they began with me.

"Margot, you could be the prettiest girl in school if only you dressed normal," said Jessica Rosenstein through hot-pink braces and Dr Pepper lip gloss. "I mean you're tall like a model, you have reddish blonde hair, blue eyes. Sure, you have gross freckles, but you could cover those up if you learned how to use makeup. Guys would love you if you dressed like a normal human being and not some freakazoid."

This wasn't fair. When you're tall, no pants fit right. I wanted to tell Jessica Rosenstein that I would look like a freakazoid no matter what. In order for pants to be long enough, you have to buy a large size, which makes you look frumpy. If you don't want them baggy, you have to buy a smaller size, which would be too short, making you look like Michael Jackson in the "Billie Jean" video. And no shirt looks hot on an extra-long, flat-chested torso. So I wore vintage clothes, yes, partially because I believed I was born in the wrong time period and would have preferred an era when flat, lanky bohemian women like Joni Mitchell were the standard of beauty. But I also wore vintage clothes because poet's blouses and bell-bottoms were extremely flattering to my shape; I immediately wanted to defend my '70s-inspired, androgynous rock 'n' roll ensemble. Somewhere there was a world where people agreed that thirteen-year-old girls looked wonderful dressed like Eric Clapton. Unfortunately that world existed several decades back.

Jessica Rosenstein continued, "Girls, do you even know what I mean? Margot's *kind of* pretty, right?"

The gum-smackers nodded reluctantly. They most certainly did not agree that I was "kind of pretty," but they knew their intervention could be next.

"But, like, where do you get your clothes? Why do you make yourself look like that? Just like get some Cavariccis, get some Skidz, and get with the program. You could even have a boyfriend."

I was at a loss for words. No one spoke and my heart started racing. I wanted to have a Spencer Tracy *Inherit the Wind* moment when I discussed tolerance and justice and made a room full of ignorant people do the right thing. Yet I knew giving an overdramatic speech would make the next few years of middle school even more unpleasant than they already were. But still. Jessica Rosenstein didn't have a boyfriend; why was she giving me advice as to how to get one? A boyfriend wasn't a priority for me in seventh grade. I had only three goals at that point in my life: I wanted to rock, I wanted to stop growing, and I wanted to get the hell out of New Jersey. I was going to be a brilliant singer/actor/dancer/fashion designer in some faraway utopia I hadn't discovered yet.

Even though Alyssa, my big-boobed neighbor, was a fun girl, I didn't need these girls' approval. As soon as they were done "helping me" and moved on to the next victim, Alyssa and I made up an excuse to leave and headed back to our neighborhood to listen to White Lion and shave our legs.

I opted out of the next few White Lipstick Posse group activities.

Luckily for me, Jessica Rosenstein was wrong, as there was one boy in my town who seemed to truly appreciate me in all my towering corduroy glory (aside from the Ecuadorian immigrant with a man-perm who had started writing me love notes in seventh grade). Jonah Hertzberg was the only guy in my entire middle school who shared my passion for classic rock. He was kind of cute, too, if you found Joe Perry from Aerosmith attractive, which I totally did. Joe Perry was a great Keith Richards to Steven Tyler's Mick Jagger. He was all right in the background to a point but also had his own following, appeal, and story to tell. This was the year that Aerosmith's power ballad "What It Takes" hit the charts (which is still my go-to karaoke song to this day), which really added to Jonah Hertzberg's appeal. "What It Takes" helped me understand that hard rockers also had a soft side, and that made me love them even more. Hearing long-haired recovering drug addicts sing about broken hearts was almost as exciting to me as Bobby Brown's "Roni" video. I couldn't help finding every hard rock/hair metal star sexy—living in the town next to where Bon Jovi grew up, and the town above the town where Skid Row was from, it came with the territory. Jonah Hertzberg also felt misunderstood and misplaced in the wrong era and wrong town. He was not troubled by the fact that I was five inches taller than he, so I decided to let it go that he was missing a finger. So what if the only guy who liked me had only four fingers on his left hand? He could still play guitar, and knew how to French kiss, and that was really all that mattered.

I was seeing Jonah here and there outside of school, but during school, I tried to keep to myself. I didn't need the White Lipstick Posse telling me that I could do better if only I dressed "normal." While I watched the other kids write I WANNA SEX YOU UP on their binders, I would think to myself, *This is a stupid era*, while drawing I ♡ LOU REED on my notebook. I fantasized about going back in time and having front-row seats to the Band's *The Last Waltz* concert.

Partway though seventh grade, though, something happened that gave me hope. A war. The Persian Gulf War. Finally there was something to give us a reason to protest and make meaningful music. Finally, my fashion choices made sense! I was excited to go to my generation's Woodstock, to be one of the willowy flower girls, and to begin experimenting with hallucinogens. Finally I would have something to talk about with my parents' cool former hippie friends. Now we were equal; we had all been through the tragedy of conflict. Except my war had trading cards with images of Saddam Hussein, George H.W. Bush, Colin Powell, and "Stormin'" Norman Schwarzkopf alongside a stick of stale, pink, sugary gum.

Jonah Hertzberg was already composing antiwar ballads and I was interested in organizing a walkout like the one I'd seen on *The Wonder Years*. Music instantly improved. Yoko Ono had made a remake of "Give Peace a Chance" featuring all the biggest names of the time: LL Cool J; Kadeem Hardison, who played Dwayne Wayne on *A Different World*; Flea from the Red Hot Chili Peppers; Lenny Kravitz; and, best of all, Sebastian Bach of Skid Row. I had fantasies about running my fingers through Sebastian Bach's long, flowing mane, which was pretty narcissistic, considering we had similar hair. Despite my proximity to Skid Row's hometown, the best my town had to offer was Jonah Hertzberg, the wiry-haired Jew who looked like Joe Perry from Aerosmith, if you squinted hard enough.

However, this remake of "Give Peace a Chance" gave me hope. I'd always felt a kinship with John Lennon, not only because he was from Liverpool like my grandmother, but also because our birthdays were one day apart. I had always wished I had been born a day earlier and shared a birthday with an icon of peace and music. Instead, I shared a birthday with David Lee Roth and *Saved by the Bell* star Mario Lopez. Whatever . . . at least I didn't share a birthday with Screech. Now instead of wearing out my father's John Lennon records, I could maintain a vigil on MTV until they played this groundbreaking song. Sebastian Bach sang the best part, of course. Sandwiched between Cyndi Lauper and Randy Newman, he got to wail the line *Amazon trees gone* in an inhumanly high pitch that made me feel alive in a place only Jonah Hertzberg and Bobby Brown had aroused.

One day, during lunch, the popular, hot boys were all sitting at the table behind me eating school pizza. Pretending to read my history textbook while poking at my hard-boiled egg and tuna sandwich,

I overheard Chad Decker ask his dumb-faced friends, "Have you heard this new song 'Give Peace a Chance'?" Chad was the most popular boy in school, but not for being particularly athletic, or smart, or even interesting for that matter. He just had an abundance of Champion sweatshirts and really nice eyes. I really wanted to correct him that it was not "new" and that he was a complete moron, but I decided to hunch over my hard-boiled egg and play cool.

"Yeah, the song is like, 'all we are saying is give peace a chance, whoooooo,' or something like that. You may not have heard it yet," said one of Chad Decker's nameless peons.

Chad Decker and his crew were so clueless and so off-key that suddenly I just had to show them how it was done. This could be the big antiwar protest I had fantasized about! Starting a "Give Peace a Chance" sing-along could be my version of a *Wonder Years* walkout. And I could school these dipshits in real music while I was at it.

I felt a force take over me. My body couldn't control itself. I had to stand up and sing, showing Chad and his boys how it was done. Maybe if I sang loudly enough, I could send out a force to help end the war. My singing would definitely cause more of an impact than those mainstream yellow ribbons everyone seemed to be donning. I was going to go for it.

I lifted up my lanky five-foot-eight-inch frame, closed my eyes, and wailed with every ounce of pent-up rock star inside of me, *"Everybody's talkin' 'bout Amazon trees gone, Middle East crazy beast rock 'n' rollers sing for peace."* I paused a moment, hoping everyone would join in, then continued, even louder on the chorus, making sure all heard me. *"All we are saying is give peace a chance!"*

A deafening silence followed my unannounced solo, rather than the group refrain I had hoped for. I opened my eyes to see that the entire cafeteria had stopped eating and was staring right at me, braces-filled mouths hanging open. I could feel the eyes of cool dudes trying to penetrate through my vintage black blazer. This was not Woodstock; this was not *The Last Waltz*; this was middle school. And apparently in my middle school, there was no room for a hulking androgynously dressed seventh-grade girl born twenty years too late. The cafeteria had previously gotten silent only when fistfights broke out. That was always scary. However, the silence my solo summoned was truly horrifying on a whole other level. Students in line for hot lunch froze holding their Styrofoam trays, janitors stopped sweeping, cool girls stopped gossiping, nerds stopped fishing through the garbage bins for their accidentally discarded retainers.

I sat back down quickly, my cheeks on fire. What was I thinking? I was *never* going to get over this. My lame cafeteria protest was probably going to be featured next to my name in the middle school yearbook. No . . . my high school yearbook. I just knew people would still be talking about this years from now. Jonah Hertzberg would hear of it by next period and stop sneaking out to French-kiss me in the vacant lot. He'd ditch me to sneak out with one of Jessica Rosenstein's clan and forget all about the antiestablishment force we had been together. Alyssa would officially join the White Lipstick Posse and abandon me. She'd stand with me at the bus stop each morning and pretend I didn't exist. And my father would hide his records from me, calling me "a disgrace to a beautiful era." This was the beginning of my demise into a hopeless, small-town loser. It was the most humiliating moment of my life.

Everyone immediately moved away from me. It was so silent that when I crunched on my carrot sticks, I swear it echoed. The cafeteria aides gathered in a corner whispering and pointing at me. Jessica Rosenstein's fashion intervention was a cakewalk compared to this. I looked around for a friendly face, but instead the silence became laughter, then conversation—about what a doofus I was for singing.

For the rest of the day, the cool guys talked to me every chance they could. "I heard you were a great singer, can I get a private solo?"

Chad Decker approached me at my locker. "Come on, Maggot, let's have a sing-along."

This was the only time these guys ever talked to me for the entirety of middle school. I had wanted their attention for having cool taste in music, not for being a horrendously awkward cafeteria soloist. There was no way I could ever return to school after this day. There is nowhere to hide when you're the tallest girl in school and you're dressed like a rejected member of Jefferson Airplane. My parents couldn't afford to send me to private school, though—this dungeon was my only option. That, or I would have to drop out of seventh grade and get a job as a Friendly's waitress, serving overpriced ice cream to these assholes for the rest of my life.

The next morning I pulled every trick Ferris Bueller had taught to convince my mom that I was too sick for school. I stayed home that day, listening to my father's records, and prayed my unfortunate fifteen minutes of infamy would be over fast.

CHAPTER 6:

Leak-Out Pregnancy

Two days after my horrifying one-person Gulf War cafeteria protest, I went back to school. My mental health day was quite enjoyable. I found a bunch of great albums in my dad's record cabinet—the Doors, Led Zeppelin, the Allman Brothers, Santana. I had my own classic-rock soundtrack as I ate lunch alone at our kitchen table and used all my brainpower to stop reliving the Gulf War solo protest over and over in my head. But alas, my vacay was not open-ended.

When I returned to school, Chad Decker and the other cruel popular boys tried to hang on to torturing me about it, but like color-changing, touch-sensitive Hypercolor T-shirts, the incident quickly faded. Besides, the war ended, before many of the baseball hats, bumper stickers, and trading cards commemorating it had even been mass-marketed. I thought it was strange to have fun wartime mementos like trading cards. Albeit brief, it was still a war, after all. And I had nowhere near the same passion to trade these stupid cards with American eagles and yellow ribbons on them as I had for the Garbage Pail Kids of my younger years.

Thankfully, the hallway discussions soon moved from what a horrible singer I was to how my classmate, B-student Teresa Carimonico, had not "gone to study abroad" but instead had a baby. It *had* seemed strange to me that Teresa was studying "abroad" yet no one knew exactly what country she had taken off to. And we were all wondering where she had gotten the money for her vague, possibly European semester away. Now it all made sense. I guess those elementary school assemblies had not properly scared her straight. My cafeteria solo abruptly became ancient history. While this was a lucky break, Teresa Carimonico's story terrified me, as I had been sneaking out on a more regular basis to the vacant lot down the street to make out and play guitar with Jonah Hertzberg. Jonah Hertzberg was amazing at guitar even though he was missing a finger. I sucked at guitar, even with a full set of fingers, and used it more as an accessory.

Surprisingly, even my make-out sessions with Jonah Hertzberg had lasted longer than the Gulf War. And still no one in school knew about us. It was for the best. We were just two weird kids born in the wrong era who had found each other. The Gulf War ended way too soon for our big plans to pen protest songs and there was no time for us to write a hit antiwar ballad in the style of John and Yoko. War *was* over. It didn't matter if we wanted it. So instead we did what we knew best—we snuck down to the vacant lot and made out and turned our discussions toward music, with frequent arguments over who was the superior guitarist: Eddie Van Halen or Eric Clapton. I voted for Eric Clapton, not because I truly knew he was better, but because my father had a lot of his records and I really admired his fashion sense. And he was hot. I didn't care that Eric Clapton was old and damaged from years of cocaine use and not cool for young girls in the early '90s to like. What were my contemporary alternatives? Was I supposed to pine over Milli Vanilli? *Puh-leese.*

I'll take an old man with a coke problem and a suede jacket anytime over some phony-baloney pop stars. Gross.

Meanwhile, the girls in school were moving forward with boys pretty quickly. They all seemed to pair off with boyfriends and many were doing things like going to second base, and even sloppy second base (where the boy touches the girl's boob with his mouth). This sex act seemed remarkably close to breast-feeding, a stage in parenting that my mother always publicly referred to as "one of the happiest times of her life." The thought of Jonah Hertzberg suckling my nonexistent boob gave me about the same level of sexual excitement as the birthing video I had averted my eyes from in health class.

I was too busy for sloppy second base anyway. I was now learning both the major and minor chords on the guitar, studying modern dance, and modeling my outfits after Stevie Nicks. No one's mouth was anywhere near my boobs, even though, thanks to my height, my barely boobs landed at most boys' mouth level.

One day, I managed to get invited to an all-girls afternoon hangout at the house of the Newly Hot Hair Girl, the one I had traumatized by making a move on during my Bobby Brown phase. Time had passed and she either had forgiven me for the incident or had been so horrified that she had blocked it out the way my health teacher told us most mothers forget childbirth. Nevertheless, my invites were few and far between, so I decided to go, even though I wouldn't have any close friends there.

When I got to the Newly Hot Hair Girl's house, she and her friends were in her wood-paneled den. Newly Hot Hair Girl's den was a cool addition that was constructed onto the back end of her Cape Cod–style house. I walked in, trying to take in the room, only to interrupt a conversation discussing bra sizes. This was not my idea of a good time, but I plopped down on the shag carpet anyway, attempting to make the best of the invite-only social hour. I suspected the bra-size discussion was really some sort of bizarre competition and I definitely lost. My bra size in proportion to my height definitely worked out mathematically to a humongous loss. I was built like Popeye's girlfriend Olive Oyl, who was not considered a sex symbol in any culture, time period, or universe. I was getting antsy when finally the conversation shifted from bra sizes to music. The Newly Hot Hair Girl put on some cassette singles, starting with FireHouse's "Love of a Lifetime." This poor man's rock ballad was a huge hit among these girls. They all gasped and screamed at the song choice, looking around the room for approval with each girly whimper. And they all sang along:

I finally found the love of lifetime.
A love to last my whole life through.

I hated this pitch-it-down-the-middle style of rock, but I looked in amazement around the room as these girls tried their best to make themselves cry. I could tell by their excessive blinking and subtle pulling on their eyelids that they each coveted the attention that tearing up while singing along to FireHouse would surely beckon. To my delight, no one succeeded. Too bad no one thought to go as far as to pull out a nose hair to force tears to fall. The best anyone achieved was Nancy, who rubbed her eye so much to induce tears that she now looked as if she had contracted conjunctivitis. The song stopped with a loud snap as the cassette single ran out of tape. Silence. All the girls tried their best to look as if they were really "taking in the moment," the way I imagined people looked at each other after a massive chant at some pretentious retreat where clueless rich people went to "find themselves."

"So, I thought we could go around the room and say who our love of a lifetime is," said the Newly Hot Hair Girl. What was up with these girls always wanting to go around the room saying stuff? I'd been awake way past my bedtime at enough of my parents' grown-up parties to see that they never stopped partying to go around the room taking polls on the "most successful appetizer at the gathering" or "who was their most influential historical figure." They were too busy drinking Rolling Rocks and having actual organic conversations. I definitely did not want to go around the room and declare who my love of a lifetime was. I was thirteen. Hopefully I had not yet encountered the love of my lifetime yet, because it was slim pickins at Matawan Regional Middle School. But much to my chagrin, all the guests at this lame-o party seemed enthused at the idea. I could see the wheels spinning as they began nervously brainstorming their list of possible loves of a lifetime. I fiddled with the fringe on my leather belt, hoping no one would notice me, again cursing my stature and knowing that it would be impossible to go unnoticed.

"Jessica, who's your love of a lifetime?"

"Oh, definitely Chad Decker," said Jessica Rosenstein through fluorescent-pink braces. "Except he doesn't know it yet." The girls all laughed. Jessica Rosenstein was killing it! She didn't have a boyfriend, so she thought outside the box. Wow. Nailed that one. What was I going to say when they came to me? I couldn't say Jonah Hertzberg, despite the fact that we were fully fledged members of the frequent-Frenchers club. No one knew about us, and that's what was exciting about it. And he wasn't my love of a lifetime anyway; we didn't even acknowledge each other in the school hallways. Ugh. *Please pick me last. I need some time here.*

"Nancy, who's your love of a lifetime?"

Oh good. Nancy. Nancy had an actual boyfriend. She wasn't secretly sneaking out to make out with him in the dark; Nancy actually held hands in the hallway with her boyfriend and stuff. This was true love. "Chris of course. He is totally my love of a lifetime. We're going to get married."

All the girls oohed and aahed at this, completely on board with Nancy's lifelong commitment to Chris, a thirteen-year-old guy who wore nothing but soccer T-shirts. Then, with the sharpness of a businesswoman conducting a job interview, Nancy turned to me, made severe eye contact, and said, "Who's your love of a lifetime, Margot?"

No! Not me! Why did I have to go next? I hadn't had time yet to aptly prepare a witty response! All perfectly lined eyes were on me. I looked at the wood-paneled walls for inspiration. Nothing. Blank. Silence.

I had no idea what to say. I didn't have enough time to concoct a lie. I turned back to Nancy and said with defeat, "I don't have a love of a lifetime."

Gasps came from the crowd of Electric Youth perfume–doused teens. What? How could that be? How could I already be thirteen and have not yet found my love of a lifetime? I was a shriveled-up old maid with an A cup and a mouthful of baby teeth. I fiddled with the peacock feather earrings my mom had let me borrow for the occasion as long as I "didn't destroy them." I sat stoically, refusing to call on the next girl and potentially humiliate her by asking her who her love of a lifetime was.

The party had hit a low point thanks to me, when finally the Newly Hot Hair Girl said, "Are we ready for the next song?" We were desperate to change the mood and we all agreed that the best thing to do would be to put on the cassette single for Extreme's "More Than Words." Everyone was so busy singing along that no one noticed me sitting in silence, desperate to get home where I had unlimited access to real rock 'n' roll and where no one questioned the fact that I had yet to meet "the one."

These girls were really not for me. They just didn't get it. I'd rather spend my spare time in modern dance classes and learning to play guitar with Jonah. And their Electric Youth perfume smelled to me like a strawberry-scented pine tree car air freshener. I didn't want that wussy smell rubbing off on me. I longed to be allowed to wear Nag Champa organic body spray, something I had seen once in a hippie store and that seemed like a "woman's scent."

And don't forget, I had a secret lover, and nothing was more exciting or illicit at the time. I was having much more fun with Jonah

Hertzberg anyway. After our jam sessions, we would make out and our bodies would get really close. I had felt something move down there, though only through clothes, and was constantly worried that something would *leak out* of him. I often wondered, while Jonah Hertzberg's denim-clad groin rubbed up against mine, did my pregnant classmate Teresa Carimonico actually have intercourse? Because according to our health classes, you didn't need to have sex to get pregnant. Our super-intense health teachers had told us a toilet seat, heavy petting, and dry humping could impregnate you. I had no choice but to believe them. And after that all-too-vivid birthing video, I certainly did not want to fall victim to pregnancy via toilet seat, or any other method for that matter.

The week of Newly Hot Hair Girl's party, I was aware that my period was a little late, but the constant chatter of Teresa Carimonico's situation made me take it a little more seriously. The next day, I turned to the free cat wall calendar I had gotten from the local Chinese restaurant and counted off, only to discover that my period was in fact a whole two weeks late. Two weeks! Never mind the fact that I'd never even seen a man naked besides that awkward time I went to see *The Crying Game* with my parents. Never mind the fact that I'd never gone beyond second base *above* the shirt. Never mind all of that; I was thirteen; I was two weeks late with my period; I was a whore.

For nearly a month I carried this weight around. I was sure I was pregnant with Jonah Hertzberg's baby. What other possible explanation could there be? Our bodies were so close when we made out, something could have leaked out. Recently, in the dark, Jonah Hertzberg couldn't see so well and he accidentally Frenched my cheek. Could the angle have affected things? He was a few inches shorter, giving his penis room to stick straight up through his jeans, which fell directly below my crotch. Had I been wearing thick-enough pants to every make-out session? Corduroy would probably have prevented any leakage, but what about my new velvet leggings? Granted, velvet is one of the thickest fabrics aside from burlap, but leggings really bring out your crotch.

I was totally screwed. I had to tell someone . . . but who? The girls from the horrible "Love of a Lifetime" circle were not to be trusted. My parents weren't even an option; we weren't *that* kind of family. We didn't have free-spirited, anything-goes conversations about our sexual journeys while passing around a rain stick. My brother, Greg, was too busy remaking Tim Burton films into his own creations, such as *Gregory Egg-Whisk Hands*. Jonah was a no—I wanted to keep my cool image with the only person who actually thought I was cool.

Finally, I came up with someone I could tell. The only person who wouldn't judge me. I could tell Alyssa, my big-boobed friend up the block. She'd know where I could get a cheap back-alley abortion with the money I'd saved from babysitting those wretched twin girls down the street.

I picked up the tan clunky telephone in my parents' bedroom to call her. I had asked repeatedly for my own line but my parents refused to cave. I had then started begging for a phone in my room, maybe a cute multicolored one like they gave out as consolation prizes on *Double Dare*, but alas, there was no phone jack in there. When I asked them to upgrade to a cordless so I could bring the phone into my room, they told me that the tan phone worked just fine and there was no need to replace it. So I was reduced to hiding in their bedroom whenever one of them wasn't lying in bed doing a *New York Times* crossword puzzle, knowing I could be walked in on at any moment.

I began to dial Alyssa's number, which I had committed to memory the second she gave it to me the first day of middle school while waiting for Randi at the bus stop. Then I remembered it was Saturday. The Sabbath! Shit! It was *Shabbos*, the Jewish day of rest. On Saturdays, Alyssa's family didn't use the phone or TV or drive or cook. Sometimes they would slip me some cash to come over and use their electrical appliances to make their dinners. I loved those nights. Being made to feel magical by simply turning on an oven was just the ego boost I needed at that point in my life. Though some would have viewed this as sacrilegious, I saw it as a great way to make a dime while hanging out with Alyssa. It certainly beat babysitting those bratty twins who wanted to watch *Look Who's Talking* every single time I came over. I'll take turning on a Jewish oven and dishwasher anytime over rewatching forced sexual tension between two puffy Scientologists.

I had no choice but to walk to Alyssa's house. The seven-minute walk felt as long as that fateful viewing of *The Crying Game* with my folks. As I knocked on Alyssa's door I thought to myself, *Please be home, I have to take care of this soon, the fetus is growing inside of me, I can feel it.* My fist trembled as I knocked, intentionally not using the doorbell in order not to show off my unlimited electrical rights during Shabbos. Lucky for me, Alyssa answered the door wearing a tight black T-shirt that hugged her C-cup boobs just so. "Can I come in?" I asked, my heart racing.

"Sure!" she said, smiling at me with those perfect teeth that didn't even require braces. She must have been relieved, I'm sure, to have a visitor from the outside world of electricity users. Shabbos always had a laissez-faire connotation to me, so I was relieved I wasn't crossing any religious boundaries by popping in during the day of the Sabbath. We sat down on the couch; I looked around for any family members lurking, then mustered all my strength to confess to her my deep, dark, dirty secret.

"Alyssa, I think I'm pregnant. I French-kissed Jonah Hertzberg in the vacant lot last month and I haven't gotten my period since. Our bodies were really close. Something could have leaked out. I'm sure I am. A woman *knows*."

Alyssa took a moment, soaked in the bomb that was just dropped, and assessed the situation. Jonah Hertzberg and I were hardly boyfriend and girlfriend; we were just two people nostalgic for a time we never experienced firsthand who liked to make out with each other. Alyssa now had to process the hot gossip that I had been making out with Jonah Hertzberg on a regular basis, *and* that I was with child. It seemed like an eternity as I sat there waiting for advice from the neighborhood sexual guru.

She let out a big sigh and then finally gave a verdict. "Well, it sounds to me like you're definitely pregnant. What you need to do is call the 1-800 number on the back of your box of Tampax and they'll tell you where to go to take care of it."

"You mean you don't know where to go?"

"No," she said, "but the ladies at Tampax will. I'm sure of it, that's why they have the number on the box. Everyone knows that. Are you going to tell Jonah?"

"I don't know, I'm not sure, I'm trying to keep him out of it, I don't want to freak him out."

"Good idea," said the object of every seventh-grade boy's sexual fantasy. "Try to remain cool with Jonah."

I left Alyssa's house and walked home, feeling my unborn child grow within me with each nervous step, sure that I was the most fertile kid in town (aside from Teresa Carimonico). At home I frantically pawed through the linen closet, searching for a box of Tampax, tiny soaps and mini shampoos flying everywhere. I never understood why my dad hoarded them if he never intended to use them. Whenever I asked, he would just say, "Someday." I felt using the soaps was a very attainable dream, but to my dismay, he never went for it. I occasionally used them, but the tiny size of the soap only made my body feel larger, like a giant in a dollhouse. I wondered if this was why no one else in my Amazonian family ever used them.

Finally, behind a universe of tiny lotions and various Ramada Inn soaps I found one box of Tampax Supers. Gross. Supers were for ladies with larger-than-average vaginas, which was the direction mine was heading if I ended up giving birth to Jonah Hertzberg's baby. I never wanted to be caught with a Super, feeding the stereotype that tall girls have big vaginas, as stupid Chad Decker had said on more than one occasion.

I found the 1-800 number on the back, snuck into my parents' bedroom, closed the door, and dialed the tan, clunky telephone. A nice operator lady picked up the call right away.

Panic-stricken, I summoned the courage to blurt out, "Can you please help me? I'm thirteen years old, my period is two weeks late, and just one month ago I made out with Jonah Hertzberg and our bodies were really close. Something must have leaked out; I'm pregnant, right?"

Silence.

I worried that the Tampax lady, like Alyssa, might have similar concerns regarding my social standing, so I said, "Don't worry, I haven't told Jonah."

"Well, did you actually have sex with this Jonah?" she asked.

"No . . . that would be gross," I said. "At one point he did French my cheek, could the angle have affected things?"

"No, the angle could not have affected things."

I let out a breath I didn't know I'd been holding as she explained on.

"Well, miss, you may not know this, but it's very common in young girls to have irregular menstrual cycles at first."

Silence. *Irregular? Whatever. Was I pregnant or not?!*

The Tampax lady continued. "Sweetheart, a 'leak-out pregnancy,' as you call it, is highly unlikely and in any case would have had to involve nudity at the very least. You're definitely not pregnant. Calm down. Everything is going to be okay."

It was going to be okay! Was it really? Was everything going to be okay? Okay to me meant happily starting my weekend over French toast with my family before socializing at the sunny park with my many, many friends who loved me. Instead, I was spending a beautiful

Saturday afternoon alone on the phone with a middle-aged stranger whose job it was to field calls about menstrual blood. Thinking about how I had managed to already be a huge disappointment to human-kind, again I had no words.

"Miss? Miss, are you there?"

"Yes," I said, clearing my throat. "I'm here." Why couldn't I just say "thank you" and hang up? What more did I want from her?

"Miss," continued the Tampax lady, "are you okay?"

This was a loaded question. On one hand, I was okay. I had gotten confirmation that I was not pregnant; I was not going to have to go "study abroad" like Teresa Carimonico. But on the other, I also had confirmation that Alyssa, the sexiest girl I knew, had no idea what she was talking about. She was supposed to know everything! After all, she did have big boobs and boys liked her. So if she was faking it, and she wasn't really all-knowing, what did that mean? Did anyone really know anything about anything? I suppose the Tampax lady did; otherwise she wouldn't have been hired as a licensed period expert. But still, I was now doubting the credibility of the entire human race. I needed to answer, so I decided to leave Ms. Tampax with a cliff-hanger.

"No," I said. "I am not okay." And then I hung up the phone so aggressively it dinged a little, a truly dramatic ending to a bizarre phone call. If I ever one day spoke of this to my brother (highly unlikely), I would certainly advise him to use the "No, I am not okay" phone slam in his next creatively licensed film. This conversation with an employee of Tampax was the most informative discussion of sex I had ever had up to this point. This anonymous call with a kind stranger was the most I had opened up to anyone the whole year.

Despite the relief I felt from finding out I was not in fact teen pregnant with Jonah Hertzberg's baby, how could I be okay? I was a gargantuan young girl, entering her teens during what seemed to be the wrong decade, in the wrong town, in the wrong state. Everyone else seemed to be reveling in Umbros, Color Me Badd, and New Jersey culture, while I indulged in bell-bottoms, Jethro Tull, and Haight-Ashbury. Something was definitely wrong with me if the *best* thing that happened to me all year had been the Gulf War. Something was definitely wrong if Alyssa, my confident neighbor whom I thought of as the next Dr. Ruth, was just as clueless as I was about sex. Something was definitely wrong with my depth perception if I believed a poorly angled, clothed French kiss could cause a fetus to grow inside me. Aside from the Tampax lady, I was pretty sure the rest of the human race was just as dumb as I was. No one knew anything about anything.

No, Ms. Tampax, I was not okay.

CHAPTER 7:

Not Exactly a Horse Girl

The phone call to the Tampax lady was truly a low point, so I decided to spend more time with live friends my own age. After spewing it all to an anonymous expert on period blood, I had the realization that I was desperately in need of more true friends. Alyssa and I hung out more and more as seventh grade was ending and summer approached, but I was itching to branch out. I also needed to figure out what I was going to do for the summer. Now that I was officially a teenager, I wasn't sure I should spend it in my usual fashion—performing in the community summer theatre review, run by failed actors with possible drinking problems. This program took place at the local high school and had just enough budget to make all costumes out of tin foil. Being one of the oldest participants, I had basically peaked the summer before, when I was cast as Mary Poppins in the Disney montage. I stood on a riser, swaying to "Chim Chim Cher-ee" wearing a large hat. I had no solo or lines but all the glory. I got to have a solo bow instead of the horrible group ones, and got "special makeup" instead of the requisite blue eye shadow and red lipstick (which also got used as blush). I had a feeling if I went back again for the fifth year, I would be spending my pre-show moments hoping that the lipstick being smeared across my mouth hadn't just been used on some sweaty kid's acne-ridden cheek. I would be back to my usual role of girl in back row wearing unflattering high-cut leotard. I was a little too old for that stuff now, and needed to figure out another way to spend my days so I wouldn't go stir-crazy inside the house. If I didn't find an activity, my mom would surely find one for me, whether it be weeding, laundry, or dusting her endless bone china teacup collection. I needed to find a new summer outlet.

I was not athletic, or coordinated, or agile, so when Alyssa invited me to horse camp, I was skeptical as to whether or not this was my true calling. I said yes, although I wondered just how fast Alyssa could gallop on a horse with her giant boobs. Perhaps horseback riding was a place where my A cups would be an asset. Alyssa's invite was my pathway to finding a social group outside of my town, where everyone knew me as the girl who has looked thirty since she was twelve.

I was optimistic about horse camp, even though I had never ridden a horse, or experienced one in person for that matter. I had barely even seen one on film. When my brother re-created the Godfather trilogy on his borrowed camcorder, we used my live dog as a replacement for the iconic horse's head scene (although I found my brother's description of that scene to be far less harrowing than the old lady chloroform scene from *Cloak & Dagger*). I had never seen the actual Godfather movies because my parents deemed them "too violent." (Yet *Octopussy* when I was a small child and *The Crying Game* as I hit puberty were perfectly appropriate.) I had an aversion to horse-centric *Little House on the Prairie*, which I thought was for choir girls and sissies. *Laverne & Shirley*, *The Carol Burnett Show*, and *Moonlighting* reruns on Lifetime . . . Television for Women never had a single horse on any episodes.

Besides, horse girls were constantly reading books like *Black Beauty*. I still hadn't moved on from my obsession with *Go Ask Alice*, the published diary of a suicidal, drug-addicted teen. I continued writing every journal entry with the intention of someone reading it, discovering I was a genius, and publishing it at a profit, which was such an un-horse girl thing to do. Horse girls sported long, straight ponytails that they brushed out frequently and publicly like manes. I did not have a long, straight ponytail. No matter what I did with my hair, I always ended up looking like an extra in a Whitesnake video. Horse girls wore clothing inspired by Quakers. I wore clothing inspired by Jimmy Page, Stevie Nicks, and Cher. Horse girls drew horses on their notebooks and wore sweatshirts with horses airbrushed on them. Perhaps the horse girls would also be misunderstood and desperate for new friends and we could bond over not quite fitting in.

Nonetheless, I was excited for horse camp. I didn't need to spend another summer singing "Home" from *The Wiz* Broadway musical alone to my own reflection in my mother's full-length mirror. (I had wanted to play Dorothy in a previous summer's production of *The Wiz* but ended up the Scarecrow. They told me it was because I moved in such a "floppy manner.") I didn't care if I'd be spending the summer surrounded by girls who would probably remain virgins way longer than most and tended to be obsessed with mythical folklore. Horse camp for me was purely a social strategy. Maybe at horse camp I could be at the upper level of social standing. Compared to these girls, maybe I could be cool.

Despite Alyssa's current interests, which included above-the-jeans hand jobs and Nair, she was an undercover horse girl. No one but I knew her dirty secret, which is how she remained so popular with boys at school. She had been going to this camp for years. This horse camp was a few towns over, where all the girls were rumored to be sluts. I had heard all the girls in that town had professional, salon-quality full-set acrylic nail tips with nail art. They chewed gum at all times and went all the way with boys behind the Gravitron whenever the ghetto carnival came to town. I was thrilled to be leaving my town on a daily basis, even if it did mean I had to spend time with sluts and spooky animals whose severed heads could be placed in one's bed if one ended up rolling with the wrong crowd.

The first day of horse camp, Alyssa's mom pulled into my driveway in her old station wagon with a FOLLOW ME TO THE HADASSAH bumper sticker promptly at 8:00 AM. My mom, being somewhat unsupportive of my new career as an equestrian, didn't have any desire to be a part of the first day of the rest of my life. Although she enjoyed betting on horses at the racetrack, riding them was something foreign to my family. We were more of a placing-bets-while-someone-else-rode-the-horse kind of family.

When we arrived at horse camp, I quickly discovered that this town had no horse girls available to run the place, so instead they utilized the local Jersey sluts. I had imagined that even in this skanky town there would at least be one or two horse girls on call—but no. These girls were not reading *Black Beauty*, they were getting finger banged by guys in jean shorts behind a Friendly's dumpster. They were classic Jersey girls with big perms, tans, spandex shorts, mirrored sunglasses, and an unlimited supply of gum. They all looked like the spawn of Tawny Kitean and Samantha Fox. Still, they had a certain cred. Alyssa immediately informed me that she had heard one of the counselors had made out with a member of Skid Row. She didn't know which guy it was, but it "definitely wasn't Sebastian Bach." Yes! This was exactly the kind of lifestyle I had been yearning for. I was under the supervision of a girl who actually knew a real rock star and had tasted his saliva! I was practically in the presence of rock 'n' roll royalty. I immediately became obsessed more with the counselor's past relations with D-list rock stars than with saddling up a stallion.

I didn't expect the counselors to make us ride on the first day. I thought we'd spend the day trading gum and swapping lip-liner techniques. But after a very brief intro, they discussed the difference between riding Western (sexy/badass) and English (pretentious/Hamptons). I tuned out and let my mind consider these options. Girls who rode Western seemed more attainable, while the girls who rode English were wealthy and wore cute helmets, beige tight pants, and fitted blazers. These girls came from old money, possibly had their own pony at home, and definitely had a country house. I had never met the type of girl who rode English, and I had high hopes to possibly encounter one during my brief stint at horse camp.

Suddenly everyone was standing up, and I snapped back into the discussion, forcing my brain away from my fantasy of going to visit a preppy girl named Tabitha in the country, to discover that the skanky counselors were making us all get on horses. It was assumed if we all went to a camp exclusively for riding horses, that we would all have a strong interest in actually riding said horses. I resented the assumption. My time on a horse was short-lived anyway. Before we even took off for our first trot, I showed my true equestrian abilities by falling off a horse that was standing still. A permed brunette counselor, noticing I was not quite at the horse camp entry level, abruptly separated me from the group and told me, "You gotta sit out." As I explained that I was just clumsy because I was so tall and not fully adjusted to my never-ending growth spurt, I saw Alyssa galloping away with the rest of the advanced riders, not to be seen again until her mom picked us up seven hours later. I was reduced to beginner's activities such as cleaning out horse's hooves, brushing horses, and learning how to put on a saddle.

It turned out sitting out at horse camp was much better than participating in horse camp. Sitting out meant I got to be a fly on the wall to these whorish teenage girls running the show. I listened intently to every single detail of their very active sex lives.

"Yeah, so we were gonna do it, but then Ritchie didn't have a condom so I was like, 'I'm not gonna raw-dog it with you just so you can give me AIDS and make me die instantly.' Right? I mean come on!"

"Yeah, who does he think he is?" said one counselor through her perfectly glossed lips.

"I mean it's not 1980 anymore, we've gotta protect ourselves," said the counselor with the biggest boobs.

"Totally," I agreed, munching on a greasy grilled cheese from the lunch truck.

I loved horse camp.

The next day, I automatically sat with the counselors. Right away we had a mutual understanding that riding horses really wasn't going to be a part of my summer at horse camp. I was too uncoordinated to even sit on a horse properly. Despite the modern dance, my inner thighs still had zero muscle tone, making it impossible for me to grip around the horse with enough force. There was no way I would face the humiliation of falling off another stationary horse. Forget horseback riding. I was there to learn all about sex from real women.

To keep up appearances, the counselors tried to find appropriate activities for me, like grooming horses. It was just an effort to save face. I was so gigantic I could have passed for a counselor, without the self-esteem and sex appeal. "So, like, when you made out with him, was it all sloppy?" I asked my counselor, desperate for a much-needed break from brushing some dumb horse's mane.

"Yeah." She snapped her gum. "Real sloppy. Like wet and all."

"Wow," I said, as my eyes widened and my horse brush dropped into the dirt.

And if that wasn't good enough, while Alyssa galloped and trotted her way through the week, I sampled the hot lunch menu from the lunch truck: grilled cheese, grilled cheese with bacon, cheeseburger, cheeseburger with bacon . . . which was all much better than my mom's usual packed lunch of melba toast and cottage cheese. This was so much better than every other summer of my life, spent learning amateur dance routines to cliché show tunes. This was teenage stuff.

When the weekend came, I got bored. I wanted to continue on my transition into cool teenager, but there were no trashy teenagers around to guide me. I slipped back into the old me: I found out what songs they were featuring in that summer's musical review and cast myself as the lead singer in all of them in my fantasy production. Alone, in my mother's full-length mirror, I sang along to the show tune recordings I found in my father's record collection and made up my own dances. Summer theatre workshop was so much better when I was in charge.

When I returned to camp, I rejoined my BFFs to gossip and sweep hay. "So, Lisa, how was your weekend?" I asked, totally proud to be one of the girls.

"Well, it was good. Frankie wanted to go past third and I was all like, 'I only do that with guys I love.' And he was all like, 'Well, do you love me?' And I was like, 'I dunno. I always pictured losing it somewhere else besides your brother's pickup truck.' So I think next weekend he's gonna put a mattress in the back as a compromise. I'll probably do it to him then. How was your weekend?" she asked, trying to be polite, while staring off pondering if giving up her v-card on a mattress in the back of a borrowed pickup truck was truly the right choice for her.

"Oh, it was awesome," I said. "I learned all the words to 'Let Me Entertain You' and figured out a killer dance routine to it. Want me to show you?"

The counselors collectively stopped sweeping their hay and stared at me. I knew right away that I had blown it. In that one summarization of my weekend, these girls all had a simultaneous realization that even though I was the same size as they were, I was not one of them. I was five foot eight, I wore short-shorts and T-shirts with the neck cut out, but I was no high school senior. I was a dorky middle schooler who spent her weekends doing very immature activities. I continued to sweep, trying to ignore the whispers.

Luckily, that same day, another girl arrived at camp named Katie. She also sat out frequently, as her horse activities were limited because she was so short that her feet couldn't reach the stirrups. Katie and I hit it off right away. She was also really into the foods with hot cheese on them from the lunch truck and I'd always felt a closeness to anyone whose size holds him or her back in any way, hence my brief telephone relationship with Paul the five-foot-tall bank teller. I couldn't participate in certain games as a kid because I was so giant—riding tiny carts for "crab soccer" in P.E., pony rides, piggyback rides. Katie and I sat on the sidelines every day, eating Cheetos (crunchy not puffy) and having heart-to-hearts. Katie was a tomboy who didn't like school. I was certainly no tomboy—I couldn't even ride a horse—but I understood not fitting in. I didn't care that Katie was only six and I was thirteen. She was a cool chick and a true friend. I told her about the middle school social cliques that were as hard to break into as Studio 54 in its heyday. Katie told me about how she was struggling with cursive. I left that summer feeling as if I had made a lifelong friendship in Katie, which eased my paranoid fear that Alyssa would be ditching me soon after, now that she knew I was so clumsy I couldn't even participate in a sport in which I was essentially a passenger. So at the end of the summer when Katie asked for my phone number to stay in touch, I was elated. I had accomplished my goal for the summer—to make a new friend!

Then, a few days later, Katie's mom called me . . . to find out if I would babysit her daughter.

Babysit? Did she not understand the true bond, the true connection we had? We both loved hot cheese, for God's sake! How many times in a lifetime would I be able to find someone I had that in common with? Babysitting cheapened the whole thing. It's not like I was going to discipline my best friend. We were equals, damn it! However,

I said yes, because it was an excuse to spend time with Katie before we both got busy with the distractions of school. I knew that in the fall my demands in eighth grade would be more than hers in first grade, and Katie might have trouble understanding if I didn't always have time to chill out with her.

The night I was scheduled to babysit, my mom dropped me at Katie's place a few towns over. I was feeling a little better about it by then. After all, given the countless weekend evenings I'd spent babysitting those wretched twin girls down the street, I was anxious to revise my clientele. The last time I watched them, their parents had gone out for the night with friends who had triplets, leaving me and some other teenage twit alone with twin five-year-olds, triplet toddlers, a yippy Pomeranian, and a howling Beagle. Again, we watched *Look Who's Talking*. I wanted out. Katie could not have come at a more perfect time.

When I arrived at Katie's, I was shocked to discover her mom was only slightly older than the Jersey-trash horse camp counselors. When she turned her back, I mouthed to my BFF Katie, "How old is your mother?" To which she mouthed back, "Twenty-five." Wow. I had never seen a mom so young before. Then Katie's mom introduced me to her husband, who was, at the youngest, fifty. He looked like a present-day James Taylor: bald with a dark ring of hair circling his skull and a face that said "I used to be hot."

I wanted to ask Katie's mom what was up with the age difference but decided to just ask Katie after her parents left. Then, instead, I drew my own conclusion: Katie's mother was probably a former babysitter herself who had an affair with the father of the very kids she was babysitting. Then she got pregnant out of wedlock and the man left his own family for the babysitter. Now I was the new babysitter and maybe she feared I would have an affair with her wrinkly husband and continue the cycle. How exciting! This house already felt like a Jackie Collins novel instead of the dirty kennel I was used to babysitting in. As I listened to this teen mother ramble on that "Katie goes to sleep at exactly eight thirty every night" and "no more than two Oreos" and "absolutely no television—books only!" I pondered how much money Katie's father's former wife must be getting in the divorce settlement.

The parents left, probably to go to some swingers' party, and I proceeded to disobey every single one of Katie's mother's rules. First we ate the whole package of Oreos. I couldn't stop myself. My mother only had Lorna Doones and Pecan Sandies in our house. Even when the Girl Scouts came she would order boxes and boxes of the toast-like Trefoil shortbreads and was the sole customer keeping the Lemon Chalet Cremes in business. If my mom ever ended up in a nursing home, she would be delighted with their cookie selection. But I would have killed for a peanut butter Tagalong, Thin Mint, or Samoa. A chance to eat Oreos unsupervised was something I had yearned for since I started eating solid food.

Then Katie didn't want to put on her pajamas. Who was I to make her? And if Katie didn't want to brush her teeth, so be it. I was only a few years younger than her mother was when she had her, so I was sure breaking a bunch of household rules was nothing compared to getting knocked up by a forty-four-year-old at age nineteen! I couldn't risk Katie thinking I was some stick in the mud when she was basically the only person who thought I was supercool at this point. I needed this friendship.

Katie wanted to stay up late, and I had become accustomed to watching *Saturday Night Live* every Saturday and was not excited about breaking my routine just because Katie was a little young for it. I could look at this as an opportunity to expose her to real culture. My brother was already recording *The Treasure of the Sierra Madre* off of TCM that night, so I couldn't risk missing an episode of *SNL*. What if Julia Sweeney debuted a new "It's Pat" sketch and finally revealed whether Pat was in fact a man or a woman? I needed to know for certain if an "It's

Pat" sketch played so I could wear my "It's Pat" oversize T-shirt to school Monday as a conversation piece. What if I missed Rob Schneider's hilarious antics as "the Copy Guy"? I loved the Copy Guy so much: I even had a Rob Schneider Copy Guy refrigerator magnet to prove it. Really I had no choice but to let Katie watch it with me.

It was a funny episode, as usual. Kevin Nealon's "Weekend Update" nailed a joke about Socks the Cat. Then there was a sketch that used the word *condom*. Katie asked me what a condom was, and thanks to my horse camp counselors, I now had a very clear understanding of how sex worked. For once, I was the cool older girl with all the answers. It didn't even cross my mind that she was too young to hear this. I was so consumed with finally feeling like an all-knowing, experienced teenager that I couldn't control myself. Even if I had, there was no need to shelter this little horse girl from the Wild West. I muted Chris Farley's antics and words just started spraying out of my mouth. I was the Tampax operator, I was the horse camp counselor, I was all-knowing Alyssa, and I was the sexy backup dancer from Bobby Brown's "Every Little Step" video. I began straight-talking to Katie as the wise, worldly teenager I knew lived somewhere beneath my layer of dorkiness.

"Well, Katie, a condom is something a man puts over his penis when having sex to prevent him from getting a woman pregnant or getting AIDS."

"What's AIDS?" Katie asked, her eyes wide.

"Well, Katie, AIDS is something you get when you have sex without a condom and then you die instantly." I was proud of myself for my honesty and for knowing the facts.

Katie continued, "What's sex?"

This was going to be a long night. I regurgitated all I could remember from my horse camp counselors. I told Katie about first base, how "If you don't need to wipe your mouth after, it's not a real French kiss." Then I moved on to second base and grody sloppy second base. Meanwhile, I kept quiet on my theory on how her parents met; I figured I should save that for next weekend when they asked me back to babysit after Katie told them how much she enjoyed spending time with me.

At some point during this discussion, I suddenly felt we were not alone. I turned around, and standing in the doorway were Katie's mismatched parents. I didn't know how long they had been standing there—hopefully they had just walked in and only heard about "sloppy second," which without careful listening could have sounded like a discussion about leftovers, not putting one's mouth on a boob. Then again, Katie's parents' relationship was clearly one of sloppy seconds, so either way it wasn't good.

"Hi, guys!" I said, doing my best impression of someone who had not spent the last ten minutes traumatizing their first-grade daughter. "You're home early." I gave them a big smile, flashing my underdeveloped mouth still containing a few too many baby teeth. "How was your night?" I asked, desperately trying to derail them into talking about the grown-up stuff like wine tasting and fondue eating that I imagined they had done on their wild adult night out.

"Katie, go to bed," said her father, in a stern tone I was sure his laid-back look-alike James Taylor had never used. Katie waved a timid good-bye to me and walked up the stairs to her room, too terrified to look back. I sat in silence, desperate to confess all. I wanted to tell them that everything they heard me say I learned at horse camp from my slutty counselors. I wanted to explain that I just wanted to feel cool like those girls for once in my life, rather than an awkwardly oversize preteen. I tried to get up the courage to explain that the only reason I heard all that sex stuff from them was that I was too uncoordinated to ride a horse and if I hadn't fallen off that horse that was standing still because my legs were too long for my body, I would have never been sitting out in the first place. I wanted to tell them that I was indifferent to horses. I only went to that stupid camp because Alyssa invited me and I thought

I'd make some new friends. But Alyssa and I were separated into different groups as soon as the counselors discovered she was ready for the Belmont Stakes and I couldn't even sit on a horse. And that's how I met Katie. I shouldn't have even met Katie in the first place.

I didn't even like horses!

But the father simply said, "Ready to go, Margot?"

I grabbed my vintage suede fringed purse and slumped out the door, not making eye contact with the young mom. As I got in the car with bald Humbert Humbert, I wondered if this was how it all started with Katie's mom. Maybe all it took was a long, late-night ride home with the babysitter of his kids from his first marriage, ending in a smooch. Maybe I was going to be part of an exciting scandal and I would have a great story to impress my classmates with about the older man who totally had the major hots for me.

Much to my disappointment, he did not try to continue the cycle by having an affair with me. Instead, he said, "So Katie's mother and I won't be needing you any longer."

I wished he had waited until the end of the ride to say that. He chose to lead with the termination, so we were left with fifteen minutes of post-firing silence. This was not my finest moment, fantasizing about a fifty-year-old bald man putting the moves on me. I wasn't even attracted to him, yet I was insulted that even I was too repulsive for this letch.

I never saw Katie again. And the next weekend I found myself back at those awful twins' house, watching Kirstie Alley and John Travolta maneuver the first year of parenting a talking baby in *Look Who's Talking*. This time I remembered to bring leftover earplugs I had from my pool club days to muffle the yaps of the Pomeranian and Beagle.

CHAPTER 8:

Sneaking Off to Church

The rest of summer passed uneventfully, and I entered eighth grade hanging on to Alyssa as my closest ally. Sadly, Jonah Hertzberg was a year older and had gone off to high school without me. I tried not to replay the untimely walk-in by Katie's parents over and over in my head, but to no avail. This summer had been a total bust. I had traumatized a six-year-old and had retained absolutely no equestrian skills. I was right back where I started: depressed, stuck, and remarkably unathletic, despite my size and stature. I didn't go through some '80s movie change where I got made over and came back to school cool. In fact, nothing had changed physically about me—even my growth had slowed a bit. I was holding tight at about five foot eight and hoping that my journey of awkwardness would end there.

I tried to keep a positive attitude as school began, but the White Lipstick Posse ruled the school even more than ever, and my fashion sense was getting more and more extreme. The Black Crowes had just emerged onto the music scene, and they were a different kind of rock. They weren't hair metal; they were more classic rock 'n' roll and they dressed the part. I immediately Manic Panicked my hair a darker color and invested in some cowboy boots to poke out under my flared jeans. I didn't care that lead singer Chris Robinson was a man. I wanted to look just like him.

Without Jonah Hertzberg around to distract me, I became more and more aware that I was a magnet for weird dudes with long, dirty hair who played guitar. There were two kinds of long-haired, guitar-playing guys—the weird dudes and the scuzzes. The basic difference was that the scuzzes always had girls (albeit trashy girls) around and the weird dudes didn't. The weird dudes were socially awkward, a little overweight, had unattractive pubescent facial hair that really should be shaved, and chain wallets. The scuz guys were left over from my brother's generation— borderline metal heads who chain-smoked, came from broken homes, and were always getting action in the school bathrooms from skanks. I do admit there were a few of these guys I found desirable; their broken homes seemed much richer with color than my parents' uncomfortably happy marriage. (I could do without hearing about their love life ever again.) But I would never think to act on my secret scuz desires for fear of catching an STD surely lurking in the inseams of their black leather jackets. But the few guys who liked me were the rejects of the scuzzes. They were too unattractive to hook up with skanks in the bathroom. They didn't come from broken homes; they were fairly decent students. These invisible, average-looking dudes, who would never be antiestablishment enough to drop out and go to vocational school, seemed to find my height desirable and my taste in music even more appealing.

Too bad I wasn't on board. Perhaps my summer with the horse camp counselors made me return to school with a newfound secret knowledge. Sure, I had minimal experience with boys, but now I knew what was out there. I knew what real teenagers were doing, and I wanted in. Just hearing the skanky counselors' stories made me feel as if I had a step up. I had learned it was best not to share my sexual wisdom with six-year-olds, but beyond that minor bump in the road I was ready for a new year. I had no interest in these ultrasafe wannabe bad boys. But I wasn't complaining—if they wanted to pay attention to me, despite taunts of "how gross" from Jessica Rosenstein, I welcomed the attention. One overweight guitar dude would buy me black T-shirts of different hair metal bands and leave them in my locker. I had two Warrant "Cherry Pie" shirts, three Poison shirts, and countless Skid Row shirts. After all, Skid Row was the ultimate success story of our area, after Bon Jovi and Bruce Springsteen of course. I didn't want to wear these shirts to school, because I didn't want this guy to think I liked him. However, I would wear them after school to impress my brother's high school friends whenever I got the chance. I wonder now if even that weird guitar dude was subtly trying to have a fashion intervention with me. Maybe he was thinking that if I wore hair metal band T-shirts, at least that would get me out of my "Female Jimmy Page" look a day here and there. Regardless, I was so not into him, or anyone for that matter. I just wanted to get through the day.

Meanwhile, it seemed as if everyone else at this time was busy preparing for a religious ceremony followed by a party where they received lots of presents and had really good cake. The Catholic kids were having confirmations, where their cakes were store-bought and filled with heavy vanilla pudding and covered in a thick coat of buttercream with roses made of orange. My mother always insisted on making all my birthday cakes from scratch, following traditional British recipes resulting in a vile brown cake filled with raisins and orange peels and coated in a glaze, never a frosting. All I ever wanted was a brightly colored store-bought cake from ShopRite with HAPPY BIRTHDAY MARGOT written in neon tones. Enough with the raisins, Mom. I was getting more than enough fiber from her black, seed-filled bread.

I went to a few confirmations, but I didn't quite understand what was happening in the ceremonies. I loved that the girls got to wear white dresses after Labor Day though. Anything that pushed the rules of fashion seemed cool and antiestablishment to me. I'd eat at least two pieces of ShopRite sheet cake at each confirmation, thinking, *This may be your last chance, eat it while you can.* Coming home to my mom's Pecan Sandies was almost tolerable after an afternoon gorging myself on cheap sheet cake in a Catholic church.

The Jewish kids were having Bar and Bat Mitzvahs with personalized party themes such as Jonathan's All Stars, Marla's Marvelous Mall, Samantha on Broadway, or, my absolute favorite, Gary's Stock Market. Somehow I had secured an invite to Gary's Stock Market Bar Mitzvah, whose party premise was, essentially, money. He had Styrofoam glitter dollar signs as a centerpiece (no doubt made by my old BFF Amanda's mother out of her garage) and fake dollar bills with his face on it. I admired his directness. When guests entered the Temple Shalom rec room, it was decorated as if to say, *Listen guys, we all know I learned that haftorah just for the money, so let's cut to the chase and celebrate why we're all really here. You're going to give me money and I am going to collect it. Sure, we'll rock out with inflatable neon guitars and cheap giveaway sunglasses, then play some classic Bar Mitzvah games like freeze dance and huggy bear, but beyond that, I'd really like to take you for all you're worth and pay for one to two years of college—and not a state school. I'm talking big-time, private college, far away from here. Got it?*

I was invited to about eight Bar/Bat Mitzvahs, most likely because I had gone to elementary school with a bunch of Jewish kids and they felt obligated to invite their "oldest" friends. I was never close enough with anyone to be called up to light a candle during the "special people" section of the party. This was when the Bat Mitzvah girl would stand in front of her fabulous, store-bought, raisin-free sheet

cake decorated with, say, a giant purple buttercream telephone for
PHONE IT IN AT ALISON's BAT MITZVAH. Then the Bat Mitzvah girl
would say something like, "I love it when we go shopping at the mall.
You always know the best bargains and that's not all. Nancy, come
on up and light this light, you always know what fits just right." Then
some gum-smacking girl in a puffy teal balloon dress would act as
if she'd just won a surprise Academy Award and come up and light
the candle, being swarmed by Jewish aunts taking photos of this special friendship that will surely last forever. Often the Bat Mitzvah girl
would get sick of writing individual poems for her "special people"
and toward the end would say something like, "I love you guys with
all my heart, you're always there for me even when I got a C– in art"—
hold for uproarious laughter because this is the funniest private joke
in history—"So without further ado, Rob, Karen, Doug, Lisa, Jodi,
Sara, Debbie, Carrie, Elizabeth, and all my art club pals, please come
up and light this candle. I love you guys!" That's when it would really
sting, when the Bar/Bat Mitzvah guy/girl would essentially pull the
original black-and-white *Gilligan's Island* opening credits technique of
"The movie star . . . and the rest . . . here on Gilligan's Isle," instead
of giving the Professor and Mary Anne their due. Why couldn't I be
clumped into some ragtag group of "and the rest" called up to light a
candle for once in my life?

I didn't have a Bat Mitzvah or a confirmation. My mother is half
Catholic, half Protestant. She and her twin sister were baptized Catholic
in honor of her father's side of her family, but one day he went off to work
at the candy factory, slaving away as usual to master the latest recipe for
chocolate turtles, when her British mother lit up a cigarette, made sure
no one was on her tail, and rebaptized the twins at a nearby Protestant
church. So I am pretty sure the double baptism cancels each individual
baptism out, making my mom unbaptized and unable to force me to
endure confirmation training.

My father was raised Jewish but is a staunch atheist. Known for his clever catchphrases like "Think about it, Margot, where do you suppose everyone fits in heaven? There's no room, it's not practical," this man would never enroll me in accelerated Hebrew school just so I could have a big party with store-bought sheet cake and foam centerpieces. Besides, what would my Bat Mitzvah theme be anyway? "I Had a Hulking Good Time at Margot's Bat Mitzvah" or "Margot's Gargantuan Good Time"? Between my two parental figures, there was no solid religious guidance. That made me nothing. A heathen. Raised without God and with no opportunity for a big theme party with tacky dresses and cash gifts. That particular year it felt really pointless when my birthday came.

My mother and I were fighting a lot at the time, normal teenage girl/mom stuff, but nonetheless unpleasant. Her mom, my British grandmother, was dying, and the stress of dealing with that huge loss and her overdeveloped daughter entering her teen years was not a good combination. I wasn't a little girl anymore (not that I was ever little), and raising my A-student older brother had not prepared her for the wrath of a teenage girl. Everything she said to me seemed so lame, and everything I said to her came off as confrontational. One Sunday morning she came downstairs and said, "Your morals are becoming fucked up. I'm taking you to church today. And don't tell your father." I wasn't quite sure how watching a big-boobed neighbor make out on a regular basis made my morals "fucked up," but excited by a Thelma-and-Louise-style getaway, I went without protest. Sneaking off together, albeit to church, would surely be a true bonding opportunity and way to reconnect after a lot of nonsensical bickering. I put on a flowery dress that landed right below my knees, that unflattering length that's too long to be sexy and too short to be stylish. Realizing I was teetering on looking Amish, I debated putting on a church hat from my childhood dress-up drawer, but I thought that would draw my father's attention during the sneak-out.

I came downstairs where my mother was waiting for me, blending in, washing dishes so as not to draw attention to the world's first church sneak-out. She saw me out of the corner of her eye, finished rinsing the chipped Smurfs mug from 1983, grabbed my arm, and said, "Follow me." We walked to the Plymouth Voyager, not stopping to say good-bye to my clearly oblivious dad, who was leafing through records for his "Sunday soundtrack," or my brother, who was filling out applications to top-notch universities, and took off. If church wasn't the final destination of this trip, this would have been one of the most exhilarating rides of my life. My mom was speeding. Fast. I rolled down the manually operated window and let the wind flow through my hair. We were rebels, sneaking off to church to fix my "fucked-up" morals behind my atheist father's back.

I didn't realize how fast we were actually going and wondered if we were going to be unfashionably late. My hat-versus-no-hat inner debate had set us back only about two minutes, but I was just noticing my mom was going eighty miles per hour when the cop lights turned on behind us. "Shit," she said, in true fashion of how she'd been acting all morning. Her sudden potty mouth was probably caused by the stress of her own mother being very sick at the time, but nonetheless, I loved my mom's new vernacular.

She pulled over to the side of the road, took a deep breath, held it in for a beat, and began to cry on cue. Never before had I seen such magic from her. 1, 2, 3, cry. Amazing. She probably used season 6, episode 113 of *Laverne & Shirley*, "Not Quite New York," as a sense memory. I blinked a few times to try to induce tears to help the cause but to no avail. The officer approached the window and my mother manually rolled it down. Just once in my life I wanted my parents to own a car with power windows, which were first invented in the 1940s . . . I know this for a fact. I looked it up. With each inch the window clunkily rolled down my mother's crocodile tears grew more and more evident.

"Hello, officer," said my mother, barely able to get the words out.

"Hello, ma'am," the officer nodded at me, "miss."

I nodded right back, eager to not disturb the awkward dynamic my mother had already instituted with her enviable ability to cry while simultaneously being chased by the cops. This was my first run-in with the law. I was loving every second of it.

"I'll need your license and registration, please." My mother handed it over, awaiting her punishment. "Ma'am, you were speeding pretty badly. Eighty miles per hour in a fifty-five zone. Were you aware of that?"

"Sorry, we were on our way to church and didn't want to risk missing the sermon." As if we hadn't missed it every single other weekend of our lives? My mother took out a used tissue from the bottom of her purse and wiped her nose with it for effect. Who's kidding who, it was probably a piece of one-ply toilet paper, as we never had any tissues in the house.

Still, my mother must have known what she was doing, because the cop softened. "I understand, ma'am. I'm a God-loving man myself. I hate missing church on Sundays."

What the hell was happening? My mother was now bonding with a cop over their mutual love of God and churchgoing habits! This would be a lovely moment if any of it were true. I sat and watched, happy to have one up on my mother for this behavior. My mother then unfolded the already snot-filled toilet paper and loudly blew her nose into it . . . again. My mom's nose blowing and sneezing were a constant cause of embarrassment. We were once in a two-level store shopping with my grandmother in Manhattan when my mom sneezed her usual overexaggerated "A-CHOO!" We were on the second floor of the store and a customer on the first floor called up to us, "God bless you!" I was humiliated. This particular nose blow in front of a suburban cop was as loud as the infamous Manhattan sneeze.

"Here's what I'm going to do," continued the cop, desperate to make her stop reusing what had now become the opposite of a tissue.

"Because I understand what it's like to be late to church," he chuckled to himself, my mom joining in as if they shared a bond over the hilarity they both knew from personal experience ensues when one walks in late to church—"I'm going to let you off with just a warning. Drive safely, and please obey speed limits in the future. Enjoy the service ma'am, miss."

I nodded in disbelief.

"Thank you, officer," said my mother, "and God bless."

God bless was a phrase she had never once used, but it rolled off her tongue with such ease that I wondered why she had chosen a career in teaching rather than three-card monte. She let out a closing sniffle and rolled up the window, each creak accenting the awkward silence. As the officer walked to his car, my mother watched him in the rearview mirror. As soon as he got into his vehicle, she quickly wiped the tears from her eyes, leaving just the smear of her Estée Lauder midnight-blue eyeliner. She sucked in her remaining mucus, looked me in the eye, and said in a tone I'd only heard previously in Clint Eastwood movies, "Jesus Christ, I thought for sure that officer was gonna give us a ticket. Let's go." She peeled out going even faster than before with no sign of having been in hysterics just seconds earlier. And my morals were "fucked up"?

We arrived late to the service, though no one seemed to mind or even notice, and sat in the back. This was a Unitarian Universalist church, and we had missed the preaching part. We arrived during a medley of pretty songs, and I couldn't tell if they were religious or not. The songs seemed to mostly be about flowers and love, which seemed remarkably similar to my father's Joni Mitchell records. Then we sat in silence for a while "meditating," during which I spent the entire time wondering about my mother. She must have been really upset about her mom. Where did she learn to cry on cue and lie like that? Did the officer think my mom was hot and that's why he let us off? Or did he really believe her Mother Teresa shtick?

Either way, between the church sneak-out and the run-in with the law, today would be a special secret day kept between only my mother and me. If her intention in taking me away was to re-create a mother-daughter bond that recently had been diminishing, she had definitely achieved her goal. After the service, we drove home at the requisite speed limit, never spoke of the day, and never returned to church. My father never found out (until now if he's reading this). But one thing was certain after our brief stint with religion: I was certainly not going to have any sort of God-infused coming-of-age celebration for this year's birthday. If I wanted one, I was on my own to figure it out.

CHAPTER 9

My Orange Unitard

Because my birthday falls in October, so close to the beginning of the school year, who to invite to a party always seemed a little shaky. Having no love of a lifetime, no style, no religious affiliation, and not really belonging to any clique, I was about to resign myself to forfeiting hope of any rite of passage. But then I heard rumblings around school and found out to my delight that Alyssa was throwing me a surprise party at her house (obviously not during Shabbos, so we could pump up the tunes). I thought surprise parties were for popular, well-dressed, normal-size girls like Jessica Rosenstein of the White Lipstick Posse. I thought girls like me were supposed to spend their birthdays alone writing tortured love ballads on their acoustic guitars. This grand gesture of throwing me a party was pretty much the nicest thing a friend had ever done for me.

The big night came when I was supposed to come to Alyssa's house under the ruse of the usual experimentations with Nair and Jolen body hair bleach. Having clear body hair still made me envious of brunettes who got to experiment with chemicals and hot waxes in order to remove unwanted hair. Pouring bleach on one's upper lip seemed like really risky behavior, and I wished I had reason to give it a try.

I walked over to Alyssa's house to "hang out for the night," making sure I was wearing my best outfit: black-and-white horizontally striped tight bell-bottoms with an oversize belt. I knocked on the door and heard a few "Shhs" and "She's heres." Alyssa opened the door wearing a tight gray V-neck over tight black jeans. She looked hot in a way that said *I spent two hours to make it look as if I just threw this outfit together.* She smiled and then flung open the door to a group of pubescents in Starter jackets and neon-colored, parachute-material Hot Dogger jumpsuits yelling "Surprise!"

I took a note from my mother's recent brilliant performance and acted incredibly surprised. I said things like "Wow! Alyssa, you devil! I had no idea! I am sooooo surprised! You guys!" I really worked my skills as an actress, marveling at how convincing I was and figuring it must run in the family. But no one bought it. Instead, everyone began yelling, "You knew, who told you? Alyssa, she knew!"

As disappointed as I was to find that I was an ineffective actress, I was elated to see how many kids showed up to my party! Granted, the guys were all there because Alyssa invited them and she had big boobs, and the girls were all there because Alyssa was indirectly popular because of her boobs. I didn't care. My friend cared about me enough to throw me a surprise birthday and people actually came. No longer would I be forced to hang out with six-year-old tomboys whose parents disapproved of me. My weekends would now be spent gallivanting around town with fun kids my age rather than babysitting big-mouthed twins and rewatching *Look Who's Talking.* Eighth grade was going to be so much better than seventh grade after all!

When I opened my gifts, I was shocked by how many kids gave me cold, hard cash. Twenty-dollar bills were shoved into free blank greeting cards from the ASPCA mailings. A few kids even had their moms write me a personal check. Imagine that! A check just for being born. At home I had to weed the front walkway to earn an Andrew Jackson. It was the closest I would ever come to that mythical Bat Mitzvah/confirmation money I had been so jealous of the legitimately Jewish and Catholic kids getting. This party was my time to get in on the money everyone else my age seemed to be getting after they read some religious speech. I was even luckier—I would still get the money ($250 total!) without ever setting foot in CCD or Hebrew school. Wow.

After the party, I thought about my options for my money. I could save it, toward a car or computer, but that would be boring. Besides, my parents didn't know about the money because Alyssa hadn't told them about the party. She got the feeling my parents didn't like her, which was kind of true—Alyssa gave off a confident vibe that lots of people, including my mom, interpreted as sluttiness. Alyssa was completely boy crazy, and the boys were crazy for her. What my mom didn't realize was that I wasn't participating in Alyssa's escapades. I was just tagging along, occasionally being forced to make small talk with a cute guy's less attractive friend while Alyssa made out with the hot guy on the other side of the sofa. But nonetheless, my mom worried that my hanging out with Alyssa would lead to me doing slutty things. What my mom didn't consider was that the only guys interested in me at this point were dirty and gross, albeit with keen musical ability, and even they were barely interested. The guy who had given me all the rock T-shirts seemed to have moved on, sensing I wasn't game. I had learned from '80s movies that playing hard to get was the best way to keep a guy's attention, but I guess it wasn't fair if you were keeping his interest for self-esteem purposes, not because you returned his feelings. He probably figured, "If this chick, who has no other viable options, isn't biting, I'll take my T-shirts elsewhere." I hope he did. Living vicariously through Alyssa's actions was much more my style.

I decided that my mom and dad didn't need to know about the party, and they didn't need to know about the money. Therefore I would have total freedom to do exactly what I wanted to do with it. The possibilities for $250 were endless.

I also decided that I would spend my unexpected windfall by going to the mall and buying absolutely everything I desired. I loved how on the old episodes of *Wheel of Fortune* the winners of each round could go shopping in the *Wheel of Fortune* rooms and buy whatever they wanted. Even though people were forced to buy cat plaques and vertical blinds in order to use up their money, I still found it exciting to be able to buy anything I desired. This is a similar feeling to the way I felt the few times my mom dragged me to the dollar store at Christmastime for wrapping paper. In Dollar Dreams, I couldn't help but think, *Wow, Margot. You really can afford whatever you want in here.*

So, when I got dropped off at the mall with Alyssa, I had an incredible rush of adrenaline. This was the Freehold Raceway Mall, the newest mall in the area. It had a lot of clout because it was in Bruce Springsteen territory, which gave it slightly more class than the Bon Jovi territory fifteen minutes away that I was used to. The people there were less likely to get in fistfights over a Black Friday Nintendo special, and walking among them made me want to rise up to their level of class. We entered a boutique and I pulled a bunch of items off the racks without looking at the price tags first and truly felt like a rock star. The shopping mall was limited in its '70s-rocker-clothing selection, but I found a bunch of impractical items to suit my needs. Poet's blouses, chiffon shirts, purple pants. I could afford it all. Shopping with money had exceeded my expectations. I felt like the youngest contestant ever on *Supermarket Sweep*. As I took my loot home, I was really excited to debut my new looks at school the next week, especially because ever since the surprise party I thought I might be teetering on being almost popular.

Sunday night I planned out my outfit for Monday. I would wear a bright orange spandex unitard paired with a mustard/orange/hot-pink zip-up shirt strongly resembling a wet suit. Why hadn't I ever worn this color combo before? The hot pink really brought out the rosy hue of my pale skin. I loved how the unitard clung to my lanky frame, giving me an androgynous look, as the skintight nature of the outfit really accentuated my lack of cleavage. I would look just like a freckled David Bowie. This outfit was going to be the start of my new social standing.

As usual, my parents had left for work by the time I caught the bus to school. There was no time to get a second opinion on my ensemble, not that I would have asked for it, since it was clearly the most fantabulous outfit ever known to man. I could even get double use out of my new orange unitard if I wore it to modern dance class. This was money well spent. I walked proudly into school strutting my stuff as I imagined David Bowie did when he first took the stage as Ziggy Stardust. If people were going to stare at me for being a head above all, at least now I was giving them something to stare at. For once, I welcomed the feeling of all eyes on me. I was ready for my new, happier, more fashion-forward life. New look, new year, new me.

I strolled down the east wing, towering over everyone as usual, but this time I stood up straight and with confidence. Everyone looked at me and whispered, and I imagined they were all talking about "New Margot." Suddenly I felt a clammy hand aggressively grab me by the arm. "Come with me," said my petite gym teacher sternly.

"What did I do?" I asked, genuinely confused. I had recently seen a special on PBS about the assassination of JFK and was fascinated by Lee Harvey Oswald's famous claim, "I'm a patsy." Watching him say this to the camera was invigorating, as I wondered if perhaps he was a patsy and more was afoot at the grassy knoll. I also (dare I admit this?) found and still find Lee Harvey Oswald to be kind of cute, so I was inclined to believe his claim of being a patsy. That being said, as this nag of a woman grabbed my arm, I hoped my call of "What did I do?" was played as effectively as my man Oswald's performance had been.

"You know what you did," said this tiny shrew of a woman.

Nice. This was getting dramatic! But then this frail woman whose ass I could definitely kick publicly dragged me to the principal's office in front of all my peers. I had hated this gym teacher ever since she wore her high school cheerleading outfit to school last Halloween and did nothing but loudly brag all day about how it "still fits." She had curly gray hair shaped like a dirty poodle's and was the same size I was in about third grade.

She told me to "sit tight" as she walked into the principal's private office. A minute later I was invited in. The principal, a dowdy woman who always looked as if she were pregnant but never was, terrified me. My gym teacher pled her case. "This outfit belongs in a nightclub, not at school. She'll be a distraction in class to the other students."

I found this statement ridiculous. As if students wouldn't be able to do their algebra equations because I made controversial fashion choices.

The dowdy principal looked at me and said, "Stand up."

Nervously, I stood my long body up and tried to salvage what little pride I had left. I tried to stand up straight, thinking about how proud my mom would be of me that I was finally displaying good posture. My mom always blamed Laverne as a bad influence on my spinal alignment. It felt as if it took three days for these two old biddies to make a decision about whether or not my ensemble was too wild for a public regional middle school in central New Jersey.

"You can't wear this to school. I agree. You are way too distracting."

Come on! They were actually saying that there was no way any students could possibly concentrate as long as I rocked this look. This was ridiculous. The drama of getting pulled into the principal's office (and missing first period social studies) was fun at first, but now things were getting real. What was wrong with these women? I had seen girls come to school in midriff tops paired with hideous oversized jeans à la Kris Kross and no one called them "distracting." I had seen guys "busting the sag" so low on their jeans that the entire backside of their underwear was showing and the principal glided right past them. In comparison, my outfit was quite tame. My risky fashion statement was just more noticeable because I towered over almost every person in the school. I couldn't slip through the cracks like those petite crop-topped girls in my homeroom. No way I was going to take this lying down. "So, my outfit is more distracting than Teresa Carimonico's pregnant belly?" I asked, using a tone I knew was going to get me in deeper. But I had a moral stand to take and, by God, I was going to take it.

The gym teacher gave the principal a look as if to say *We got her. Self-expression will remain illegal in school. Book her.*

"Call your mother. You're going home," said the principal.

What? What? I never in a million years thought that the bizarre response to my risky new look would be so extreme. And I didn't even get to claim that I was a rebel, a member of the noble youth, speaking out for justice against the establishment, because they didn't suspend me. No. I was officially being sent home "unfashionable."

The gym teacher went back to work, teaching pimple-faced kids to square dance, and I was left alone with the principal who dug in my file for my mother's contact information.

"She's at work and so is my dad," I said, hoping to get out of this one. "My dad works in the city, it's too far for him to come. And my mom is a teacher; she can't come to the phone. She can't leave her classroom."

"Well, we'll just have to call her then and make her leave, won't we? Next time think about that before you leave the house like this. What did your mother think of this outfit?"

"She didn't see it, she was at work. But I'm sure she would love it." Even though I had been bickering nonstop over nonsense with my mother in the past few months, I knew when it came to the big stuff she would be on my side. No one was going to tell her that her daughter was too weird-looking to be in school. I pled my case again. "She's a teacher at a school forty minutes away. You won't get her on the phone."

"Well then, we'll just have her paged."

The principal dialed my mother's school and asked for her snidely, staring at me the whole time with the same look Jessica Rosenstein gave me before my ill-fated fashion intervention in seventh grade. She flipped through my file, disappointed to find nothing else on me, as the receptionist explained my mother was working and could not be disturbed.

"Well, this is an emergency situation. I am the principal of her daughter's school," she said, giving me another look to say *See! See how much power I have? See what you've done?*

The principal waited as the receptionist paged my mother, then waited for my mother to get coverage for her class, then waited for her to make the trek to the other end of the school to answer the phone. At least ten minutes passed as she sat on hold, angrily shuffling papers to make herself look more important.

"Mrs. Leitman," said the principal, sneering at me to show she was winning, "I'm afraid you're going to have to come get your daughter from school today. She is wearing an ensemble inappropriate for a learning environment . . . Yes, she is fully covered . . . No, there are no curse words on her clothes . . . It looks like she's wearing some sort of leotard."

"Unitard!" I called out, correcting her ignorant mistake.

"Unitard. She belongs in a disco. A nightclub. A rock concert. Not school."

"So what?" I thought I heard my mother say. Her voice was getting progressively louder on the other end.

"So what? She cannot possibly stay here dressed like this."

"She's a free spirit!" screamed my mom. I heard her loud and clear that time.

"Mrs. Leitman, I repeat, this is not optional. You must come pick up your daughter at once."

I heard rumblings of my mother screaming things like "coverage" and "substitute" and "not using up vacation days for this crap."

Then the principal stood awkwardly repeating, "Hello? Mrs. Leitman? Hello?"

My mom had hung up on this wretch of a woman.

Badass.

"You know," I said, "she has to get a substitute teacher for the rest of the day, and drive forty minutes to come get me now."

"Well, then maybe she'll learn to pay closer attention to her daughter's choices from this point forward," she retorted.

This really got me going. She was attacking my mother's parenting! "It's called being a working mom. You work. Do you have kids?" I subtly glanced at her bulging, faux-pregnant gut, knowing full well that she did not have any children.

"That's none of your business. You can wait out there until your mother comes. And when she gets here, send her my way." She opened the door to her private office and shuffled me out.

I sat there in my unitard waiting for over an hour in silence for my mom to save me. When she finally arrived, it was a grand entrance.

"Mom!" I called, and jumped up out of my seat to greet her.

She looked at my outfit and said with rage, "You look fine."

"Mrs. Leitman, can you please sign your daughter out right here," said the receptionist, passing over a clipboard and a Bic ballpoint pen.

"I have my own pen," said my mother with a scowl, as she took out a keenly polished sterling silver Cartier pen my grandmother had gotten with her employee discount. She angrily signed her name with perfect penmanship and slid the clipboard over to the receptionist staring at her with a look that screamed *Don't fuck with me.*

"Let's go," she said, and gestured for me to get up.

"Mom, the principal wants to talk to you," I said meekly, feeling as though even relaying this message was accepting defeat.

"No thank you," she said, throwing her JanSport purse over her shoulder and guiding me out the door.

And on that note we busted out. Two tall ladies walking arm in arm, feeling stronger than ever. Once we got into the car my mom gloated, "I'm not speaking with that woman. I won't give that bitch the satisfaction."

As we stayed home watching *The Price Is Right* together I had a feeling the bickering was going to ease up between us. She even let me keep my unitard on all day. My mom had never had my back more.

CHAPTER 10

A Dangerous Camper

As eighth grade continued, word spread about me being sent home "weird." There wasn't much hope that things would improve. I had basically peaked at the surprise party in October, and my social status had tumbled downhill from there. Bored and anxious, I begged my mom to send me to a performing arts high school in Red Bank, a few towns over, where I was positive I would fit in. The high school allowed you to pick a major from the most awesome subjects ever: creative writing, dance, drama, vocal performance, photography—all the stuff my heroes excelled in. I imagined it as a land of freakishly tall girls who had a flair for the arts, like Theodosia from my modern dance class. People seemed cooler in Red Bank, as if they wrote Beat poetry and talked about "society." I had purchased all my vintage dresses for the seven Bar/Bat Mitzvahs I had gone to that year in Red Bank. I would go into Backwards Glances on Broad Street and stare at all the vintage clothes while waiting for my mom to pick me up from dance class. She was always late and blaming my father for it. "Well, I would have been here ten minutes earlier but you know, your father." My father what? She was always vague enough for me to ask no questions. What my mom didn't know was I liked the extra time I had alone after dance class. Looking at Pucci prints and leisure suits, I would dream of what it would have been like to be alive at a time where bright orange unitards were celebrated rather than oppressed.

I slipped hints here and there about how much I wanted to go to school in the cool town. "You know, I could just go straight to dance class from school if I went to the Arts Academy. Wouldn't that make your life easier?"

"It's no trouble for me to drive you. The only reason I'm ever late is your father," my mom would respond, not picking up on the hint.

I also tried a more practical approach. "You know, Mom, the sooner I get training, the sooner I can start making money for the family."

"Make money doing what?" she asked, her ears perking up.

"I don't know . . . recording my first album? Designing my first fashion line?"

"Margot, you're scared to sing in public, and you refuse to learn how to sew. Have you noticed I've stopped offering you sewing lessons? I've given up. But you are welcome to get a job when you start high school. I'm sure there are plenty of local businesses that would welcome a hard worker like you."

Ugh. Making clown sundaes at Friendly's was hardly the career path I was hoping for.

When the end of the school year approached and it came time to actually enroll in the cool school, my mother told me that she was sorry, but it was just not possible for me to go. There was simply no way to get me there every day. I was too young to drive and had two working parents. I figured as much. My brother was going off to college at an out-of-state school and there was no money to spare. She reminded me that the public regional high school was free and just a two-minute walk away. It's true that the public regional high school was just behind my house, but to get there you had to traverse a path populated by broken beer bottles, cigarette butts, and high school delinquents (a.k.a. scuzzes) who hung out there before, after, and during school. Deeper in the woods, just off the path, girls with low self-esteem gave blow jobs and hand jobs to popular boys like Chad Decker.

Although my mom clearly lived her own high school experience to the fullest (I would often sneak peeks at her high school yearbook, filled with inscriptions from cute 1960s boys who were all openly in love with her), she sensed my lack of excitement about the four years that lay ahead. Once the logistics of my brother's college tuition were all taken care of, my mom offered me a compromise.

"Margot, your father and I thought, since we can't send you you-know-where"—my mother delicately avoided mentioning my dream school by name—"we could at least send you here." She then passed me a brochure for what was essentially a Disneyland for weird kids: Camp Wallobee, a place for "Youths Who Excel in the Arts." I opened it up to find a summer curriculum that was every artsy-fartsy kid's wet dream: dance classes, music classes, a radio station, theatre, video classes, and horseback riding. What was up with summer camps' fascination with horses? Eh, well, at least there would be other things to do than ride horses. At Camp Wallobee I would *make art*. It actually looked amazing.

* * *   I counted down the days until it was time to go off to sleepaway camp, renting relevant movies from the local video store for research. I watched films like *Sleepaway Camp* and *Friday the 13th*. So many great horror films took place at camps. In these movies, teenagers

were always sneaking off to the woods to go neck while a man with a mask and a chain saw lurked in the bushes. Living on the edge like that was just the spice my life needed.

About a month later, my mother and father drove four hours with me to rural Pennsylvania—destination: Camp Wallobee. We pulled in off a winding dirt road to pure heaven. From the car window I could see depressed-looking kids in tie-dye, shaggy-haired boys sitting under trees with guitars, girls in leotards practicing a modern dance routine in the trampled green field.

Camp Wallobee was going to be awesome.

"Well, here we are," said my father.

As he put the car in park, my mother had already begun tearing up.

"We're going to miss you so much, sweetie," she said.

I grabbed my duffle bag and they walked with me to bunk 9, where the older girls resided. We were greeted by my bunk counselor, a young Brit named Agnes. My mother immediately bonded with her over their shared heritage.

"How are you liking America? Are you missing anything from back home?" my mother asked, desperate to rehash some of her favorite vile British traditional foods with her new BFF, my counselor.

"Oh, it's nice so far. But it will be hard to go a whole summer without my Yorkshire pud."

Oh no! Seriously? One minute into camp and my mom is already discussing my least favorite food with my cool older counselor?

"Oh, Margot hates Yorkshire pudding. In fact she even claimed to be allergic to it to get out of eating it!"

"Allergic?" squealed the counselor. "To Yorkshire pud?" Agnes let out a cackling laugh, which my mother all too quickly joined in on. While they had a good hardy-har-har at my lack of love for beef-flavored pudding, I became anxious to unpack my 1970s wardrobe onto my bunk shelves. Eventually she hugged me good-bye.

"You'll be in good hands," said my mother, glancing over at my British counselor.

I didn't care if I was in good hands or not. I just wanted to be among my people.

Sure, the summer in between eighth and ninth grade was an odd time to *start* going to sleepaway camp, but I didn't care. It was a new experience, and I was open to wherever it took me.

I opened the creaky screen door to find a bunch of teenage girls with funky asymmetrical haircuts, almost all in vintage clothing and '70s prints. Most of the girls in my bunk seemed mildly depressed, like me. They wore combat boots in the summer, had journals by the side of their bunks, and dried flowers in pretty blue bottles. I had found my element. These girls were the misfits in their hometowns, but at Camp Wallobee, they were cool. I quickly gravitated toward the saddest-looking girl, a morose teenage rebel named Jackie Angel. Jackie had a hippie mother, dyed black hair with bangs, and dark circles around her eyes, which made her truly the embodiment of cool chic. Even better, she was a whole year older than me. "Wanna listen to some music?" she asked, in her deep monotone voice.

"Sure," I said, as Jackie Angel took out some homemade mix tapes.

"My mom loaned me some stuff—she's got great taste. We could maybe, like, perform one of these songs in the talent show this week."

"Totally!" I said, and we quickly got to work. Jackie Angel was a good singer, unlike me. She seemed to understand what it meant to harmonize, while I just sang more quietly on the hard parts. On the second night of camp, we snuck into the costume shop and stole some cool outfits for me to wear that fall to high school. Somehow having a black-and-white embroidered jacket from Guatemala made me feel less scared to walk down that skuzzy path in the fall. By day three, Jackie Angel had convinced me to become a vegetarian. I discovered new foods like sprouts, chickpeas, and bulgur and I looked forward to using my dietary restrictions as an excuse for my paleness back home at the Jersey Shore.

A few nights later I performed an obscure antiwar ballad with Jackie Angel in the camp talent show. I was disappointed that the Gulf War had ended before I had a chance to really protest, but this performance was a nice compromise. Afterward, we sat back down in the audience next to an Argentinean boy with long hair, who leaned over and said, "I like your song. It has good message."

Finally, I was getting discovered.

"My band meets at east field tomorrow at noon," he continued. "We like it if you ladies join."

Jackie Angel squeezed my hand.

"Sure, that sounds cool," I said, all aflutter.

"Nah man, that's cool, but thanks," said Jackie Angel. She smiled at me. I realized she was letting me potentially be the star of the band, and she was okay with that. I'd known her for three days and already she seemed to care about me more than any friend I had met back home.

The next day I joined the Argentinian boy's band, PBJ. We were supercool because everyone thought PBJ stood for *Peanut Butter and Jelly* but it actually stood for *Psychedelic Blow Jobs*. We did only covers, no originals; we were saving those for our big-time record deal.

That night I auditioned for a play. Camp Wallobee seemed to have a dozen plays rehearsing at all times, and most of them held no appeal for me. There were old-timey musicals and dramas and silly children's theatre. But one play was perfect for me: *Little Nell*, an over-the-top melodrama about a damsel in distress. I was far from "Little," but I thought it might be funny to put a now five-foot-nine-inch camper in the title role. Rodreigo, the youngest counselor in training, had already been cast as the male lead, so he got to sit in on the auditions. I looked around at all the petite girls auditioning before and after me and prayed the director would get my little joke. Thankfully, I aced the audition.

I improvised a line at one point, saying to one of the shorter girls I was reading with, "You're not short, you're vertically challenged!" All the short girls were in stitches. When we finished the scene, Rodreigo pointed at me and said, "I want her."

I thought I had peaked singing my antiwar ballad a few nights before, but boy was I wrong. I had finally found my groove at Camp Wallobee. Perhaps if I lived there all year round, I could be happy. Jackie Angel and I stayed up almost every night in our bunk, having serious talks about kissing and boys and parents, developing a deeper connection. I practiced with PBJ for our final performance and rehearsed with Rodreigo for my play. Rodreigo and I never got anything done; we laughed and goofed off and rarely got around to rehearsing. There was only one other camper in our play, an odd quiet boy with glasses, and he was too busy strategizing his next move on his everlasting game of Risk.

Rodreigo was only slightly older than I, but he seemed very worldly. He was smart, bilingual, and well traveled, and was like no one else I had ever met back home. On the other hand, our director seemed right out of *Meatballs*; she was more concerned with her days off and who was hooking up with whom to focus on staging and character development. We spent the majority of our rehearsals gossiping about staff hookups, which felt fun to be on the inside track of. It turned out the Shakespeare director was shagging the costume designer. There were hardly any camper-to-camper hookups, as only about fifteen boys went to this camp, many of them were under twelve, and most of them were gay.

The night of the show I got a little nervous. I had been there less than two weeks and was about to go onstage in front of the entire camp in a leading role. This was the first time I'd be the one making a public mockery of my size. In the past I had fallen victim to public taunts, but here, at Camp Wallobee, I knew that wouldn't happen. At least, I was pretty sure. I was cool. I was cool at camp. I just hoped that the audience would get the joke when my character was introduced as "Little Nell." Also, there was the small problem of me not knowing any of my lines due to incessant gossiping during our valuable rehearsal time. I'd never been the lead in a play before. In the summer theatre workshops back home it was all done musical-review-style. There were no words to remember. Just some kick ball changes while singing the hits of Andrew Lloyd Webber. This was big-time. I took solace in the fact that Rodreigo didn't know his lines either. If we were going down, we'd go down together.

The curtain opened. He delivered his opening monologue and then introduced my character, "Little Nell." I took the stage in a pink and white puffy dress with a giant pink bow in my hair . . . and the crowd went wild, laughing in hysterics at the ultimate sight gag. It didn't matter that we didn't know our lines. They were enthralled by our genius hilarity. We plowed through the general idea of the script, basically improvising the entire thing and receiving uproarious applause at the end. This was the first time I had a little humor about my size. And giving the audience permission to laugh felt really badass. I friggin' loved it.

Rodreigo and I hugged at the end of the play, laughing at what we had just gotten away with. "You are so funny!" he said, after our embrace. "I couldn't have gotten through that without you. It would have been a total disaster."

I didn't need four years at an expensive arts high school. A week and a half at Camp Wallobee among my people was enough to make me begin to understand life beyond my small town. With one oversize pink bow I had proven myself as funny to a group of artsy teens, and most importantly Rodreigo, who I thought was just the greatest person. We looked around for our director so we could celebrate, but she was nowhere to be found. "She's probably off giving a handy to the soccer coach," said Rodreigo, cackling with laughter at his own joke. "Let's go meet our fans." He grabbed my hand and we went out to accept the uproarious accolades from the brooding teenagers waiting at the stage door. I lost Rodreigo somewhere in the shuffle, but it was okay. This kind of attention I loved . . . attention for an accomplishment, a talent (and I use that word loosely), not a crazy outfit or embarrassing moment. I was on fire.

Camp flew by. I wished so bad I could have stayed there all summer—all right, more like the rest of my life. For my final performance with PBJ, I sang lead on a bittersweet "November Rain" and played tambourine on "Paint It Black." I'd be lying to say anything less than "I nailed it." I wore one of my father's oversize white button-down work shirts with the sleeves cut off. I laced my combat boots over my Lee Relaxed Fit Extra-Long Riders and sported a backward white sailor's hat. I had never felt sexier. Kids in the audience took pictures of me on their disposable Kodak cameras so *they* could remember this moment. Wow. I had wanted to rock for so long; now I finally was a rock star, not to mention a hilarious leading lady with a cool best friend, and it was time to go.

PBJ decided to make the most of our last night at camp, sneaking out of our bunks to have a wild last night in the woods. Maybe we would even be chased by a dangerous masked man lurking in the woods. Unfortunately, the actual sneak-out proved uneventful; we mostly ended up walking in circles around the woods, trying to scare one another. The members of PBJ didn't have much of a personal connection beyond the music, and truthfully that night made me doubt that we were bound strongly enough to ever get that record deal. I wondered if legendary bands like the Who were actually friends offstage. Surely Roger Daltrey and Pete Townshend would find something to talk about deep in the woods. PBJ did not. We reviewed our last performance at the talent show, but beyond that we really had nothing else to talk about.

"Good job, Margot."

"Thanks, Ben, good job on the guitar."

"Way to wail on that high note."

"Yeah."

No one even had weed, and this would have been the perfect night for me to try it. The girl who played tambourine had a bottle of Diet Coke from the canteen, but that was about it. If Jackie Angel had been there, we would have had some sort of be-in, but this sneak-out was for the birds. I made out with my Argentinean bandmate just because I was bored.

Just before the sun started to rise, I arrived back at my bunk to find my British counselor, Agnes, wide awake, pacing with her arms crossed. She didn't even give me a chance to attempt immunity with her by engaging in a discussion of traditional British foods. Before I could utter a word about blood pudding and Cadbury Flake candy bars, she brought me directly to the camp advisor's office, where the rest of PBJ were also incarcerated. The camp advisor had already been informed there were campers on the loose. He seemed excited that he got to flex his barely used authoritative muscles. Artsy kids were so used to being teased that we rarely caused trouble. In camp horror movies, it's always the hunky sports counselors and the big-boobed swim instructors that are first to die after they have sex in the woods. My kind of folk would simply lock the door and continue reading their novel by candlelight if there was a killer on the loose. As the sun came up, I listened to this man's prewritten sneak-out lecture. Finally, he got to break out that old chestnut.

"We have no tolerance for deviant behavior at Camp Wallobee," began the aging camp advisor, who had clearly been smoking since he was fifteen. "I have alerted the local police, just in case." I looked around at the other deviant campers, who all seemed to be stifling laughter. I was fairly certain he was lying about alerting the police. There were no cops anywhere to be found; he didn't call the cops to tell them we had turned up; and I was fairly certain that even if he had alerted the cops, they had worse crimes to deal with than a few rebellious weird kids hanging out after hours. The camp director continued, "You will be stricken from our camp records; we don't want alumni like you destroying the Wallobee name. You will be put on the Dangerous Camper List."

Dangerous Camper? I liked the sound of that. Jackie Angel hadn't come with PBJ on the sneak-out, so I was thrilled to be more dangerous than she. I walked out of the camp office excited that I had made an impact. The sun was shining and all the campers were saying good-bye. I would not be allowed to return to Camp Wallobee, but it was just as well. Because of my age, next year I would have to be a counselor in training, and I had no interest in disciplining anyone, especially a bunch of flamboyant campers only slightly younger than me.

My dad arrived to get me, conversing with the mole bunk counselor who had turned me in. He also got the same speech from the camp advisor regarding sneaking out against the rules. I wasn't sure, but I thought I detected a smirk on his face when he was told I was on the "Dangerous Camper List." There was no time for good-byes: My dad wanted to get in the car quickly to start the long drive home. I had already gotten Jackie Angel's and Rodreigo's info to keep in touch. Although I was a little disappointed I wouldn't get to give them good-bye hugs, I'd rather a quick good-bye than brew on the fact that I was leaving the only place I ever felt at home. My new, delightfully weird friends from camp were going to be my social circle and ticket to a new life. I was absolutely going to stay in touch with Jackie Angel and Rodreigo. So what if I had no driver's license and Jackie lived in Pennsylvania? So what if Rodreigo lived in Puerto Rico and there wasn't a shot in hell I'd ever visit there? I had just experienced three weeks of bliss and was headed home in high spirits about my future.

My father sped off in our Plymouth Voyager down the long dirt road in silence. He had spent about fifteen summers of his life at camp, as both a camper and a counselor. In every childhood photo I had ever seen of him, he was wearing his camp uniform. Most of the people at our house parties drinking endless Rolling Rocks were his friends from camp. My father was the king of camp. I was terrified he would be mad at me for dishonoring the institution of camp.

When we got to the highway, he finally spoke. "I'm proud of you, Margot. Nights like that are what camp is all about. You'll remember last night more than any other night you've had here for the past three weeks. Live your life."

I smiled. I was finally cool, and my dad was, too. He understood our need to rebel against the rigid establishment of camp schedules and bunk rules. I decided not to tell him that last night was pretty tame compared to his swinging '60s sneak-outs. I let him think I was a dangerous camper.

CHAPTER 11:

The AIDS Cookie

High school was to begin a month after Camp Wallobee ended, and this year, starting school again was a little more tolerable knowing I had cool friends just a few hours away. A few weeks later that summer (though it felt like months), Jackie Angel invited me for a weekend in her hometown in rural Pennsylvania. To be honest, Jackie Angel's invitation both terrified and exhilarated me. She was wild, she was older; her long dark bangs gave her a Demi Moore in Striptease vibe. And she was really into boys. I could tell guys liked Jackie Angel even though she was tall, almost as tall as I was. But it was clear that Jackie Angel was tall in a sexy way, not a gargantuan way like me. I imagined Jackie Angel could slink into a room, light up a cigarette, and strike up a conversation that would have every horny boy in the vicinity fighting for her approval.

Jackie told me she dated older guys who actually remembered the '70s. These were borderline-men who didn't have to stand on a few phone books to make out with her. The guys at my school all seemed to be the size of Webster compared to me. Already I had begun to fantasize about going to a battle of the bands at the local VFW where an older, tall, long-haired guitarist would notice me from afar while he strummed along to U2's "All I Want Is You." Instead, still the only guy who ever came close to that back home was Jonah Hertzberg, the guitar player with the Jew fro. Seeing another world at camp made me realize that options are truly limited when you're a gigantic giraffe in a school full of Shetland ponies.

It was just as well. I was still recovering from the damage that years of elementary and middle school health classes had bestowed on me. What I had taken from these lessons was that if I came into contact with a penis, I'd immediately die of AIDS. I knew I'd have to experience contact with a genital at some point or another, but Jackie Angel's invite made me fear it would happen sooner than I expected. Out of all my many health classes, the elementary school ones were still by far the worst. Amid all the other assemblies that tried to prevent us all from ever tasting alcohol or puffing a joint, it seemed every month of fifth grade our teachers would bring some guy into the cafetorium who actually had AIDS to scare us straight. Somehow my school never had enough pencils, milk, or substitutes, yet they had the budget for an endless supply of men with AIDS. I remember one particular guy would walk through the crowd of distracted, bad-mannered fifth graders and tap a select few on the head, saying, "You, you, you, you . . . you've got AIDS. Statistically, that's how many of you have AIDS." I almost had a full-blown asthma attack from the expectation of being tapped on the head and told I had AIDS. Even though I was in only fifth grade, I had to question his wisdom. *Really?* I'd think to myself. *Five out of 75 fifth graders in middle-class New Jersey have AIDS?* But nonetheless, as a horny teenager in the making, I was listening. I believed the words of every man with AIDS who came to our school. I believed that my raging hormones would eventually kill me and that it would be best to assume that everyone had

AIDS and not act on the sexual desires building up in my pubescent mind. Besides, I didn't want to have to call that Tampax operator again in a panic; the first time was humiliating enough.

I knew my weekend at Jackie Angel's could be a disaster in the making. Chances were high that in due time, rolling with a girl like Jackie Angel, I would come into contact with a genital. Nonetheless, I wanted to extend my camp experience, so with my parents' permission, I boarded a train to Pennsylvania. "Have fun, Margot, but not too much fun," my mom instructed. She was too distracted by the recent death of her mother to see the one thousand red flags about this trip. I was fourteen, traveling alone, across state borders, to visit an older girl with bangs she had never met. Instead of a lecture on safety, she gave me a hug, sent me on my way, and went back to knitting her forever-unfinished afghan.

Jackie Angel's house was exactly as I had imagined it. It was a home run by an aging hippie—very wooden with glass Mason jars filled with lentils, raisins, and almonds all around. My mother, being a fellow tall girl, kept no glass anywhere in the vicinity of a hardwood floor. She knew better. Did Jackie Angel live in a world where tall girls didn't shatter every breakable they encountered? That summer alone I had destroyed a glass coffee table, my mother's antique teacup, and a Precious Moments figurine (okay, that one was on purpose). I had managed to shatter all that even with being gone for three weeks of summer. Jackie Angel lived in a tall girl's parallel universe, and I wanted in.

She took me to her attic, which smelled musty and was covered in tapestries. She blasted the Guess Who and offered me a joint. I had been so preoccupied with my fear of genitals that I hadn't had time to worry about drugs. I said yes, of course, and as "These Eyes" played I put the soggy joint to my lips, the whole time thinking, *It figures I would turn to drugs. All the greats have.* I knew everyone in my father's record collection had smoked pot, including his dream girl Joni Mitchell. I wanted to rock too. After a laughing fit in the shower, and the amazing discovery that plums "taste soooo friggin' good," I decided that I liked marijuana and remained stoned for the rest of my trip.

My second night there, Jackie Angel took me to a party at one of her cool guy friends' houses. I don't know where his parents were; for all I knew he might have lived there alone! "Hey, Margot, this is my friend John. Man, John, I haven't seen you in like ages!" Jackie Angel and John embraced and then he came over to me. John looked as if he could be one of the guys she knew who remembered the '70s.

"What's up? I'm John," he said, flicking his cigarette into an open can of Natty Light.

"What?" I asked, losing focus and staring directly at his tattoo, a skull on his left bicep with the word *Dad* underneath. The only people I knew with tattoos were my parents' Vietnam vet friends. I had never met someone close to my age who was already inked up. Didn't you have to be over eighteen to get a tattoo? And if you were under eighteen, didn't you need parental permission? John seemed like he was neither over eighteen nor under any sort of parental supervision. He had definitely gotten that tattoo illegally. Wow. I was playing with the big boys.

"I said, I'm John. You're a friend of Jackie's?"

I nodded, my eyes wide.

"Cool." John smiled, just long enough to show the gap between his two front teeth. Hot. He lit up another Marlboro Red, gestured for me to sit down, and then ran his fingers through his long brown hair. He had the same dirty, dangerous, and deviant vibe as Sebastian Bach, and I instantly fell in love with him. And he was taller than me! This was my first opportunity to make out with someone who didn't need to stand on a bleacher first. Next to John, I actually felt small, the way a girl really wants to feel. I could act tough, tortured, and misunderstood all I wanted, but really I just wanted to feel small and dainty and to be swept up in the arms of some big strong man who could make me forget for just one moment how self-conscious I really was. Staring into John's eyes, I knew this moment could actually happen with him. Then, in the next instant, I remembered from my school assemblies that he would definitely give me AIDS. But talking had to be okay, right? We chatted for a bit and I found out that John was seventeen years old, a high school dropout who had been kicked out of his parents' house. Now it was confirmed that the tattoo had been acquired under illicit circumstances. Nothing was sexier to me than a guy who tattooed the very name of the person who threw him out of the house on his bicep. The second his dad saw that skull tattoo, he'd surely offer him his room back. When Jackie Angel and I finally left, we stood in the driveway saying our good-byes, and John grabbed me and kissed me passionately in front of the entire party. I had to stand on my tippytoes to kiss him! Something shifted in my burgundy velvet pants stolen from the camp costume room. This wasn't love; this was lust. Only this time Bobby Brown was nowhere in sight. John was a real-life person, not a music video, and I lusted for him.

I proceeded to spend the rest of the weekend smoking weed with John and Jackie Angel. On the second day we helped Mrs. Angel clean out the attic. She asked me to carry down the antique glass Christmas ornaments that had been given to her by her grandmother so she could put them in a safer place. Honored that Mrs. Angel trusted me with her most prized possessions, I carefully stacked the boxes and headed down the stairs, making sure to look back at John sexily on my third step, the way I had seen Greta Garbo do in one of the black-and-white movies my father forced me to watch while my brother took copious notes. I gave John the eye, making sure to blink twice, and then slowly turned my head back so my hair would swing as if it were in slow motion. Unfortunately, my left foot missed the next step, causing me to fly down the stairs on my bony butt. Crashing down a flight of stairs is quite possibly the least sexy move a girl can make, aside from stepping in dog shit during a first kiss.

I stood up when I reached the bottom, shouting, "It's cool, guys, it's all good. I'm fine. Really. I do stuff like this all the time."

No one cared if I was all right. All eyes were on the bloody glass ornament massacre I had created. Not one antique had been spared. This was total annihilation. I had ruined all their Christmases forevermore.

Right then I knew I was in no position to be running with a crew as hip and coordinated as Jackie Angel's friends. Everything Jackie touched and everyone she knew was the embodiment of cool. John was no exception. Somehow, though, John and I pretended we made sense for the rest of the trip. My final night there was spent making out with John under a completed afghan while a group of Pennsylvania stoners sat around watching *Streets of Fire*. I knew they could hear us, but I liked pretending that the colorful yarn was just as good as a wall.

I was really into the heat of the moment. This was the furthest I had ever gone with a guy, and John seemed to have all the right moves. His *Dad* tattoo was uncovered, our pants were half off, and underneath the multicolored afghan, I felt a genital move toward me. It didn't come too close, but it definitely brushed my thigh, and I just knew I was milliseconds away from contracting the AIDS virus. What if it came closer? Being a high school dropout, John probably had a lot of time on his hands to gain some heavy-duty sexual experience. I had basically none, so I thought back to my school assemblies for guidance. I could hear that scary man with AIDS threaten me, "You, you, you . . . you've got AIDS." I took both hands and pushed it away. No! No AIDS! No penis! I would not be a statistic!

Then the fear set in. Oh my God! Pre-cum! Pre-cum! Overheard conversations from the descendants of the White Lipstick Posse as well as my horse camp counselors had taught me all about pre-cum. In a large coat closet during a Bat Mitzvah at Temple Beth Ahm, Jessica Rosenstein had lectured several of us girls on the dangers of hand jobs.

"I'm just saying, the second you touch it, even though you can't see it, pre-cum just leaps onta you. It's, like, microscopic. Don't say I didn't warn you." I was positive that AIDS had come out in John's pre-cum, and in that moment of pushing his penis away, it soaked into my bloodstream through my hands and destroyed my life.

Seconds after this thought, I heard, "Margot, time to go, girl!" Jackie Angel's hippie mom was coming to drive me to the train station to go home. There was no time to wash the AIDS off my hands; we were running late. THERE WAS NO TIME! I unfolded myself from the afghan, quickly said good-bye, and then raced upstairs—weaving among Mason jars, a disgraced, terminally ill whore on her way back to meet her parents in Jersey.

I ducked into the back of Mrs. Angel's station wagon as we headed off to the train depot, both terrified and secretly pleased with myself for having such a wild weekend. I stared at the slender hands that had just touched their first genital and feared for my life. I didn't want to say my thoughts out loud for fear of losing both Jackie Angel and her mom's respect. Theirs was the only place I could go to escape my mundane existence. If they knew I was freaking out, I could lose essential cool points with the coolest girl ever and the tallest and baddest boy I had ever met. John was the only guy who ever liked me besides Jonah Hertzberg and the weird guy who gave me T-shirts.

Just before my heart leapt out of my chest, Jackie's mom made a brief pit stop at 7-Eleven. She returned to the car with a box of Entenmann's soft-batch chocolate-chip cookies. I loved soft-batch cookies, but we never had them at home. My mom had moved on from Pecan Sandies and now stocked the house only with Lorna Doones, a cookie reserved exclusively for British hags over seventy. The Entenmann's looked and smelled especially good to me, considering I had been stoned for three days straight and just finished a hearty dry-humping session. At the same time, I was positive I would accidentally ingest AIDS via the cookies. I didn't care anymore. I wanted to taste them so badly I was willing to become a statistic. When Mrs. Angel tossed the open box into the backseat asking in what seemed to be slow motion, "You want some?" I knew I was screwed.

I looked down at the box, tempted by chocolate and sweet satisfaction. What was she doing? She was offering me a box of the most delicious cookies in the whole entire world. The temptation was killing me; I was staring death in the face and it smelled magnificent.

Like a savage beast, I tore into the box, holding nothing back. Well, Margot, are you happy now? If there was a shot in hell that you didn't get AIDS before, you have blown your chances now. Enjoy your cookies, slutsky.

I savored every bite of the twelve soft-batch cookies I consumed in that backseat, licking the crumbs off my fingertips. I knew when I got home I would only have stale Pecan Sandies to gorge myself on. Plus, after being stoned for the past three days, they tasted extra, extra delicious. I wasn't sure if AIDS could be transmitted via pre-cum from a penis brush-off onto an unwashed hand into a soft-batch chocolate-chip cookie into the bloodstream. My teachers never mentioned it.

I never uttered a word to anyone about my inner fears—I hoped I was just being neurotic. Eventually the terror wore off and I fantasized about turning the whole experience into a possible cash cow. I contemplated writing a letter to Entenmann's telling them my story as a testimonial to how much I loved their cookies. I fantasized about getting my big break when they made a commercial of my risqué tale starring me. But alas, I never wrote that letter to Entenmann's, but instead wrote letters to John.

CHAPTER 12:

Lesbian Shoes and Baby Teeth

High school began the day after my trip to Jackie Angel's house, and from the start it was nothing but stress. Right away there was a blood drive, which I opted out of on the off-chance I had contracted AIDS from the penis brush-off/cookie ingestion. I looked like a real jerk for refusing to give blood for sick people, but I blamed it on my vegetarian diet, claiming I had no blood to spare. Medically it made no sense but I couldn't handle the pressure of possibly infecting innocent people after eating all those possibly pre-cum–infected cookies.

Also, I was getting weird bruises all over my body. There were purple and blue marks on my upper arms and thighs, giving me a Courtney Love/punk rock look that I loved to admire in the full-length mirror in my parents' room. Bruises gave me a damaged look that really aided me when pouring my soul out into my journal alone in my upstairs bedroom. However, the bruises were for my eyes only. Considering I was into a rock 'n' roll man's look, I didn't often show any skin. My long-sleeved butterfly-collared shirts were usually worn with a tank top underneath, paired with jeans, and usually with a scarf to accent. I had learned a little about fashion while watching Roger Daltrey in *Tommy* one afternoon on HBO and knew that less is more. So there were no rumors going around regarding my bruises about me being beaten at home and/or having an abusive boyfriend. Of course, in order to have an abusive boyfriend, one must have a boyfriend in the first place, which I did not.

But the bruises persisted, and after rocking a black tank top à la Joan Jett one afternoon at home, my parents got worried. One day I left school early so my mom could take me to the doctor. It turned out I was severely anemic. This meant that I had very low iron count in my blood, probably due to my sudden and strict vegetarianism brought on by trying to emulate Jackie Angel at camp.

When the doctor offered his diagnosis, my mom had trouble controlling her glee. For her, this was a tiny victory, as she believed I had quit eating meat just to make her life more difficult. It must have been a hassle for my mother to have to make a separate meal for me each night, but I felt like meat was something I just had to take a stand against. I wasn't sure exactly why, but it felt good to be actively protesting against something.

"So, Doctor, this means that Margot will have to reintroduce meat back into her diet, then?"

"Not necessarily," he said, and I watched my mother's face fall. "She just needs to eat foods high in iron, like spinach and beans. Here's a list of some good vegetarian options."

My mom scanned it, looking disappointed.

The doctor continued: "And she needs to take iron pills. But with the pills and an altered diet, the bruises should clear up quite quickly."

We left the office mostly feeling relieved that nothing serious was wrong. Although she was uninterested in making burgers out of lentils, she was especially happy nothing major was ailing me. I sulked a little on the car ride back knowing that without my punk rock bruises I would no longer resemble a more articulate Nancy Spungen. At home, the phone was ringing, and it was my friend Derek calling to see if I was okay. Derek was a fun guy whom I'd known for years and often paired up with on class assignments because he, too, valued the social rather than the academic aspects of working as a team. He was in the class that I was taken out of to go to the doctor's and had seemed concerned when I'd left early. Usually anytime Derek or I left a class it was to fake sick to get out of an exam. We even had prewritten cues to back each other up. For example, if I faked a headache to go to the nurse's, as I walked out the door Derek was always supposed to ask, "Wow, Margot, what's with all these headaches?" This was to reinforce that my headaches were a recurring problem, not an isolated incident, to add to their believability. So when I left early for a real doctor's appointment, Derek was taken a little aback.

"Are you okay?" he asked, prepared for the worst. "What did the doctor say?"

"It's nothing. I was diagnosed with anemia, and I'm being treated for it."

"Oh," he said, sounding serious. "Will you be in school tomorrow?"

"Yeah, of course, it's no big deal. I'll see you then."

"Okay," he said. "Good-bye, then, Margot."

It was a weird call, and it seemed overdramatic. Well, at least he cared.

But the weirdness continued. At school the next day, a lot of people welcomed me with hugs instead of ignoring my presence as usual. All through the day, people seemed to be speaking to me more slowly and, strangely, more loudly as well. I sort of enjoyed the kind attention, though it felt as if something was up and I should probably figure out what. Finally, I got to seventh period, my class with Derek. He had saved me a seat next to him.

"How are you feeling?" he asked as I sat down, making very sincere eye contact with me as if to say, *I know what's really going on.*

"Fine," I said. "I had some spinach last night and took my iron pills. I should be on the mend."

Derek looked confused. "When do you start the real treatment?"

"That is the real treatment."

"No, I mean . . . ," Derek leaned in real closely and whispered, "the hospital treatments."

"Why would I go to the hospital?" I asked, now super confused.

"Because you have leukemia," said Derek, looking around the room for eavesdroppers as he said the word *leukemia.*

"What?" I said, practically shouting. The rest of the students turned around and stared at us. "I don't have leukemia. I said I had *anemia.* It's a minor problem, an iron deficiency. Did you tell the whole school I have leukemia? Is that why everyone is being so nice to me today?"

I looked around and a few of the other students mumbled yes and nodded their heads.

"Derek, are you serious?"

Derek stared at me, silent. Clearly he had no idea what to say. Then he burst into hysterics. "I am so sorry, Margs," he said through laughter.

I wanted to stay mad at him for creating unnecessary drama, but I couldn't help the fact that I'd loved the attention I'd received all day. How could I stay mad at Derek? He was my accomplice to many a fake illness. Now he had bestowed me with the Cadillac of fake illnesses. Watching him crack up, I couldn't keep a straight face. I started laughing too.

"I'm glad you're okay, and I'll try to clear up the rumor . . ."

I controlled my urge to tell him to wait a few more days so I could milk the schoolwide sympathy. Instead I said sarcastically, "Yes, the rumor, the one about me being terminally ill? That rumor?"

"Yes," Derek laughed. "That rumor. I'll try to clear it up."

I shook my head at him as we went back to our studies. I did like the way people treated me that day, but I didn't like that it was because they thought I was really, really sick. But just as the rumor died down, lucky for me, I got mono and got to miss an entire month of school.

Mononucleosis, also known as "the kissing disease," was the be-all, end-all of high-school illnesses to get. I got it from being run-down, but no one needed to know that. Everyone would assume I had kissed someone to get it and would be speculating about who it was! Yes, I had kissed John in Pennsylvania, but no one at school, not that anyone needed to know that either. My rep was ready for some rumors about whom I had kissed. I hoped in my absence classmates would be too distracted by solving the puzzle of my secret love life to finish that stupid homecoming float. Even better than that was how bad everyone felt for me. I reveled in pretending to be asleep on the couch while my mother stroked my head, saying things like, "Poor thing, she doesn't know how sick she is." And, the best part was, the doctors had to do a massive amount of blood tests on me while I was sick, which put a halt to my assuredness that I had contracted AIDS that fateful weekend when I came into contact with a genital at Jackie Angel's house. To add to the awesomeness of being AIDS-free, rumored to have been kissing someone, and having my mom feel sorry for me, Amy Fisher had just shot Mary Jo Buttafuoco in the face, and I got to watch *all three* made-for-TV movies about the scandal. We're talking *The Amy Fisher Story* starring Drew Barrymore, *Casualties of Love: The "Long Island Lolita" Story* starring Alyssa Milano, and *Lethal Lolita* starring some other chick. Each one was more brilliant than the next, and it saddened me to know that one day this scandal would die down. What I didn't know is that just around the corner Tonya Harding would bash in Nancy Kerrigan's knee and I would be able to get my tabloid fix once again.

Another great thing about mono was that the kids at school actually took a break from purposefully mispronouncing my name as

"Maggot" and instead began worrying about my health. Sometimes, because I lived so close to my high school (just a quick trip through that skuzzy path), kids would stop by after school to see how I was feeling. Of course, nobody cool like Chad Decker would come. I was mostly visited by kids like Larry—the lone senior in my otherwise all-freshman French 101 class. But still, people actually felt *sooo* sorry for me. I went from being visible only when I was being teased to the person people were rallying for to get back on her feet. Life was pretty good.

When I returned to school I was about five-foot-nine and down to 120 pounds from my illness. I borrowed my father's red sweater, to match my red lace Betsey Johnson tights (bought on clearance at Macy's), and wore it with a black skirt and black combat boots. I still wasn't back to my full strength, so I hoped that red (which I read in *Glamour* magazine was a "power color") would make me look less gaunt and sick. I was ready to get back to life. The timing couldn't have been better. I was just turning an age when being a giant girl was considered Amazonian and sexy. After six years of feeling too tall, at fourteen it was suddenly sort of okay to have some height. At school, Frankie Patucci, the only out-of-the-closet person at my school, told me I looked like model Kristen McMenamy. I wasn't sure if I actually resembled her or if he was just comparing me to a model due to my mono-induced weight loss. Either way, I took it as a compliment, even though I had no idea who Kristen McMenamy was. She wasn't included with the majorly big-time fashion models of the time: Cindy Crawford, Christy Turlington, Linda Evangelista, and Naomi Campbell. But if she was a model, she had to be tall, thin, and beautiful, so I was flattered nonetheless and imagined one day coming into my own enough to walk a runway like my doppelganger Kristen. For the first time I felt redemption for all the awkwardness my size had caused me. But then I read an article about Kristen McMenamy in a magazine in my orthodontist's office, which said she was "known for her unconventional, androgynous gender identity." Basically she was famous for looking like a dude. So much for flattery. *I've got news for you, Frankie Patucci*, I seethed silently. *No tall girl wants to be told she looks like the model that looks like a man. Next time go for the generic Claudia Schiffer if you want to compliment a hulking blonde woman.*

Meanwhile, my mom was a little on my case at home regarding my fashion choices, which she famously referred to as "free spirited" to my middle school principal. A week after I started working at a low-budget drugstore on Main Street, I went to a teacher awards dinner for my mom at an Italian restaurant about twenty minutes away, wearing black-and-white-striped thigh-highs, a baggy black sheath, and "Coffee Bean"–colored Revlon lipstick. I felt like the belle of the ball in my bedroom, but when we got to the event, my mother had a different opinion.

"Margot, please," she hissed in a volume just short of a yell, finally taking a break from studying her acceptance speech to notice my outfit. "I can't believe you're wearing those lesbian shoes to my big night."

I looked down at my shoes. I always donned a pair of authentic combat boots, purchased at the army/navy store, to complete my teenage antiestablishment look.

She hissed some more. "You're tall already, and those clunkers add an extra inch and a half. You'd have a lot easier time at school if you wore cute flats like I did."

Now I knew I was in for it. *Here it comes.*

"I would never have been crowned runner-up for Snow Queen if I shopped at the army/navy."

I was about to explain for the eightieth time that I had no interest in ever being crowned anything as mainstream as Snow Queen, when I was cornered by a stout yenta just dying to know the pleasures of being tall.

"Oh, you must be Pam's daughta. You're so tawl, just like her. Do you play basketball?"

"No."

"Volleyball? Beach volleyball. You couldn't live in a more perfect area to play beach volleyball."

"I don't play volleyball. I'm not good at sports."

"Oh, well then, do you model? You should!"

"I can't model, I'm uncoordinated." *And apparently I resemble a woman who looks like a man*, I didn't tell her. "And also there's this problem." I showed the yenta the mouthful of baby teeth behind my recently adhered braces. It had just been determined that I was unable to produce adult teeth for some of my pearly whites. Lucky for me all the missing teeth were located right in the front of my mouth, and for the meantime I still had the baby teeth. Meaning that when I smiled, I resembled a killer whale. The orthodontist decided braces were the best option to move my non-baby teeth into the right places so we could eventually pull the baby teeth and one day implant permanent fake adult teeth. This lethal combination of braces/baby teeth and with a few crooked adult teeth was enough to convince her that my height served me no real advantage. You can't be a model if you look like an orca. She seemed disappointed, and I understood. I wasn't so happy about it either. After all, right when I became old enough to no longer be viewed in the same category as André the Giant, I got my braces *on* as everyone else was getting them *off*. I couldn't win.

My dental defect was my deep dark secret in high school—as if being asked repeatedly by Chad Decker if tall girls also had huge vaginas wasn't enough. Plus, I'd finally been freed from the fear that I had AIDS from my encounter with a genital in Pennsylvania, and now my orthodontist refused to switch gloves between patients. I'd lie in his squeaky chair in the middle of a row of miserable, brace-faced teens, and watch effeminate Dr. Clott go from patient to patient wearing the same blood-stained gloves. I'd learned in health class that we were *extremely* likely to get AIDS from a dentist, and if I was the next statistic, I knew Dr. Clott himself would be solely responsible.

At least he gave me choices for the style of braces I'd wear. I opted for the "clear" braces, enamel-colored squares adhered to the front of my teeth with the optional neon rubber bands. In elementary and middle school it was the cool thing to get red- and green-colored bands around Christmastime, orange and black for Halloween . . . you get the gist. Nothing says *Happy Easter* like cheese-stained pastel rubber bands in an acne-faced teen's mouth. I'm sure that's exactly how Jesus would have wanted his resurrection observed. I opted for the "tooth-colored" rubber bands, which yellowed as soon as they hit the air. My teeth looked like the fangs of a chain-smoking vampire.

By my sophomore year, I was so unfortunate-looking—tall, gangly, braces, baby teeth—that I faked sick on picture day. I wanted no proof that I ever looked or felt like this, no preservation of this memory for years to come. Strangely, when the yearbook came out, all the other missing people were listed as "not pictured," except for me. In place of my photo was just a blank space. No name, nothing. It was as if I didn't even exist.

When I finally got my braces off during sophomore year, there was no time to celebrate, because they then ripped out the baby teeth and gave me a retainer with removable teeth on it. This was another step on the way to my permanent fake adult teeth. In order to eat, as with any other retainer, I would have to take out my front teeth—only, of course, after making very sure I was alone. This worked fine at home, but in the cafeteria, surrounded by upperclassmen discussing dieting and Boone's Farm strawberry-flavored wine products, I attempted cold grilled cheese on pumpernickel with my retainer still in, allowing the food to rot up there for sixth through eighth period. It was more important to have bad breath and be mistaken for normal than to let anyone know I was a giant girl in lesbian shoes with missing teeth. And despite having to endure history class with cream cheese stuck to the roof of my mouth, for the most part it worked.

However, I *would* take the retainer out when I ate dinner at the drugstore where I now worked. Here I toiled alone at the back lottery counter, where I sold scratch-offs and Pall Malls to loyal local customers such as Squirrel, the town pimp. I always ate between 8:00 and 9:00 PM, right before we closed and I knew no customers were coming in. The pharmacist worked the front counter and was too busy to notice the toothless teenager chowing down in between selling losing lottery tickets. The entire shift I looked forward to the eggplant parm sub from Vito's Pizza next door, the hottest hangout in town. Vito's wasn't only a pizza place; it also doubled as a marijuana delivery service. The pizza department was run by two smokin' Italian brothers named Vito and Vinnie. The pot department was run by a few thugs from school who made no attempt to be inconspicuous. I didn't think much of it. Considering that just that year ago a girl had given birth in the school nurse's office, and that kid in my homeroom had been arrested for murder, I figured Vito and Vinnie's pot/pizza place was the least of this town's problems.

So nobody seemed to mind the fact that Vito and Vinnie were also running a marijuana ring out of their pizza parlor. They were still legitimately running a pizza business anyway, so who cared? Every night, for a year of high school, I would place my order, then put on a coat of tinted Blistex before Vito or Vinnie stopped in. Even though Vito and Vinnie weren't my type—for one thing they were both under five-foot-eight—they had great smiles and didn't know what a freak I was at school. It was all that kept me going, a smile from a cute Italian drug-dealing brother, right before I took my teeth out to eat dinner alone at the drugstore lottery counter, five nights a week, longing for my days at camp.

One particular night, Vinnie brought me over the usual eggplant parm sub, hold the weed. As usual, I made sure the coast was clear, popped out my food-crusted moldy retainer with three fake teeth on it, and took a gummy bite. Just then, Cecelia Rios, the hot, big-boobed cheerleader from my school, came up to the counter. How could I have missed her? Shit! Now, towering over her with my retainer in my hand, it was too late to put it back in. I tried to play it cool, clenching my saliva-ridden, halitosis-stanked retainer with falsies and smiling at her without opening my mouth. I had gotten really good at the tooth-free smile lately.

If Cecelia finds out I have a dental birth defect, my future is fucked. I'll end up working for the town pimp Squirrel and giving birth in the nurse's office.

"Hey, Cecelia, how's it going?" I said, speaking as if I'd been in a horrible car accident and my jaw was wired shut.

"Good, Margot," she said, looking at me suspiciously, her back arched, huge breasts sitting pertly under her size-small MATAWAN HUSKIES sweatshirt.

"Just this?" I asked, desperately hoping that she was buying something embarrassing like Imodium A-D or a pregnancy test, so when she told everyone I had no teeth at least I could retaliate by saying, "Well, she's knocked up and has runny poops." But no, she was just purchasing a greeting card.

As I rang up her card, clenching my teeth in my right hand, I thought, *The gig is up. She's going to know, you've got to pop your teeth in quickly before she figures it out. Just pop in your teeth, give her the change, end the transaction, and she'll be none the wiser.*

My heart was racing. My whole life could come crashing down at this very moment. If I didn't do something fast, Cecelia would see that I was toothless and tell everyone at school, including Chad Decker. He would now have the fact that I am without teeth to add to the relentless cafeteria Gulf War protest teasing and ruthless claims that I have a huge vagina. Word of this would spread faster than Teresa Carimonico's pregnancy and the reveal of Milli Vanilli's lip-synching combined.

I was shaking, and the moment seemed to last an eternity. Cecelia Rios was staring at me strangely, eager to get home and retrieve her phone messages from various hot guys or do whatever it was popular people did. It was time to make a move.

I took a deep breath, faced Cecelia, threw all her change in my mouth, and handed Cecelia Rios my fake teeth.

As soon as it happened, I knew I was dead. I stared in horror at Cecelia as she looked down at the fistful of falsies I'd handed her. Utter repulsion registered on her face a full beat before she could speak.

"Ugh, ugh!" she gasped, disgusted. I couldn't blame her. I was pretty grossed out, too, and they were mine.

Still, I couldn't believe it. I had mixed up what was in each hand. I actually handed the captain of the cheerleading squad my teeth. I had put in her hand the single most prominent reason why I would never, ever be cool. I had to act fast or this would only get worse. There was no time to strategize, so I did the only thing I could: I snatched back my teeth, spit the 93¢ out into her hand, popped in my fake teeth, and said, "Thanks, Cecelia!" with a smile.

"Whatever," said Cecelia, horrified, and she shook her head, her perfectly conditioned hair swinging as if it were in a Pantene commercial, and walked out the rickety door.

It wasn't until then that I completely freaked out. She was going to tell everyone! I was absolutely positively never, ever, ever going to be cool! How would I be able to go to school the next day? I imagined it spreading like wildfire that I had a dental defect, that I had dentures at fourteen, and that I was a humongous freak. That I would be selling lottery tickets and Pall Malls to the town pimp for the rest of my life. That no one should ever love me and that this would forever be my life: the pharmacy, eggplant parms from Vinnie or Vito, and my vague resemblance to a she-male. I was nothing.

I tried to stay home sick the next day, but having just faked sick from the school photo, my mom was on to me and made me go (after my morning tea and biscuit, of course). I arrived at school and tried to blend into the crowd—which was difficult being almost five-foot-ten and owning nothing but crushed velvet attire. But to my surprise, nothing happened. Beyond the usual purposeful mispronunciation of my name as "Maggot" and being told I looked like "Girl Eric Clapton," no one said a word about my teeth. *Cecelia must be absent today*, I thought.

But the following day nothing happened, either. Then a week went by, and then a month, then two months, and still, no one said anything about my teeth. My nickname did not become "Gums," Chad Decker didn't wait by my locker mischievously asking me to flash my "pearly whites." No one left me those windup 1950s teeth toys in my desk or offered me gummy candy teeth for dessert at lunch. Cecelia Rios, surprisingly, never told anyone about what happened in that drugstore. How could that be? I figured she just didn't know what to say. After all, how could she explain it?

"Uhh, she, like, gave me teeth and ate my change. I dunno, she's weird."

To comprehend this one would need a full understanding of orthodontics at a Dr. Clott level. Cecelia didn't have time to ponder how exactly my teeth ended up in her hand and then back into my mouth, giving the impression that they were somehow connected at the root. She was too busy cheerleading, dating, and having a real social life that didn't involve Vito or Vinnie from the pot/pizza parlor.

But on the other hand, maybe she was just a nice person. Maybe she had been embarrassed some other time and understood. Perhaps even cool girls faced humiliation from time to time and weren't necessarily mean-spirited. Maybe underneath it all we were all hiding embarrassing secrets, and some of us just kept them to ourselves while others blatantly placed those secrets in the hands of others. Maybe underneath that tight-fitting sweatshirt Cecelia Rios was stuffing her bra like the rest of us. And for some reason, that thought gave me just enough hope to get through that year.

CHAPTER 13:

Subsidiary Acid Tripper

S adly, my dating dry spell continued for about two more years. The most recent notable experience I'd had with a boy was my penis brush-off in Pennsylvania. I was now a junior and had no interest in anyone from high school, which worked out well because the feeling was mutual. Tan girls of average height with straight brown hair seemed to be the standard of beauty. *Friends* had started airing, and no one seemed to be lusting over Phoebe. I identified with Phoebe. We lengthy, pale vegetarians who bruised easily were on the outs. I needed to find other venues to meet people like me. My father's classic rock record collection and my brother's VHS tape of the Woodstock documentary were swiftly becoming my best friends, so I decided to branch out and start seeing live rock shows. Luckily my town was situated near two major concert venues so there were many options to see rock 'n' roll in the flesh. After all, what's the point of being a teenager in New Jersey if not to at least attempt to re-create the nights Bruce Springsteen sang about?

The best venue was the Garden State Arts Center (now the PNC Bank Arts Center), which was about ten minutes from my house. This was a humongous concert venue with stadium seating and lawn seating and it could hold 17,500 people. Huge acts like Metallica and Phish would play here during their concert season. During the off-season it was home to large-scale events like the Holiday Spectacular, something I never attended but imagined was filled with tiny dogs in Santa costumes and lots of flavored hot chocolate. The Arts Center would announce their spring-fall programming, and I would scour the long paper calendar circling all the shows I wanted to see: the Moody Blues, the Allman Brothers, the Indigo Girls, Santana, and anything that relied mostly on kick-ass guitar solos (acoustic or electric).

I didn't have a driver's license, so I had to arrange an early ride to the box office the day tickets went on sale. My friend Eli, a short boy with long hair who occasionally wore skirts to school, got himself a ride with two seniors and offered to take me along. I was never sure as to why he wore skirts sometimes. My guess was that because this was during the horrific Guns N Roses *Use Your Illusion* era when Axl Rose began wearing kilts, Eli may have misconstrued Axl's fashion statement and thought the door was wide open for women's wear in general. Eli was a great guitarist though, and lucky for me, because he was friends with the other musicians in school, he had an in for a ride. I was ecstatic; I was going to get to the Arts Center on opening day and get lawn seats to every classic rock show available. My life was changing! I had listened to rock music alone, and I had tried to play rock music—but now I was becoming a full-force live rock music connoisseur.

I even had my own money to buy my tickets. Thanks to the raise I had gotten at the drugstore (I was now making $6 an hour), I no longer needed to moonlight by babysitting those vile twins. Finally, I had watched *Look Who's Talking* for the very last time. And due to a miniscule social life, I was working around the clock. I was making the equivalent of the cash windfall I had received years ago at my surprise party. I could definitely afford a few concert tickets. Once I got these tickets in my hands, my boring '90s teenage life would be more like the '80s debauched youth I had always fantasized about. I'd worry about who would join me at these shows later. For now it was all about the music.

The morning of opening day, I waited by the bay window at 6:30 AM sharp so all the seniors would have to do is honk. I didn't want anyone knocking on the door, causing my embarrassing dog to bark at them and then hump them gently as he escaped out the front door. I also didn't want my mother coming down in her bathrobe and offering the seniors tea. I waited eagerly until a dented black 1982 Camaro pulled up with Led Zeppelin blaring. The brakes screeched to a halt as they honked the horn a little too loudly for 6:30 AM on a Saturday morning. Luckily my dog, and mother, didn't notice. I quietly exited the house, opened the car door, flipped the front seat forward, and tried my best to ease my too-long legs into the pint-size backseat.

"What's up?" said one of the seniors. These boys were remnants of the '80s New Jersey hair metal heyday and had long hair and black leather jackets and Marlboro Red cigarettes dangling from their mouths. They didn't give a shit about grunge music, and they'd certainly never seen the movie *Singles*. They were from the time when Skid Row and Bon Jovi hit it big and put Central Jersey on the map, before bands like Soul Asylum and Soundgarden took over and we all started dressing like high-class lumberjacks. Before I could answer their question of "What's up?" they turned up the radio, Jimmy Page blared a perfect riff, and they sped off. Eli gave me a look that said *You can thank me later.*

During the ten-minute drive to the Arts Center, I thought I was going to die about seven times. The seniors ran red lights, slammed on brakes, drove up on curbs, each time laughing harder than the last. Apparently slamming on the brakes in the middle of a four-way stop sign intersection is friggin' hilarious. I clenched my fake teeth and did kegels so as not to pee my pants and wet the already-stained backseat. I could only imagine what the previous stains were from, and I tried not to let my mind wander too much, as I'd finally recovered from the penis brush-off.

At least the ride was invigorating. I told myself that this was probably how girls like Tawny Kitean and Jessica Hahn rolled in the '80s. I was truly living on the edge at last! And it being 6:30 AM on a weekend in a small town, almost no one else was on the road. We soon arrived at the venue and the senior with the long black hair parked in a manner that somehow made the Camaro take up three spots.

We climbed out of the car to a reasonably empty parking lot, and to our surprise there was hardly any line. I got the feeling something was wrong, like when the Griswolds finally arrive at Walley World in National Lampoon's *Vacation* and pull in to an empty parking lot. I worried the Garden State Arts Center might also be "Closed for Renovations." But luckily, there was no automated moose telling us we were screwed. Like the Griswolds we were the "first ones here . . . first ones here," but unlike the Griswolds we walked up to an open ticket counter. We each purchased our tickets for the season and sauntered back to the car, feeling excited about what was to come. No major disaster, just some overzealous planning on our part. I couldn't believe there wasn't a line around the block for those Moody Blues lawn seats but no one else seemed fazed.

The drive back was equally terrifying. These guys drove like they were being chased by a 'roided-up Loch Ness monster. By the time they pulled into my parents' driveway, Eli and I were clutching each other's hands in anxiety while holding on to the "oh shit handle" usually reserved for hanging dry cleaning. The car screeched to a halt and Eli and I finally allowed ourselves to breathe. "Wow, you guys are really driving like crazy this morning, aren't you?" asked Eli, in a brave attempt to address the elephant in the Camaro.

"We are?" the senior driver asked sincerely. He then looked at his friend and they both started laughing a little too hard and a little too long. "Sorry, guys," said the last remaining die-hard fan of hair metal, "we're on acid!" The two seniors looked at each other and laughed in a way that would only make sense if one were on acid. They got louder and softer completely in synch, pausing for seconds at a time, then starting all over again in perfect harmony. I wanted to get out of the Electric Kool-Aid Acid car, but there was no way I could sneak my giant frame out without getting one of these spawns of Timothy Leary to stop his hysterics to flip my seat forward. I had seen movies where people smashed car windows with their bare fists in order to break free from scary people like kidnappers and jewel thieves. If only that kid in *Cloak & Dagger* had thought of that, he wouldn't have gotten chloroformed by the three-fingered senior citizen.

Finally, in complete synchronicity, they stopped laughing. The driver calmly turned to the backseat to say, "We took it late last night and haven't been to sleep since. At least we were on time, right, bro?"

"Right," I said, not sure if it was Eli or me that they were addressing as "bro." "Thanks so much for the ride, see you around," I said, hoping that was enough of a hint for the guy in front of me to move so I could get out. He didn't move, though, so I began pushing the passenger seat forward, along with the tripping passenger in it. At last he understood and got out of the car, allowing me to exit in a less humiliating manner than unnecessarily smashing a window with my bare fist. I looked through the backseat window at Eli just before they sped off, and he stared back with the look of a kid being shipped off to Jesus Camp for the summer. His pressed his hand against the window as one does when talking to a loved one on a prison phone, and as the car took off I hoped for the best. Now that I was safe, I was exhilarated. Being a subsidiary acid tripper was just the jolt I needed to start living the rock 'n' roll lifestyle I so desired.

The concert season started soon after and I loved finally having something to look forward to during snooze-fest civics class. The only problem was, between my drugstore salary of $6 an hour and whatever extra I had saved up babysitting the twins down the street, I actually didn't have enough money to see every single concert I had hoped to. Taxes and hidden fees had jacked up the prices just enough that I would have to cut a few out. I wanted to be hearing live classic rock music every single week—I needed the escape from the present-day trends of Counting Crows and hemp necklaces, and the weeks I didn't have tickets to a show were depressing. More and more, though, I was hearing about people I knew from school getting summer jobs at the Arts Center. If only I had been smart enough to apply for a seasonal position there. I wouldn't have had to take that ride with the acid trippers for tickets because I would be able to see all the shows for free, albeit while wearing a horrendous canary yellow and navy blue uniform. The weeks I didn't have a show to look forward to, I sat alone in the dreaded third-period lunch (who wants to eat mass-produced sloppy Joes at 10:00 AM?), writing in my journal about how I wanted to be anywhere but here.

Then I discovered that my favorite substitute teacher, Mrs. Bernstein, moonlighted at the Arts Center as security. I loved Mrs. Bernstein. She seemed smarter than the majority of my full-time teachers, and her hard-assed-ness somehow seemed comical to me. I guess any shake-up from the day-to-day ritual of high school made me slightly happier. I bet she was great at her Arts Center job. She was short and built kind of like a potato, and I was sure that with her self-confidence and sassy sense of humor she could overcome that grotesque yellow and navy uniform. In fact, I was sure she could rock it. It seemed an appropriate position for her, as she took school security very seriously when she subbed, interrogating anyone who asked for a bathroom pass to determine whether or not he really had to "make" or if he was going to "smoke on her dime."

In between accusing students of faking coughs so they could go to the nurse and hiding gum underneath their tongues, Mrs. Bernstein mentioned while subbing in my psychology class that she would be working security at that weekend's Tom Petty concert. I was over the moon. Tom Petty was on my B-list of acts to see, and so I hadn't sprung for a ticket, but I had been regretting that decision for weeks. Now I had hope. I knew Mrs. Bernstein liked me, as neither of us really belonged at this school, and perhaps she would sneak me in the door. I didn't want to be so gauche as to ask her ahead of time, but I thought surely she would have my back when I hit her up for a favor on the sly.

That Saturday, I went to the Arts Center along with a cute female friend I'd known since elementary school. Lucky for me the cute girl had fabulous taste in music and was not a member of the White Lipstick Posse. After the Cecelia Rios incident I now understood that some cute, cool girls were also nice and high school would be a more enjoyable experience if I let go of the assumption that everyone was out to get me. Sure, some people were out to get me. The girl who waited at my locker every morning to ask me, "What the fuck you wearin'?" certainly was not looking to be friends. But the quasi-popular girls who kept their opinions to themselves about my flared orange pants were just fine to socialize with. This old friend of mine was short and pretty, and liked by most, so surely Mrs. Bernstein would also fall under her spell. Neither of us had tickets, so the cute girl was game to attempt to get in via Mrs. Bernstein.

We cased the joint until we found Mrs. Bernstein's entrance. We waltzed up with the confidence of high rollers walking into a casino. Mrs. Bernstein stood proudly in her yellow security jacket, eager to check tickets and enforce rules, her favorite pastime.

"Hi girls, got your tickets?" she asked, somewhat rushed, and a little less happy than we had hoped she'd be to see us.

"Mrs. Bernstein, hi! I didn't know you worked here!" said the pretty girl. I loved the way pretty girls always snuck lies in for no reason, just because they could. I was always trapped by the truth, feeling like there was no such thing as a "little white lie" coming from a "gigantic white girl."

"Yup, I do. Every weekend, all season. Tickets?"

"Well, that's the thing, we don't exactly have tickets and we were hoping you'd help us out," said the cute girl as she stroked her hair, checking for split ends.

"Nope, sorry girls. No can do! Next! Tickets!" she called, eager to dismiss us. I could tell from her tone we weren't the first high school kids to try this amateur move on her tonight. I turned to go. At least we tried. Even though tonight was a bust, it was better than staying home watching *All About Eve* again with my parents.

"It's just that we couldn't afford them, we don't have a lot of money," continued the pretty girl. I began pulling at her arm, signaling to just give up and leave.

"Yeah, well neither do I," retorted Mrs. Bernstein. "Why do you think I'm working here? For my health? I have bills to pay, and I'm not about to get fired on account of youz two. So beat it!"

"Did she just say 'beat it'?" mouthed the pretty girl, clearly in shock over Mrs. Bernstein's outdated lingo. This night was not going as I had planned. Listening to a substitute teacher/security guard's outdated catchphrases was not exactly how I wanted to spend my night.

"Thanks anyway, Mrs. Bernstein, see you around." I pulled the short, pretty girl away, which was fairly easy considering I had about nine inches on her.

"I have a better idea anyway," she said. "Let's go back to the car."

We walked back to her mom's minivan, and the concert started. I could hear "Yer So Bad," one of my favorite Tom Petty songs (not too overplayed, but just popular enough), opening the show. I hoped the pretty girl had a real idea. I wanted so badly to get inside. She dug around in her car and pulled out two super tampons. Oh no!

Not another super tampon! Super tampons still terrified me. They still meant to me that you had a massive amount of blood gushing out of your lady parts and that you also had a wide vagina in order to hold the enormous thing in place. Knowing full well how many times I had corrected Chad Decker that tall girls do not have larger vaginas, I always made sure to buy "regular" tampons, hoping someone would see me ring them up at the counter and learn to rethink their closed-minded views.

"Here, take this," she said, and handed me the super tampon, which I held suspiciously. "I have a plan." She walked back toward the Arts Center with purpose, clutching the super tampon as if it were a baton she was eager to hand off at the end of a long lady trek. I followed her lead to the opposite gate from where we had failed to break Mrs. Bernstein.

We approached a large, male security guard, who had no line and clearly hated his job. "Tickets," he stated, visibly disturbed that we were coming in so late.

"Hi. We don't have our tickets. But our friend inside just got her period." The macho guard visibly flinched, and the cute girl took this as an encouraging sign. She continued, "She got it real bad. And we had to go back to the car to grab super tampons so she didn't bleed all over the place." The guard let out an audible "Ugh" at the word *tampon*. The pretty girl then brought it home: "Our friends and our tickets are inside." The pretty girl then held out her hand to reveal a super tampon and nudged me to do the same. Now the guard had a visual of a bloody girl somewhere within the venue just waiting for her super tampon to plug up her extra-wide, blood-spurting vagina. It was more than enough to make things happen.

"Alright, alright! Just put those things away. Go in, find your friend." The guard looked traumatized. His giant hands appeared to be trembling at the mere thought of menstruation. He wanted us as far away from him as possible, and he wanted to forget the image of the super tampon as quickly as he could. That we had in common.

"Thanks!" she said, and gave a cute wave back to him. She grabbed my arm as we walked in to "Don't Come Around Here No More" and said, "I tried that a few weeks ago and it totally worked. So far a fool-proof method."

I tossed the super tampon in the first trash I found and went from disgusted to thrilled. The tampon scam was the coolest thing I had ever pulled off, and the biggest success I had ever achieved in terms of manipulation. The pretty girl certainly knew how to get things done, and she majorly schooled me in the art of exploitation for the sake of music. That night, we chatted up some cute long-haired boys who seemed to dig me. By going to concerts so frequently I was discovering that while at school I was an undateable, gargantuan freak, at concerts I was a rock goddess. Guys at concerts complimented my outfits rather than making fun of them. Sure, maybe it was because concerts were always dark, but still, guys seemed to respond positively and that was enough for me. I had extreme confidence in dark, loud, crowded environments filled with people I would never see again. It was the day-to-day encounters with schoolmates under fluorescent lighting that I needed to work on.

CHAPTER 14:

Bubble Seduction

After the tampon incident, I was inspired to come up with a concert manipulation of my own. I wanted to meet long-haired rock 'n' roll guys and have a deep connection with an inevitable time limit à la *Before Sunrise*. What I came up with was pretty close to genius, as it worked almost every time. I would sit listening to the music, blowing bubbles I had gotten with my 25 percent discount at the drugstore. Then, hot, tall, skinny stoner guys with long hair (who all looked like me without the estrogen) would follow the trail of bubbles wondering, *Who is the rock goddess responsible for this simple pleasure?* Then, like a stoned Hansel meeting his doppelganger Gretel, the guys would follow the soapy spheres to me, the source, and I would greet them, rechanneling my *Octopussy* voice, and say, "It's me; I'm blowing the bubbles." Then they would stay and talk to me for the rest of the concert.

It was never a romantic connection, no numbers were ever swapped or awkward first kisses exchanged, but knowing that there were guys out there who enjoyed my company, albeit under a cloud of weed, kick-ass rock music, and manipulative bubble seduction, was just enough to get me through my week at school. After a concert, going to school to find that same bitch-faced bully waiting at my locker to say "What the fuck you wearin' today?" seemed almost tolerable. Listening to the tables of upperclassmen discuss their amazing futures that were just around the corner for them next year at college while I gnawed on a hummus-and-sprout sandwich all alone in the cafeteria wasn't so bad after a deep connection the weekend before over a joint and some Santana.

A few weeks after the super-tampon success was the They Might Be Giants concert at the other local venue, the Count Basie Theatre. Not wanting to be seen with a super tampon ever again, I decided it would be best to just purchase my ticket the old-fashioned way. The Count Basie Theatre was cheaper anyway, so I only had to work a few extra hours at the drugstore to afford the ticket. They Might Be Giants were in a different category of music than my usual straight-up rock. But they were a soundtrack to the outcasts, using unusual instruments like the accordion and pushing the rules of music by doing innovative above-the-law experiments like ten-second songs. They were music for nerds, and although I was not a nerd by traditional standards, I certainly understood how it felt not to be cool. These guys were alright by me, and I had copied all my brother's They Might Be Giants CDs onto cassettes when he went away to college. This was going to be a great night.

I packed my bubbles, borrowed my mom's special suede fringed vest, and headed out for a night of nerd rock. Even though this was an indoor venue, I figured my bubbles would still flow freely through the concert hall. And it being a more intimate setting, I figured the process of bubble seduction would work at a much more rapid pace. I arrived at the venue, found my seat, and just as the show began, with "Ana Ng" pumping through the giant speakers, I took out my secret weapon of suds. I blew those bubbles like it was my job, only running out of breath as the final chord of TMBG's most rockin' song came to a close.

A long-haired boy approached. Another successful bubble seduction! He was tall and thin, but his hair was dark, therefore making it slightly less narcissistic for me to be attracted to him. Corey was a little older, lived a few towns over, and had cute dance moves. He bounced up and down, keeping his arms restrained, unlike me, who flailed them around like I was the ghost of Isadora Duncan. He had good rhythm and wasn't trying too hard, which attracted me to him. Somewhere between "Particle Man" and "Birdhouse in Your Soul" he asked me where I was from and what my name was. We hung out, danced, and talked a little bit after the show ended. Corey even kissed me in the lobby at the end of the show. It was just a quick peck—no tongue, lasting a little longer than one would kiss a relative, but still further than anyone at school had attempted—and then he left. We didn't exchange contact information; emulating those hotties in *Before Sunrise*, the night was left as just a moment shared between two teenage misfits at a concert. No need to keep it going beyond that; it was what it was, and somehow the fantasy of wondering *what if?* was more exciting to me than any reality of seeing Corey ever again.

Two days later, a card arrived for me in the mail. It was from Corey. It said something about how he couldn't stop thinking about me since the concert. Then the phone rang. It was Corey. I said, "Uh, hi! I'm holding a card from you in my hand right now. How did you get my address? How did you get my phone number?"

"Easy," he said, in a voice that seemed much whinier than I remembered hearing when we shouted to each other over some badass accordion rock two nights before. "You told me what town you lived in and what your full name was. So, I looked up possible spellings of *Leitman* in the phone book until I arrived at one that matched your hometown."

What? I had only a few make-out sessions with Jonah Hertzberg and a brush with a genital with Jackie Angel's friend John as my previous experience, but I knew something was very wrong here. Sure, I had an affinity for horror movies after seeing *Chopping Mall* (tagline: "Shop till You Drop . . . Dead") at way too early an age. I also loved the thriller genre, having seen *The Hand That Rocks the Cradle* five times in the theatre, despite being under seventeen and it having an R rating. So maybe my alerts were slightly heightened, but I needed to trust my gut on this. Something wasn't right.

At the same time . . . I'd be lying to say that the thought of Corey turning into a creepy killer didn't excite me a little. How dramatic! This would truly be something to write in my journal about. Maybe this would build to him chasing me through the woods with an ax until I fell backward into a pile of muddy leaves screaming "No, no!" I thought back to the concert. True, he hadn't just asked me my name, he'd asked "What's your full name?" And I had said "Margot Leitman." To which he probably thought, *Okay, mental note, possible spellings: L-I-T-E, L-I-G-H-T, L-I-E-T, L-E-I-T . . . I will hunt her down and I will find her!*

I'd thought at the time that in asking for my full name he was just curious about my ethnic heritage. Because of my fair skin and height, people often thought I was Scandinavian. Maybe he was just checking to see if his hunch that I was from an adorable sweater-wearing culture was right. I had no idea he was going to use my last name as a tool in his overresourcefulness at staying in touch. Why didn't he simply just ask for my contact info? I would have given it to him. As creepy as this was, I didn't have any other options for love interests. No one else was into me; at school I was still thought of as a hulking weirdo, so I had to take what I could get.

Corey was still talking. "I was hoping to call first and then have you get my card second, but damn, that postal system is faster than I thought! I am impressed!"

"Yeah," I said, attempting to remain agreeable with this teenager clearly in need of a deeper connection. I tried to focus on what Corey was saying, but as he rambled on about America's underappreciated postal system, I became keenly aware that we really didn't have anything to talk about. Corey was like a vacation friend: fun to swim with on a deserted resort in Aruba, but beyond that fun in the sun and those piña coladas, there was no reason to stay in touch.

After a few moments of awkward silence, and a few more accolades about the U.S. postal system, we hung up. I figured that would be it. Hey, at least someone liked me! But a few days later another card arrived, then a letter. I made sure to start grabbing the mail as soon as I came home from school so as not to have my parents find it and wonder what was going on. Plus I've always loved mail. As a kid I would call 1-800 numbers to request brochures specifically addressed to me. My mom used to tease me when my monthly brochures for Craftmatic Adjustable Beds and the Raquel Welch Wig Collection would arrive, but I loved the thrill of something arriving addressed specifically for me.

Besides, I was kind of excited by Corey's pursuit. Yes, sure, it was strange how Corey got my info, but I admired his persistence. After being called "Maggot" and "Girl Eric Clapton" all day at school, I found it refreshing to come home to a letter from a weird boy a few towns over who thought I was "the hottest being on earth." I didn't need to actually see him; just knowing that *someone* out there liked me A LOT was enough to give me a twinge of hope that I could one day find the one.

Interspersed between the letters were phone calls, which I found less old-timey and exciting. We would hang up and then two days later I would receive a brief letter commenting on something he had forgotten to mention when we talked. He would take the time to handwrite things like "I forgot to mention, I also think Bonnie Raitt has a good singing voice," put it in an envelope, seal the envelope, address the envelope, stamp it, and find a post box to mail it to me. This guy was really dedicated to his correspondence. And slowly becoming obsessive.

Corey kept wanting to hang out, and I had a gut feeling that was a bad idea. He was becoming less like a vacation friend and more like a prison husband—fun to receive letters from, but if we ever met in person, he just might kill me. His initial search through the phone book to find the right Leitman scared me a little. Did he send letters to the other Leitmans and call them as well until he finally got to me? Was I being paranoid? He hadn't done anything dangerous, but why did he have to contact me every day? The more he asked about getting together, the more I started dodging his calls and not writing him back.

This only made him persist more. Never before had I been in a position of having the upper hand with a guy. I wasn't playing hard to get; I really didn't want to get gotten. I wasn't all that into Corey to begin with. My parents still had no idea Corey existed. I thought about telling them but worried I would be sad if it all came to an end. If Corey stopped calling and writing, I would be back to looking forward to a "hey" from Vinnie at the pizza/pot store as my only male attention.

Meanwhile, Corey's letters were becoming some bizarre meta experience, in which he instructed me how I should write him. They would be filled with sentences like "I am writing you to remind you that you should write me a letter. Stop reading this right now and start writing me a letter. Still reading? What are you doing? Start writing me!" And so on. I didn't find this desirable. But then again, I wondered if anyone would ever like me this much again, and if not, I should make the most of this. I began looking at my somewhat scary correspondence with Corey as a once-in-a-lifetime experience in being aggressively courted. Girls like me may never have another opportunity to be loved quite like this. I wasn't Alyssa with big boobs. I wasn't Jackie Angel with a cool swagger. I was Margot, or "Maggot," and in the same way that "boys seldom make passes at girls who wear glasses," boys also seldom made passes at girls six inches taller than them.

So I ignored his instructions for me to reply by mail, but I never told him to stop writing, either. Corey, in turn, resorted to writing right on the envelopes, in case I wasn't opening them. The envelopes would be decorated with "write me" or "call me" written over and over on the outside. Sometimes he would even start the letter on the envelope as a teaser both to me and the dozen or so postal workers who had handled the letter before it reached me.

Then, finally, came the coup de grace . . . the ultimate serial-killer envelope. This envelope was covered entirely with the phrase *CALL ME*, all caps, written in pencil hundreds of times in perfect penmanship. Then, erased into the hundreds of *CALL ME*s was a giant *CALL ME*. Then, on the back flap of the envelope, was a large *CALL ME* in which each letter was formed by a series of individual *CALL ME*s.

This wasn't fun anymore. Well, actually it sort of was. Sure, he had my home address and phone number, but he was *obsessed* with me. Me! A girl who once had a rumor spread about her that she had a penis! Some lonely teenage boy a few towns over liked me enough to spend hours decorating an envelope just to get my attention!

I put the envelope away and looked at it again after a good night's sleep. The next day it didn't seem flattering or fun. It just looked scary. I knew it was time to tell Corey to go. I opened the envelope anyway. I mean, who could resist? Inside was a Valentine card that read "Valentine, I think of you day and night, night and day, even when I'm asleep." Well, no one could question this card's authenticity.

He called later that day. I answered the phone, and told him I really wasn't interested. I tried to explain it was just a concert boyfriend/bubble thing, but he didn't understand. Apparently the four seconds we were able to chat in between "Istanbul (Not Constantinople)" and "The Statue Got Me High" was a deeper connection than he had ever felt. I tried to be nice and not hurt his feelings, but I don't think it made him feel any better to learn that for me he was just another concert boy to make my dreadful days of suburban high school more tolerable.

A few days later I received a letter from Corey while my parents were out running errands. The letter was full of graphic language that at the time seemed shocking, especially after the sweet, romantic letters he'd been sending. He wrote, "I thought we had something special, that doesn't mean we have to fuck or anything . . ."

Fuck? He said *fuck!* What? Wait! I was in shock! I didn't know you could mail that word! I stood by the bay window clutching the pornographic letter in horror. My mother's handmade rust-colored drapes captured the light in a way that made this moment extra dramatic. This would be a great closing scene to a horror movie, I thought. After the lead heroine thinks she's safe, a letter comes in the mail. The camera zooms out as she clutches it in the rust-colored lighting by the bay window . . . I really soaked in the moment. Just then, as I clutched the letter in my perfect cinematic lighting, I noticed my parents were home way earlier than I expected. I looked out to the driveway to see the Queen of England and my academic dad with the hood of the car open. This was a sight I had never seen—the two of them seemed to be working on the engine. Noticing that the car was smoking, I went outside to investigate.

"It's the strangest thing," began my mom, careful not to get grease on her cute denim jacket. "We found a block of wood in the engine next to the fan belt, where it almost caught fire. It looks like it was purposely placed there. *Maaargot*, do you know anyone who might have it out for you? A boy you may have rejected perhaps?"

I paused for a moment, gathering up the courage to tell my parents this was all my fault. I wanted to tell them how I was lonely at school and all the other girls had boyfriends and the only guy all year who seemed interested in me was Corey from the concert. I wanted to tell her my self-esteem was at a low point, that a girl waited at my locker every day to bully me about my outfits, that I'd sunk so low that I'd rather be stalked than invisible. But before I could even speak my mom apologized for suggesting such a terrible, impossible thing.

"Sorry, honey. Of course no one would do this to you."

I stood, mouth agape, insulted! I knew full well my mother was actually saying, *Sorry, honey, we know no one would ever like you enough to try to kill you.* There was no need to tell her about the stalking. I was dealing with a former runner-up for Snow Queen. My cute mom had probably been stalked by loads of guys dying to be her man. Even if I told her all, she would barely be impressed. I kept my flattering murder attempt by Corey to myself and went back to being ignored by local guys.

All communication from Corey abruptly stopped after that. I'm pretty sure it's because he thought he had succeeded at killing me. But I was right about something. I can safely say, no one ever did like me *that* much ever again.

CHAPTER 15:

He Looked Like a Man

Junior year continued, and after the stalking drama died down, I got a little stir-crazy. Nothing else eventful had happened to me all year. I was still sitting alone during third-period lunch, I was still working at the drugstore, and there were no other romantic prospects since Corey tried to set our car on fire. Also, I didn't have my driver's license yet, so I had to walk everywhere. Every day before I left the house, my mother would say, "Be careful, Margot! Be careful walking!" Be careful *walking*? Sure, tall girls are garishly clumsy, but every time my mother told me to "be careful walking," she might as well have said, "I didn't raise you to be a gawky klutz. Your grandmother was five-foot-eleven, carried a set of twins, and she never fell once in her life." I detested my daily walk to and from school, down the skuzzy alley past chain-smoking guys in Megadeth T-shirts, each of whom had everlasting hickeys on his neck.

At school if you were good at math, science, football, or band you had an automatic social circle. Those kids had it made with their math competitions, science fairs, football games, and endless group practicing of their brass instruments. The rest of us were left to fend for ourselves. I started writing innovative poetry instead of listening in pre-algebra class or participating in pep rallies. To my dismay, no one ever picked up one of my journals, purposely left open on my school desk when I left for methodically planned bathroom breaks, hoping to return to class to overhear classmates declaring me the next Sylvia Plath. Sadly my musings of the struggles of being young in the '90s were for my eyes only. My poem "Sick of Sixteen" was just begging to take over the poetry scene where Allen Ginsberg left off. I did my best to draw attention to myself whenever I was writing alone. I wanted someone to ask, "What are you writing?" so I could show him or her my feelings on paper. Then surely someone would read my poetry and be so deeply moved and inspired that he or she would say, "I have big-time connections in the poetry industry. Would you mind if I shared this book of original poems with my major-league colleagues and made you a star?"

My favorite poem in my collection was "Help."

I don't need your help.
It's useless.
Don't use that word for me.
Help.

I also sucked at poetry. It was yet another thing I wasn't good at.

Maybe it was because I was date-deprived. Beyond my brief seventh-grade romance with Jonah Hertzberg, the one peck with the They Might Be Giants–loving stalker, and Genital John from Pennsylvania, there was no action to be found. It's not that guys didn't want to hook up with me; I'm pretty sure they did. But they were interested in me in an "isn't that weird girl wearing men's pants kind of fuckable?" voyeuristic, Andy McCarthy, *Pretty in Pink* kind of way. Instead I wanted a guy who liked me in an "I identify with that girl with the Manic Panic–dyed hair and I, too, often feel like a misfit," Ethan Hawke in *Reality Bites* kind of way. I wasn't into brain-dead morons, so I chose to fantasize about Vito and Vinnie from the pot/pizza parlor and stay solo. I knew no world beyond the natural deodorant–wearing Blues Traveler fans, sloppy French kissing, and meat-headed boys who were curious about me for the novelty of it.

College still seemed like light-years away. I knew if I kept my grades up, I would have a lot of options for schools all over the country, but somehow that didn't seem real to me. I was a so-so student for my first two years of high school. I didn't care too much about grades, but I wanted to go to college as far away from my high school as possible and I needed the best score possible to make that happen. My brother, a straight-A student, had his pick of top-notch schools. Three years ago, after weighing his scholarship options, he left for Northwestern University in Chicago and was having a blast. My grades were more erratic, always As in English and writing classes but solid Bs and Cs in math and science classes. I wanted to go to a large, big-city school like NYU or Boston University for college, but my grades wouldn't be enough for me to be accepted. So I was banking on my SAT scores and extracurricular interests to get me in the door. But at a year and a half away, it just seemed like ages to me. I couldn't really picture my life beyond high school. I felt stuck. Jackie Angel and her family had now moved far away, so even escapes to rural Pennsylvania were no longer an option. No more weekends in her Mason jar–filled home. Additionally, my glamorous city-gal grandmother had passed away a few years ago, so going off to New York City on weekends didn't really happen much these days. Sure, my family and I would go on day trips here and there, to see a play, or to shop the holiday market at Christmastime, but we'd always come home right afterward. Going back to camp was not an option, and I started to regret my uneventful, anticlimactic sneak-out that had put me on the "Dangerous Camper List." Was that night of making small talk in the woods really worth causing me to never be allowed back to the one place I was truly happy?

I began writing depressive letters to Rodreigo, the young counselor I was in the play *Little Nell* with at Camp Wallobee:

"No one understands me here like you did. And to make matters worse, I don't think my band, PBJ, is staying together. The distance is killing us!"

He would respond with cheerful notes about his life in sunny Puerto Rico:

"Sorry to hear that, Margot. Today I went to the rainforest and caught a salamander!"

All this is to say that midway through my junior year, when my parents gave me some good news, it was much needed.

"*Maaargot!*" called my mother.

I sighed, reluctantly, put down *Go Ask Alice* (which I was reading for the third time), and headed down the stairs to find out what she wanted.

My mom finished making her perfect cup of black tea in a floral bone china cup, carefully stirring in the few drops of whole milk and then removing the tea bag and placing it on her sterling silver used tea bag depository (another Cartier castoff from my grandmother).

"Have a seat, honey."

I sat down nervously in one of our awful wicker chairs. This one was ripped, causing half your butt to sink through the saggy seat. It was pretty much the opposite of a chair—it actually made you less comfortable than standing up.

"Well, as you know, your father has a new job, and we are doing a little better financially."

My father, who had had a very modest upbringing in the Bronx, had been working his way up in the big-city world. I never fully understood what my father did for a living, but I knew he commuted to the city, worked late, and got to stay in glamorous chain hotels like the Radisson. Recently he had taken a new job where he was the boss and we were all really proud of him. Now he brought me back tiny soaps and lotions from even more luxurious hotels like the Hilton and got home a little earlier.

"Um hmmm," I said, wondering how much better we were actually doing if we couldn't afford chairs that actually served their purpose.

"Oh—I can't keep it in any longer. We are going on vacation! Just the three of us!"

Awesome, I thought. *Camping, again?* We had spent vacations roughing it in New Hampshire when I was a kid, and I wondered how quickly the novelty of three five-foot-nine-inch-plus people, including one snorer, in one tent would wear off. On the other hand, my brother was away at college, and being an only child on a vacation could have its advantages. I could have double the amount of virgin strawberry daiquiris without anyone complaining that I was running up the bill. I decided to contain my lack of excitement and just wait for my mother to continue.

"Margot, don't you want to know where? I mean, the *where* is *where* the excitement lives." My mother's catchphrases never made sense to anyone but her.

"Sure. Where?"

"Okay . . . *dum da dum dum* . . . drum roll, please . . ."

"Uh, you just did the drum roll yourself."

"Oh, for God's sakes. We're going to Saint Thomas in the Virgin Islands, Margot! For spring break! *You're welcome!*"

My mouth dropped. Never in a million years did I expect this. We were going on an actual tropical vacation! And I would be really close to Rodreigo in Puerto Rico! Maybe I could even visit him there. I

knew nothing about Puerto Rico but I imagined it was a place of dash-
ingly handsome tan men and also a place where I could temporarily
alter my pasty, vegetarian complexion. People on *Hollywood Squares*
were always winning trips to "sunny Puerto Vallarta" (announced by
hottie Shadoe Stevens) and seemed overjoyed at the prospect. I wasn't
sure what *Puerto* meant, but I was pretty sure *Puerto* was a good thing,
whether it be *Rico* or *Vallarta*.

Wow. Suddenly life seemed a lot better, and that night I decided
not to finish my chapter in *Go Ask Alice*, even though I found Alice's
state of depression riveting. Alice was contemplating suicide again, but
really it was just the drugs talking, which she would soon figure out for
herself. I let her be; I could always come back to the book later if I really
needed a fix. Instead I pasted together some semblance of a tropical
spring-break wardrobe out of my crushed velvet '70s attire. I was so
excited I even made a spring-break mix to play during the flight on my
brother's old Walkman he forgot to pack for college.

★ ★ ★   On our plane to Saint Thomas, my highly intelligent
father couldn't wrap his brain around volume control when it came to
speaking with his headphones on. We had a real bitch of a stewardess,
who had an unironic beehive hairdo, even though it was the mid-'90s.
When asked for a glass of water, she said, "Ugh, I guess so," and then
huffed and puffed to the flight attendant station two feet away. So you
can imagine what happened when it came to be four o'clock and my
first-generation faux-British mother absolutely *had* to have her cup of
tea, as she had every other day of her entire life.

"Excuse me, miss? Uh, miss? Yes, may I have a cup of black tea?
Just milk, no sugar. Milk, not cream please. Not cream. Okay, miss?"

Beehive lady grunted at my mom (as I had wanted to every time
she requested a stupid tea from me) and stormed to her station. My mom
quietly seethed.

My father, not seeing how close the stewardess was, took note. Headphones still on, he whisper-screamed, "WHAT? THE BITCH WON'T COOPERATE?"

My mom whisper-shouted back, "*Bo-obbb!* Shh! She's right there!" and then pointed at her so the rest of our cabinmates could see whom they were complaining about. At that moment I knew, sunshine or no sunshine, I wasn't going to make it through seven days with these doofuses. I knew I should have brought more than that one mix tape to tune them out.

Upon arrival, I spent the first two days lounging on the beach studying manically for the SATs. However, forty-eight hours of studying on the beach made me a little antsy. My parents were on their first real vacation of their marriage and I felt like my being underage and angsty was weighing them down. While I was lying in a shaded lounge chair doing algebra equations, they were frolicking in the ocean, drinking mojitos, and refusing to wear sunscreen. I needed to do something fun, and I really wanted to go see Rodreigo, but I didn't know how my parents would react if I asked to go off to Puerto Rico on my own. I hadn't asked Rodreigo yet if he was game for a visitor, but I assumed his island lifestyle would be adaptable to a drop-in from an old friend. I rehearsed a few times in the bathroom mirror, making sure to sound as though I was doing them a favor. Then I entered their suite with a fresh coat of aloe vera on my shoulders, took a deep breath, and began my plea for freedom.

"Guys, my friend from camp, Rodreigo, lives in Puerto Rico. It's just a quick puddle jumper away. I was wondering if maybe I could, like, go there and visit. I'd be doing you a favor I think, really. You guys could do grown-up stuff without having to worry about me."

My parents rejoiced a little too quickly. "Yes! Absolutely! Please do! We'll look into flights tonight!"

Never in my wildest dreams did I expect them to say yes. Fifteen hours later, my parents waved good-bye to me at a sketchy, tiny airport with a dirt runway.

"Have fun, *Maaaargot* . . . but not too much fun, hahaha!" my mom singsonged. "Be careful flying! Be careful driving! Be careful walking!"

My dad was calmer. He remained relaxed at all times, actually, except when he was behind a wheel. There he clenched his teeth and called people "assholes." He kissed me good-bye and said, "See you in a few days. You'll be fine."

I thought to myself, *Duh, of course I will be fine,* and waved good-bye to my parents.

I ducked my head as I entered the tiny propeller plane, which was clearly not designed for people my size. No sooner did I squeeze into my seat than I looked out the window to see them racing away at top speed to go get drunk and probably have sex. Ewwww.

The flight lasted about thirty seconds. There was no drink service, no peanuts. No one checked to see if my seatbelt was buckled properly. There was just one seat per row on each side of the plane, so I didn't even have a seatmate to avoid making small talk with. I didn't even have time to write in my journal! As we landed in bustling Puerto Rico, I wondered if it would have been more cost-efficient to take a paddleboat.

When I stepped off the plane, I suddenly felt flustered. I didn't speak Spanish and I had never traveled alone before. People were racing around speaking very rapidly, wearing a lot of linen and floral prints. I felt extremely out of place. This was a far cry from Newark International Airport. And everyone in Puerto Rico was so short! Why couldn't I have visited Rodreigo somewhere I would blend in better, like Sweden or Norway? Would I remember what Rodreigo looked like? Would *he* recognize *me*?

Sure enough, I walked out of the terminal and there he was: in a lavender collared shirt with denim shorts and black sandals, his dark hair tossed right in front of his eyes. He seemed to have a more mature vibe than the silly boy I had stumbled through a melodrama with onstage at Camp Wallobee. And even though he was only about two years older than I, he looked like a man.

"There she is!" he shouted theatrically. How could he miss me? I looked like a gargantuan albino compared to the airport locals. I was elated someone was so happy to see me, especially after being the third wheel on my parents' second honeymoon for the past few days. We got in his Jeep Cherokee and took off through the streets of Puerto Rico.

Puerto Rico was much more action-packed than Saint Thomas. Stray dogs ran free everywhere and I was called an "amateur" for getting excited over a lizard sighting. I was completely unaware until this point that in terms of driving, Puerto Rico is a lawless island with anarchists behind the wheel. My driver's ed teacher would have a heart attack if he ever came here and saw people turning left *without* using their blinkers! When Rodreigo drove through a stoplight at about eighty miles an hour, wind whipping through his black hair, I knew this was going to be the most amazing weekend of my life.

First thing, he took me to a restaurant called Mona's, where it seemed all eyes were on me. The patrons and staff seemed to be monitoring my "careful walking" a little too closely.

"Why is everyone looking at me?" I asked.

"You're blonde, you're tall. You have blue eyes and freckles. Here, you are an exotic woman," Rodreigo explained.

An exotic woman? Yes! This was unbelievable. It took only two airplanes and a language barrier for me to become an unattainable goddess. Here, my hair bounced in the same way Cecelia Rios's did. My blonde half–Jew fro didn't look like a wet David Coverdale wig; it looked like an exotic mane to be copied in salons everywhere. I sat taller than ever, suddenly proud of my size and willing to accept the attention I was getting for it. I never wanted to leave Puerto Rico.

After a fun night of catching up and a good night's sleep, the next day I got back in the car with Rodreigo. He drove me through winding unkempt roads at top speed, and we came millimeters away from hitting multiple cars. But it was all worth it, because we were going to a rainforest. An actual rainforest! I had spent many hours in school staring at burnouts in various hemp T-shirts advising me to save the rainforest, but I never thought I'd actually visit one.

We survived the car ride, disembarked, and began our hike. I could barely talk because I was so struck by the beauty of it all—I had never seen a place so green. I had never smelled air so clean. The freshest air I had ever smelled before was at the top of the hill at Camp Wallobee. This place took nature to a whole new level. Rodreigo's letters had been true; there were salamanders everywhere! There were also brightly colored birds squawking and wildlife so green it looked as if it had been colored by a child in art class. I felt completely calm and forgot all about the jocks, dorks, skaters, and scuzzes back home, lost in my new jet-setting lifestyle. Until . . . I looked up to the top of a small hill and saw a familiar face. It was Floyd Barstow, the blond kid in high-waisted jeans who played the trumpet from my music appreciation class. Back home we were hardly friends; he was really into his trumpet and often shot me dirty looks in class, as I was one of the many B students taking the class for an easy A. But we were in Puerto Rico in the middle of a rainforest, what were the chances? I called out, "Floyd! Hey Floyd!" and waved manically so he would notice me at the bottom of the hill. Already I was planning that when we returned to school Floyd and I would be forever bonded by the fact that we were both now world travelers. Floyd and I would have private jokes, saying things like, "Sorry, man, I'm still on island time," and would peel the skin off our sunburns whenever we got bored in class. I waved again, bigger than before.

"Floyd!!"

Floyd stopped walking, saw me waving and yelling, and then walked away at a faster pace than he'd been walking before.

What the—? Floyd wasn't even one of the cool kids, like Chad Decker. He played the trumpet, for God's sake! And he's blowing me off? Even in friggin' Puerto Rico, I was too weird to say hi to? Even in a *rainforest*?

My spirits dropped. I was hiking in a tropical island alongside a handsome Hispanic man, but I was still a gangly girl from Jersey nobody wanted to talk to.

Rodreigo put his arm around me and jokingly said, "Close friend?"

I laughed it off and we kept walking. I wasn't going to let a band nerd ruin my adventure.

That night, Rodreigo took me to this beautiful old castle in Old San Juan. This was pretty much the coolest way to spend a spring break ever. Not only was I in a castle, but also I was now a tropical island beauty. Rodreigo walked proudly with me, and I felt like one of those girls who just expected to be prom queen. I was on top of the world.

Then, without warning, Rodreigo ever so slowly touched my freckled face with his tan hand, leaned close to me, and kissed me. This wasn't a sloppy middle school kiss or an awkward seven-minutes-in-heaven kiss. This was a slow, romantic kiss like I'd never experienced before. I was kissing a man—a man who had seen the world and been with a bunch of girls already (but hopefully used condoms because I couldn't chance it with AIDS again). This was no lame hookup with some dimwitted Jersey thug; I was passionately kissing an exotic man who appreciated theatre and wore denim shorts unapologetically. I'd finally made it.

It didn't stop there. The kissing continued until we were on the ground outside in front of the castle. Things were moving quickly, clothing was shed. I tried not to think about the possibility of a foreign insect crawling up one of my orifices and laying eggs inside me. Things were going to a whole new level here; Rodreigo was the first guy ever not to struggle with the clasps on my bra. When his shirt came off, my velour pants came off too. It became clearer we were heading toward something intense. I did not want to become a statistic, so I stopped everything and said, "If you're gonna do something, you better have something!"

Realizing he didn't have a condom, Rodreigo ceased all heavy petting and we were on our way back to the car.

I knew the evening was probably heading toward sex. I had just come to visit an old friend, but I didn't want to pass on this major opportunity. At home I would have been skittish and nervous, but being so far away and completely separate from all the high school bullshit (Floyd Barstow aside) made me feel relaxed and like a whole new person. If I didn't act on this now, I would probably end up losing my virginity in my twin bed to some desperate dirty rocker weirdo virgin back home, while my parents were at a jazz concert in the city. Who knows? If Corey hadn't tried to kill me, maybe he would have eventually won me over and I would have had awkward first sex with him. I'm sure he would have been game. But instead I was in Puerto Rico with a foreign, older man. I was rolling with the new me.

Then a second thought occurred. *I hope I don't die in the freakin' NASCAR race I'm about to enter in Rodreigo's car. I'd really like to lose my virginity to an older Latino boy on a tropical island. I'd really love to have just this one night. Universe, if I can get safely through this one night, I promise to fight less with my mother and to quit my kicking-holes-through-walls-with-my-lesbian-shoes fetish cold turkey. I promise.*

As we swooshed through three red lights and passed in a no-passing lane at eighty-five miles per hour, I wondered if all Puerto Ricans were on their way home to get condoms mid-hookup. When we finally got back to his house, I noticed for the first time how lavish it was. The house was entirely white without a speck of dust anywhere. They had a beautiful outdoor porch for doing fancy things like drinking cocktails with a tan group of dignified friends. I had never seen anything so tropical and extravagant in New Jersey, and I wondered how every single flower around the house could be blooming in full color at the same time. Back in Jersey my mom was always ranting about her uncooperative "paperwhites" or "pointsettias."

I let Rodreigo take the lead on the bedroom stuff. I was too neurotic and inexperienced to make any moves and was trying to let myself go for once. I didn't want this night to end with a frantic call to a Tampax operator or be the cause of me skipping future blood donations. He asked me if I had done this before. I said, "Yes, once . . ." I didn't intend to lie to him, it was just one of those things that slipped out of my mouth and it would have been really dorky to take it back. I decided to let Rodreigo think I was cooler than I was—John's penis in Pennsylvania came really close, and that was probably the same thing, right?

WRONG. Wow. Super wrong. Wow. As things started for real, it was way too late to stop and say, "Actually, Rodreigo, I haven't done this before. My mistake." So I just kept going with the charade that I was an experienced woman, which was a nice distraction from the hugeness of losing my virginity under these fantastical circumstances.

"We're such good friends, we do *everything* together!" joked Rodreigo when we were through. I laughed, which was a nice relief after living in a Spanish soap opera for the last few days. I had seen people smoke cigarettes and take swigs from bedside whiskeys in this postcoital moment on film, but this wasn't like that at all. I just lay there thinking how it was odd that a few years ago we were friends at camp and for this visit we decided to suddenly be lovers. I looked forward to showing photos of Saint Thomas ocean views to classmates and slipping a photo of Rodreigo in there.

"Who's that?" the classmate would ask.

"That?" I'd giggle. "Oh, that is Rodreigo . . . my lover."

Did my life really just get this awesome?

I was in a great headspace. I knew I didn't want him to be my boyfriend; that would be way too complicated. But I also didn't want to leave it as just this night.

Rodreigo seemed to be reading my mind. "Let's promise to see each other again, at least one more time."

"Pinky swear?" I asked.

Rodreigo stuck out his pinky and said, "Yes, pinky swear."

We fell asleep and the next day he drove me to the airport. He held onto the wheel with one hand and my hand with the other the whole time. He could barely watch the road for wanting to look at me, and suddenly I no longer cared about traffic safety. He passed three cars in a no-passing lane and I didn't even fear for my life. This time I just knew somehow I'd be safe. At the airport we made out for a long time. I felt a crowd gather, gawking at the young lovers, but maybe that was in my head. What wasn't in my head was that I missed my plane. It's hard to miss a plane when you are standing in the terminal as it takes off behind you. This was just about the most careless thing I'd ever done, but I didn't care. *Whatever,* I thought, kissing Rodreigo again. *My parents can have an hour more of alone time. That's what they want anyway.*

Finally we separated. Lucky for me Rodreigo stuck around for a bit and was able to speak to the gate attendant in Spanish and get me on the next plane. The gate attendant had surely just watched me miss the plane due to our very public make-out session but tried to remain professional. Whatever. I wasn't embarrassed; it's not like I would be seeing that gate attendant ever again, so who cared?

I stared out the window on my plane ride home wondering if my parents would be able to sense something different about me. Sure, I had lost my v-card, but something else happened on this trip. I understood how big the world was, beyond my small town, beyond high school, beyond Chad Decker's taunts. All I had to do was get through the next year and a half and then real life would be waiting for me. I could start over and meet people I really connected with and pursue whatever it was I really wanted to do. There was a whole other world out there and I would be living in it soon. My dumb high school issues seemed so small now that I knew they didn't really matter.

When my plane landed back in Saint Thomas, two frantic parents greeted me. My dad angrily clutched his newspaper that I had now delayed him from reading on the beach. My mom's midnight-blue eyeliner looked smeared, her hair undone, and her lips dry. There was no time for her to apply gloss because she had been so terrified something had happened to me, causing me to miss my plane. I'm sure she worried that I had sprained an ankle from not walking carefully enough. Perhaps she envisioned me laid up in a remote Puerto Rican hospital with my ankle elevated unsuccessfully trying to fill out medical forms in Spanish, which I didn't speak a word of despite her repeated suggestions that I enroll in a Spanish class after dropping French.

"*Maaaargot! Thank Ga-odd!*" My mom was in hysterics. She let out all the pent-up fear in one grand old cry. My dad was comforting her, shaking his head at me as he hugged my mom to soothe her.

"I'm fine guys, I just missed my plane."

I missed my flight for a great reason, because I didn't want to leave a place and a person who made me feel content. They looked so concerned, but really there was no cause for it. I wasn't hurt or kidnapped or lost or scared. Their daughter was just off on a Caribbean island losing her virginity. *Calm down, guys!*

I was happy for the first time since I started high school. They missed me.

CHAPTER 16:

My Little Ben Franklin

For the rest of my junior year, happiness and a new kind of calm settled in. I now was content to ride out the rest of high school, knowing that when I left for college, there would be men like Rodreigo out there in the world—men who treated tall women like goddesses and were unafraid to wear pastels. I had the confidence to make a fresh start senior year. I had permanent teeth implanted, so no more falsies, too.

I even got a new job. I quit the drugstore and was now working the counter at a bakery. Despite having to sometimes be there at 5:30 AM, I loved my new job. I found it less depressing to sell Boston cream donuts to local residents than to watch Squirrel scratch off nonwinning lottery tickets every day and say to me, "Next time, right?" And who doesn't like being surrounded by baked goods? Aside from the embarrassing rule set that I was the only employee not allowed to write on cakes due to my left-handedness smearing away each letter of HAPPY BIRTHDAY the second after I wrote it, I enjoyed the job.

Usually I worked with a chain-smoking senior citizen who stood outside smoking the majority of her shift. I enjoyed the alone time. Although I missed interacting on a daily basis with my #1 customer, Squirrel, I enjoyed the free brownies I got at my new job. Anything deemed "unfresh" or broken was up for the taking. I lived for the good stuff to break like éclairs, rainbow cookies, and chocolate-chip cookies. My mom liked it too. Now I could bring her unlimited day-old apricot linzer tarts and apple turnovers for her high tea time.

At school, college application deadlines were coming up soon, and I joined every activity possible in an attempt to boost my chances of getting into good schools. I'd never done any sports, due to my inability to run down a field without falling, so my mom encouraged me to join a church volleyball league where everyone who signed up made the team. Never mind that my father is Jewish and my only stint at church was the day I witnessed my mom cry on cue as she sped like a fleeing convict to take me to a Unitarian service that seemed more like a bunch of people in handmade shawls just chillin' out.

The season didn't start off as well as I would have liked. No one on the team listened to my suggestion of bright orange uniforms with purple lettering. Instead, we went with heather gray, a color that made my vegetarian skin look even more gaunt. I hoped people mistook my complexion for illness, which might provide a less mortifying reason why I warmed the bench at every game. Crowds of onlookers would stare, wondering why the tallest member of the volleyball team, now holding tight at five foot nine and a half, wasn't being utilized. At least if I were sick I would be slightly less pathetic than just sucky at all things physical.

My parents attended zero games for support, quite aware that I was just going through the motions so I could check off an additional box on my college applications that didn't involve a brooding artsy activity like creative writing or modern dance. The team didn't suffer for it. We became intramural champs, no thanks to me, and my mother was thrilled that I could now add "volleyball star" to my college applications. "Maybe you'll even play for the college team," she purred, knowing full well that having an athletic father, mother, and brother did not trickle down to me and there was no way this would ever happen. I took her little fantasy as a compliment on my potential and went on my way to get back to my normal life of defacing plain T-shirts into works of modern art.

* * * Life carried on nicely like this for some time. Then, somewhere around mid–senior year, everything at school changed. Previously, my public regional high school was broken down into the same typical cliques you'd find in other schools: jocks, skanks, skaters, pregnant girls, thugs, guitar-playing pot smokers wearing T-shirts with messages about saving the environment, and nerds. The nerds were a tight-knit group of straightlaced boys who all shared the same jam-packed schedule of AP classes and resumé-building extracurriculars. They were all fighting to be valedictorian and to get into the best colleges in the country and therefore never really hung out with us civilians.

The nerds had all applied early decision to Ivy League schools and been accepted way before we B+ students even finished our last applications. I was still battling my father and his never-ending game of solitaire for an hour of home computer time to finish my college essay about how babysitting those twins down the street taught me the "value of sisterhood."

And once they got those letters of admission? The nerds. Went. Wild. These dudes who had spent the last three and a half years candy-striping on Friday nights had seven months to catch up on everything they had missed. And they weren't wasting a minute of it. I would go to use the bathroom and there would be a nerd smoking in the stall.

I'd come to school and all the nerds would be cutting classes to go to the beach. They started throwing parties, and not just beer parties, but acid parties. Even I had never done acid, despite my Vietnam War–chic clothing and my wild weekend in Pennsylvania. This was awesome!

Best of all, the boy nerds started having sex—full sex, not just oral sex, which I now knew was way different than talking on the phone *about* sex—with moderately hot chicks. When I heard that, I knew I had to get in with a nerd. After Rodreigo, I no longer stank of rejection. I was an experienced woman. Rodreigo liked me and not in that creepy killer way that Corey did. I stood up a little straighter since my trip to Puerto Rico and felt better about life.

I already had a long-standing promise to go to prom with Eli, the short guy I shared the car ride to the Garden State Arts Center with. Ah, that ticket-questing Camaro ride that turned into the Willy Wonka acid trip . . . the memories . . . Since that fateful ride, Eli and I had become close friends, and a lot had happened to him over the years. He literally had been struck by lightning while hiking alone in the woods during a storm, and if that weren't enough, he had to have intense surgery on his jaw, which was not going to be fully healed in time for prom. We were a perfect match.

If I didn't already have a friendly date with Eli, I would have totally wanted to go with Adam Sizemore, the second-hottest nerd. The first-hottest nerd was Michael Goldstein, whom I determined to be undateable when I watched him Windex the windows during a wild drug party he was hosting. (Eventually Mike Goldstein ended up with another girl who I heard had a lot of sex with him in the shower. Which was perfect for Mike, who could now orgasm and clean up the mess at the same time.) Adam, on the other hand, was a hot nerd who didn't care about anything once he got into Brown. I had never noticed how good-looking he was until he started partying harder than Grace Jones in 1981. And he was really funny. Not in a funny nerd "Steve Urkel" kind of way but in a legitimately funny Bob-Saget-after-dark kind of way. Considering Adam and I barely spoke until the end of the year, there was no chance we would have gone to the prom together, but it was fun to wonder what if.

Still, I was happy to go with Eli. I just refused to give in to the stupidity that was expected to go along with attending a New Jersey prom. I was not interested in the local traditions, such as trial nail art before deciding on your real nail art and spending upwards of $1,000 on a Jessica McClintock prom dress. I didn't understand how girls whose parents couldn't afford to send them to college could suddenly afford prom dresses that cost as much as a used car. But none of that mattered. What my prom date Eli lacked in funcional jaw and height, he made up for with attitude. He felt that the prom was just as stupid as I did, but he also didn't want to miss it and always wonder what if. So we decided on a compromise: We would go to the prom, as friends, and wear Elizabethan attire. We would be making a social commentary on how stupid this all was, but we would still be noticed à la Madonna's live performance of "Vogue" at the 1990 Video Music Awards. I searched high and low and finally found a gold ball gown complete with a bustle, corset, and petticoat. Eli had trouble finding his outfit, so we decided to rent a Ben Franklin costume from Backwards Glances and not wear the glasses or powdered wig that came with it. I loved that Eli was my prom date, as we were not into each other at all beyond friendship, and that took the pressure off the whole night.

Meanwhile, the nerds continued to rock out. I understood where they were coming from. Not that I had spent four years studying and not enjoying high school. But I had spent the majority of the past four years either working at the drugstore, wishing I was at camp, or writing in my journal during third-period lunch about how depressed I was. Now I had just a few months to enjoy myself before high school ended. I was so close to getting out, having made a decision on college. I ended up getting into all five schools I applied to (not sure of what I wanted to do with my life, I applied to half as a fashion design major and half as a theatre major). I decided to go to Ithaca College for theatre because Ithaca had some amazing vintage clothing stores and the college seemed the least excited to have me as a student. The other four schools really courted me, following up with phone calls, some even offering scholarships. However, I've always agreed with Groucho Marx, who said, "I don't care to belong to any club that will accept me as a member."

And once I accepted Ithaca College's offer, I too wanted to make up for lost time.

Prom night came, and Eli a.k.a. Ben Franklin picked me up in his maroon 1984 Chevy. Everyone else was going in a limo. On my way out my mother reminded me for the four-hundredth time, "Don't forget, Margot, I was runner-up for Snow Queen. This could be your night!" I groaned and headed to the beat-up car as she called out, "Have fun!"

I climbed in the car and we headed out. Before we went to the prom, we stopped for some photo ops at my new bakery job. It seemed like the avant-garde choice to make, and baked goods are so timeless that they seemed a perfect backdrop to our prom costumes. At the bakery, we took photos in front of cream pies and Black Forest cakes dressed as a lord and lady. There was no way we were going to do some cheesy traditional pre-prom shots in front of a stretch limo. Besides, we didn't even rent a limo, claiming it was stupid, but really no one had asked us to go in on one with them.

Half an hour of bakery photos and we arrived at the prom, in an excessively air-conditioned wedding factory a few towns away, which was themed "Sweet Sweet Fantasy Baby" after the Mariah Carey/Ol' Dirty Bastard song. As we entered the overcrowded banquet hall, heads turned to see gargantuan me, arm in arm with a short kid dressed as Ben Franklin. Some kids snickered and I tried to ignore them, but as we entered the main dance floor, heads turned. After years of no one noticing anything I ever did—stealing a song from Wham!, seducing a thirty-year-old bank teller at age twelve, finding a faux crack pipe on the beach, starting a protest against the Gulf War in the cafeteria, even handing the coolest girl in school my teeth—suddenly everyone wanted to know who I was. Whispers could be heard: "What the hell?" "Who are they?" "Once a freak, always a freak." Eli and I proudly danced to "Gangsta's Paradise" and then walked through the judgmental crowd to sit at our table. Well, Eli sat—I had to stay vertical due to my oversize bustle and petticoat.

While we ate a few too many dinner rolls at the table, I watched the nerds cut loose. Mike Goldstein was grinding with a slutty hippie, the valedictorian was making out with a skater chick, and Adam the second-hottest nerd appeared to be obliterated on one too many swigs of Mad Dog. I thought to myself, *Let's have some fun.* I grabbed my date and hit the dance floor. "Be My Lover" by La Bouche played and we rocked it. We partied all night, and I even got to slow-dance with Adam Sizemore.

Halfway through the night, I had to pee, and knowing it would take a little while to disengage from my bustle and corset, I headed for the bathroom right away. While attempting to fit a modified hoop skirt into an extra-small stall inside the restroom I bumped into the school Spanish teacher. She also moonlighted as the performing arts teacher, but we weren't that close. As she leaned into the mirror to apply a thick coat of lip liner underneath a maroon lipstick, she said, "You and Eli are the best dressed here. I have total respect for what you've done tonight. I've admired your originality your four years here. A lot of us have. You've really made a statement tonight. Go out with a bang, Margot."

I was shocked. This cool teacher had noticed me for all the right reasons. We had that one class together but I figured she hadn't given me a second thought after that. I didn't know she remembered me. I had never even taken Spanish—I had taken two years of French, mistakenly thinking I would be a natural at it due to the fact that I have a silent *t* at the end of my name. Was it possible I had silent fans all along? There was no time to think, though; I had to undress, pee, and re-dress quickly because I heard the prom advisor/math teacher begin to announce the prom court. I wanted to get back in there so I could see which member of the White Lipstick Posse would be selected to be queen for yet another day. I also wanted to see if a nerd gone wild could break the barrier and get on that court.

I returned to the banquet hall just as the prom advisor was announcing the winners.

"Second runner-up for prom queen is . . . Jessica Rosenstein."

Big surprise. Jessica had been so kind in seventh grade to tell me I could be pretty if I didn't dress like such a freak. I guess she followed her own advice, because she looked like she was on top of the world. I guess Jessica didn't peak at her Bat Mitzvah after all.

"First runner-up . . . Dawn Riser."

Another big surprise. Dawn was so pretty, of course she was up there curtsying like the royal subject she always knew she was.

I was spreading a tiny chunk of butter on the last dinner roll when the prom advisor turned back to the microphone. There was one more title to declare before the queen.

"First runner-up . . . and our prom princess . . . Margot Leitman."

What? WHAT??? There was a pause, long enough for me to hear people say "What the hell?" and "Who?"

Eli gave me a push. "Go up there! Congrats!"

I looked out into the crowd. A few were clapping, mostly teachers and nerds gone wild. There was a lot of whispering and a lot of frowning girls wearing Jessica McClintock dresses with matching nail art. I guess runner-up ran in the family; my mom would be so proud. I took a few strides, remembering my mother's words, "Posture, Maaargot, posture!" I stood up proudly and went to collect my tiny Claire's Boutique rhinestone crown and medium-size bouquet.

Then the prom advisor/math teacher announced the prom queen . . . dragging out the moment for dramatic effect. What member of the White Lipstick Posse was she going to call? Finally she spoke a name. Her own daughter. The crowd cheered, feigning surprise as her fairly popular daughter took the crown with very little excitement on her face.

After the nepotistic crowning, the male court was announced, filled mostly with hot drug dealers teachers were scared of and jocks they wanted to sleep with. Then they announced the prom king. As I tried to pull the crinoline out of my underwear without anyone noticing, I heard the advisor say, "And your prom king is Eli Rothberg!"

Eli! Eli! I couldn't believe it! My little Ben Franklin, fresh off of jaw surgery, was the king! Eli stood up proudly and danced his way to get his crown. Everyone seemed confused at what was happening. The freaks were getting some recognition just as we were all out the door. Eli didn't care. He reveled in the moment as the crown was placed on his head.

There was moderate applause and then "Fantasy" by Mariah Carey started blasting. Eli tried to dance with the queen, but she wasn't interested in dancing with him. Despite their equivalent crownings they were still in vastly different social circles. I didn't want Eli to be left up there all alone, so I danced with him.

It was turning out to be the best night ever. I guess lightning can strike twice! Hey-oh!

We left the prom to discover that Eli had left his lights on all night. Which really worked out for the best, because as we were stuck in the parking lot waiting for a jump, we were able to receive repeated congratulations from sneering seniors as they piled into their limos empty-handed. Waiting for the jump was like an impromptu receiving line for Eli and me, though I imagined everyone who congratulated us was secretly planning our demise. Maybe this was what it felt like to have a Bat Mitzvah.

Finally we got a jump from the banquet staff and headed home. "This was fun," I said as I climbed out of his car, and I meant it sincerely. I waltzed in the door and ran up the stairs to tell my mom about my night. She was waiting up for me in bed, in a silk negligée, knitting that same afghan, with her glasses tipped over her nose. My father was snoring next to her.

"Well," she said, as she peered at me over her glasses, "did you win?"

"I didn't win, but I was the princess. I am so stoked."

My mother sighed and said, "Well, if anything happens to the queen . . ." and went back to her knitting.

CHAPTER 17:

Less of a Nerd Than I Thought

Prom weekend wasn't over. Parties would continue all weekend, and my class was divided into two party stations: Wildwood and Ocean City. I had heard that the nerds gone wild were all opting for Ocean City, so I went there, in hopes that I would see Adam, the second-hottest nerd. My title of prom princess was giving me the extra adrenaline to go for it. I had nothing to lose, there were only a few months left of school, and Rodreigo had given me the go-ahead to explore my options.

That weekend, most kids were hooking up in the pool and drinking Natty Light any opportunity they could get. I wanted to explore a true beach town. I knew I'd be leaving New Jersey soon, and this quaint tourist town made me nostalgic for a place I hadn't yet said good-bye to. I took a long walk on the boardwalk and stumbled upon The Fudge Factory. I had to go in. My grandfather was a candy manufacturer, and I had always been jealous of my mother's stories.

"And don't get me started on Easter, Margot. We would wake up to chocolate eggs with our names engraved on them. I have five fillings because I lived on a steady diet of caramel for the first twelve years of my life." My mother's all-candy childhood diet explained my all–melba toast childhood diet. And even though I never got a few of my adult teeth, I also never got a cavity.

And while The Fudge Factory was hardly a real factory like my grandfather worked in, I was still curious as to how candy was made. My grandfather died when I was four and my one clear memory of him was him coming to our house and making grape bubble gum from scratch in our oven! Working in the bakery had shown me the in-depth process of making donuts, hard rolls, and cheesecakes, but it wasn't the same as learning the process of making candy.

I strolled in and watched a demonstration of how fudge was made. I lurked in the back of a crowd of tourists and watched silently as a smiling teenager poured a hot chocolate mixture on a cold marble slate. I found myself fascinated by the process of making fudge. After the demonstration most of the crowd made their purchases of rocky road and maple fudge and headed out. I lingered for a while. The staff of The Fudge Factory asked where I was from and what I was doing in town. I told them I was with a crowd of high school seniors staying nearby.

"Why don't you bring some of your friends by after we close tonight and we'll have a dance party?" asked a perky guy in a chef's hat.

"Sounds like a plan. Will do," I said, as he rang up my selection of fudge, gummy bears, and chocolate candies.

An after-hours dance party at a fudge factory seemed like a perfect first date for Adam and me.

I went back to the motel with a new understanding of the fudge-making process and bags of candy, which got me a plethora of attention from all the nerds gone wild. As Mike Goldstein, the first-hottest nerd, washed his hands thoroughly before gulping down a handful of chocolate-covered gummy bears, I told them all, "So, the staff of The Fudge Factory invited me to this rager they're having tonight."

"I don't know if I'm up for a rager," said Mike Goldstein, already thinking about the dust residue a party in a fudge factory could cause.

"What do you mean, 'rager'?" asked Adam. Here was my in. He was interested.

"You know, like a dance party in a candy store after hours. That's all."

Adam chomped down on a chocolate turtle and said, "Sure. I'll go." And that was all it took. Adam spread the word about the dance party to all the nerds gone wild and that night we all set out to The Fudge Factory. There were about twelve of us in total; Adam walked by my side the whole way.

"Congrats on the win, Margot. You deserved it. You looked hot."

Hot? I wasn't going for hot . . . I guess Adam had an affinity for Queen Victoria types. Either way, I had gotten his attention; I was on my way. I walked into The Fudge Factory to scope things out just as they closed.

"You came!" said the perky guy, removing his chef's hat to indicate he was officially off fudge-making duty.

"Yeah, and I brought some friends." I gestured to the group of classmates outside.

"Well, get in here then! We're just about to start."

Everyone filed in skeptically. The staff locked the door, turned the sign to CLOSED, and blasted Quad City DJs' "C'mon N'Ride It (the Train)." The party was on. The Fudge Factory staff all started shaking it; they clearly did this every night after closing. They were having so much fun we all just had to join in. I thought I had seen nerds gone wild, but I had never seen them dance like this. The staff of The Fudge Factory were pretty much the most awesome people I had ever met, and they spent their days making candy. Amazing. I made a silent vow to myself to never forget the spirit of those candy kids. I wanted always to remember to save time to let go at the end of a long day. I thought about this on the walk back to the motel as Adam and I held hands.

★ ★ ★ The following Monday at school I waltzed into homeroom ready for the endless congratulations I was about to face. I was ready for the revenge moment Sandy had at the end of *Grease* when she was suddenly cool and all the fifties greasers thought, *"Wow, I didn't know she had it in her to wear those pants!"* I sat down right next to the prom queen/prom advisor's daughter. I figured the royal court should remain together whenever possible. The queen turned to me and whispered, "Did you hear what happened?"

How could I have heard anything? I had been away for the weekend dancing in a candy store and holding hands with a nerd. "Kelly's mom came to my house and threatened my mom."

"What do you mean? Why?"

"'Cause she was in charge of the prom court; that's why. Kelly's mom spent $1,100 on her prom dress and she wanted her daughter on that court. She was all like, 'How dare you waste a crown on some humongous freak in an ugly-ass ball gown who made a mockery out of the prom? That crown should have gone to Kelly. You better make this right.'"

"Well, why is Kelly's mom spending $1,100 on a prom dress anyway? You can't buy your way onto the prom court," I said, acting as if I was a girl who was used to getting crowned in front of her jealous peers.

"Exactly," said the prom queen/prom advisor's daughter.

I sat in homeroom waiting for the bell to ring, wondering if the prom advisor/prom queen's mother/math teacher was going to get punched over my gold ball gown. I was really flattered that people suddenly cared about me. I'd take notoriety, even as a villain. Anything was better than Floyd Barstow ignoring me in the rainforest. I couldn't believe that someone cared enough about what I was doing to send her mother to kick a teacher's ass. Sure, my dress was ugly in a fabulous sort of way, but it was nothing for grown women to fight over. Or was it? How exciting. Finally, high school was getting interesting.

I saw Kelly, the girl so enraged at my crown that she sent her mother to kick ass on my behalf, in the hall later that day, but she wouldn't look me in the eye. In fact she never had. I don't think Kelly was aware of my existence until I was crowned royalty instead of her. I thought, *Well, if a math teacher has to take a punch in order for justice to prevail, then that's a lesson for us all.* My mom was too busy working, brewing tea, and knitting the afghan to fight my battles. If Kelly had a problem, she could take it up with me directly, which she never did, of course. Wuss.

Eventually the prom scandal died down, and unfortunately it didn't spread around school the way I had hoped. So far the only really successful rumor spread about me during high school was that I was dying of leukemia, and that wasn't very fun. Besides me, Kelly, and the actual prom queen, it seemed no one knew that a fight almost broke out between two grown women over my gold ball gown. But it made me happy to know that it had happened, and that it was completely ridiculous.

A few days later, hot off my prom-princess buzz, Adam asked me to hang out. He no longer cared about his homework, and I never did in the first place, so we decided not to wait until the weekend and go out that very night. We went to an empty playground and talked for a while about the end of school and our mixed emotions. We were both making up for lost time—his lost to studying and mine to brooding and feeling self-conscious.

"I feel like I'm just starting to enjoy myself and now I have to leave," I said, my feet trailing in the dirt while I swung on the swing.

"I know, I didn't breathe for the last four years," said Adam, as he stopped swinging and began to pace. "It's Tuesday night, right? Why can't we be out? Why haven't I ever done anything but study on a

Tuesday night?" Adam started to walk toward the lawn, so I hopped off my swing, careful not to fall as usual, and followed him. "It feels good, you know? I mean, I got into the school I wanted, which is great, but I missed everything."

I had missed everything too. I was too engulfed in my very own *So-Called Life* to ever enjoy high school until this point. I had hated my teachers, my classmates; I was even angry to be young in this time period. I did anything I could to be anywhere but here and now. But at the park, sitting on that playground lawn, on a Tuesday night with bookish Adam, I was in the moment. In the spirit of seizing the day, he leaned in and kissed me. As our lips touched, I wondered if he was less of a nerd than I thought. He seemed to know what he was doing. Adam was a really good kisser. Then when he removed my bra in one fell swoop, I thought, *This is no nerd you're dealing with here.* From that night forward, it was on between Adam and me. I tried my best to keep things at a "fling only" level. I was trying to be realistic. Our entire last-few-months-of-school relationship was like an '80s movie—the artsy girl and the nerd with confidence having one last fling before they left town forever. Except this movie would feature music from Chumbawamba instead of Wang Chung.

Right before graduation, my parents went away on vacation for a week. I took on extra hours at the bakery in their absence so as to minimize my hours at my now-empty house. It was so quiet there without them, my dog even barked less without my mom (his one true love) there to protect.

Working in the back of the bakery was a cute guy in his twenties who resembled Chachi from *Happy Days*. I barely got to work with him but with the extra hours I took on, our paths crossed a little more. He was fun and flirted directly with all the other bakery girls except me and the chain-smoking senior citizen who worked the twelve-to-seven shift. I didn't care. He was fun to look at and I had newfound game now that I was dating Adam. One night, while my folks were still out of town, I went to punch out, and Chachi poked his head into the office and said, "Margot, can you . . . uh . . . come back here for a second?"

I walked to the back, having a vague memory of Lyle Lovett's creepy baker performance in *Short Cuts*, which I had just rented from Blockbuster. "Margot, I . . . uh . . . understand your parents are away this week."

"Yes," I said hesitantly, wondering if he also knew where I lived.

"I wanted to give you this." He handed me a five-gallon bucket of buttercream. I had recommended the buttercream frosting over the whipped cream frosting to customers when they asked. He must have overheard. Maybe he wanted me to ice some cupcakes with my favorite frosting in my downtime at the counter. He looked me up and down, then continued, "Promise me you'll tell me everything you do with it."

I extended my hand and took the bucket. Chachi must have heard me tell my coworker that my parents were away. I looked over my shoulder to see if she overheard this random and perverted offering, but she was outside putting out a cigarette while simultaneously lighting up another.

Equally as flattered as I was freaked out, I asked, "Everything?"

"Yes, everything," said Chachi.

Weird and fetishy, yes . . . but Chachi was finally flirting with me. And who was I to judge if someone was a little weird? I once wore an orange unitard to middle school (and still stand by the fact that it was a killer outfit). Standing tall, buttercream in hand, I walked out of the bakery, anxious to call Adam and tell him the insane thing that had just happened. A few hours later Adam came over, we had a buttercream fight in the backyard, and that night I shaved my legs with it. As the pink Gillette Daisy disposable razor hit my pale, long, freckled leg, I thought to myself, *I have arrived.*

When my parents returned to town, they noticed a strange rotten dairy odor coming from the backyard. I provided no explanation for it, because even if I did, it would have left them even more confused. After my folks returned, Adam and I went back to spending our nights at the deserted playground.

School was about to end, and although no one seemed to know that Adam and I were seeing each other, no one would have cared anyway. All the nerds were paired off with last-minute girlfriends, and everyone else was cool enough to have their own thing going on. As graduation approached I was happy to finally be having fun. Adam was great, though I was more intrigued by him than in love with him. I was searching for excitement, not a relationship. Adam was going to major in politics at Brown while I was going to major in theatre at Ithaca College. Our lives were about to go in completely different directions.

Beyond the connection we had over finally enjoying high school (and some good sexual chemistry), we really had almost nothing in common. Even though Adam had some majorly hot moves, like walking his fingers up the back of my thigh while making out with me, I was getting anxious to go away and study theatre. When I would talk to Adam about this, he didn't understand. Adam was practical and had a nice future ahead of him in politics. I wanted to live a life like Rodreigo—nontraditional, sexy, adventurous, and free. I didn't really want to lead a conventional life like I could see Adam having, even though those last few months were the only part of high school I actually truly enjoyed.

"Adam, I really don't know what's going to happen to us when we go away to school. I don't want to make a false promise to you," I said one night while sipping peanut butter mocha at the local Main Street coffeehouse.

"Well, we can meet here. You'll come visit and stuff, right?"

"I don't know how much time I want to spend here once I'm gone."

"It's not so bad, Margot," Adam said as he nervously munched on his biscotti and tried to clean up the mess of crumbs he had just created.

"I know it's not. You just don't get it," I said, as I smiled and took

his hand across the table. I was really eager to go somewhere and rein-
vent myself. I didn't want to visit a place where I would always be known
as a gargantuan freak. I wanted to leave, start over, make friends with
people who appreciated intricate tie-dye patterns, and never look back.

A few days later was graduation. I was graduating sixty-seventh
out of a class of about 190. "Top fifty, Margot. I thought we were going
for top fifty. Too much daydreaming." My mother was not pleased,
my older brother having graduated in the top fifteen four years before.
"Well," she sighed, "at least you were recognized in the yearbook. You
know I was voted—"

"Friendliest," I cut her off. "I know, Mom, you've told me a thousand times." My mother's win as "friendliest" often made me wonder if
she had a slutty side in high school, but I never dared to ask. I, on the
other hand, tied with the prom queen for "Most Involved" due to my
mad-dash senior year to join every activity possible to get into college
and make up for three years of brooding.

The other superlative I won was "Most Unique," an honor I shared
with Eli, my prom date. "Most Unique" really was just a nice way of saying "weirdest," but I took it as a compliment. It helped, actually. When
graduation day came, I felt as if I had had a true suburban high school
experience, albeit in the last few months of school. Between prom princess and the yearbook, I would be remembered for being weird . . . not
gigantic. And I liked that.

On the day of graduation, my brother was away in Chicago
for the summer but my parents both came. Greg had just graduated
from Northwestern film school where *Friends* star David Schwimmer
gave the department graduation speech and big-time hottie Robert
Redford was the school graduation speaker. My high school ceremony
was far less star-studded—featuring two nerds gone wild giving the
keynote addresses. After rolling with the big boys in Chicago, I worried my folks had gone Hollywood on me and would be disappointed

in my public regional high school's inability to produce even one B-list celebrity speaker.

As Floyd Barstow and the rest of the band played "Pomp and Circumstance," I walked slowly in line with the other graduates. I sat down in my itchy polyester robe on that football field, realizing that in the past four years I had barely even attended a game. As I looked at my mom, who was weeping, of course, I wondered if she was ever going to bring up the fact that she recently found and then neatly folded the boxers Adam left in my bedroom. As the valedictorian rambled on about "following your dreams," I deduced that I was not in trouble and that my mom had decided it was easier to pretend she didn't find them and to not tell my dad. I knew when I went away to school that she would fondly remember me as Senior Year Margot, who participated in after-school activities, school dances, fudge factory parties, and beach weekends. She would be happy to forget Freshman–Junior Year Margot, who sulked around like Lurch from *The Addams Family*, smoked too much pot, and played variations of the same four chords on her guitar. The beach was twenty minutes away, the next town over birthed the great and powerful Jon Bon Jovi, and the big city was an hour away. But here, at home, to me there was nothing to offer but a town full of people constantly misunderstanding me and wanting to fight each other when I was awarded a tiny rhinestone crown. Until now. Things were finally working out, but I was out of time. I had counted down to this moment, now it was here . . . and I wasn't so sure I wanted to leave after all.

★ ★ ★ That night we drank on the football field, laughed as Eli streaked around the track, and stayed up until dawn. I went straight to work at the bakery the next morning, waltzing in at 5:30 AM and proudly announcing to Chachi, "First of all, I'm a little bit drunk." I used a grand hand gesture I imagined Mrs. Roper on *Three's Company* might use to emphasize the word *drunk* and began crookedly arranging the donuts for the crew of obese truckers about to enter the premises at 6:00 AM on the dot. Between this entrance and the buttercream incident, Chachi was beginning to think of me as a real wild broad. I liked the new me. I was growing into myself finally. Maybe it was finally time to spice things up and order a wig from my Raquel Welch Wig Collection catalogue.

The night before I left for college, Adam and I drove to the shore and hooked up on the beach, which I really do not recommend. There is still sand lodged somewhere in my cervix from that fateful night. While picking a piece of seashell out of my belly button, I wondered how the hell I could incorporate Adam into this faraway place I was about to go to. I wanted to start fresh. If I was going to say good-bye to home, I was going to leave all of it behind, as I had been planning on doing ever since I saw season 6, episode 113 of *Laverne & Shirley,* "Not Quite New York," where the girls pack it all up and head off to Hollywood. Sure, Carmine a.k.a. "The Big Ragu" joined them, but they also made new friends like Rhonda the busty blonde. I wanted to head off and meet my Rhonda.

Then we made out in front of my house in the front seat of his Toyota Corolla and kept accidentally honking the horn, because girls my size really need at least an SUV to have ample room for the front-seat make-out. As the horn kept honking, I wondered if my mom could hear it. Then I hoped she would categorize this moment with the time she found Adam's boxer shorts in my room. She definitely heard it but would pretend she didn't, because that was easier than admitting that her teen/almost-adult daughter was hooking up on a hot New Jersey night in a vehicle right under her nose.

We promised each other we would try our hardest to make it work while we were away at school, but there would be no commitment. I had a sinking feeling about that.

"Okay then, well, I guess this is good-bye," I said.

"I'll try my best to stay in touch while we're away."

"Okay, but remember, no promises, right, Adam?"

"I know, no promises. But when are you coming home to visit?"

"I'll be home for Thanksgiving."

"November, Margot?"

"November. Until then?"

Adam kissed me good-bye and I exited the car, feeling more free than sad. I entered my house and waved good-bye to him as he drove away. I walked up the stairs and noticed my parents turning off the light just as I got there. They were pretending they were asleep so they didn't have to acknowledge why exactly I was in a parked, honking car outside the house for over an hour. I went into my room and looked around at the now-bare walls, just specks of Fun-Tak and tape stains in place of all my posters of middle-aged rock stars. Perhaps my mom was right in her initial insistence that I just use magnets to hang posters on my metal closet doors. The tape and Fun-Tak did ruin the walls. She was right. I took out my bags and finally began to pack, something I had avoided doing since my college acceptance letters came in.

I slept about two hours that night because I gravely underestimated just how long packing up a closet full of vintage clothes would take. The next morning I opened the door to start my travels to Ithaca and found a handwritten card on my doorstep from Adam telling me how much this summer together had meant to him. He must have gotten there really early to leave it. As I opened it I thought about his commitment to romance, and how much more sleep he would have gotten if only he had simply given it to me the night before.

My parents and I headed off in the jam-packed Plymouth Voyager for the five-hour trek to Ithaca. I clutched Adam's card the whole way there and thought about how lucky we were that Corey the stalker had not succeeded in blowing up that car. If we had to take my mom's sedan, I definitely wouldn't have enough room to take my entire handmade paper collection.

CHAPTER 18:

Good Old Maggot

I have heard that college is a place where fitting in doesn't matter and one can completely revamp him/herself, like on *The Facts of Life* when Beverly Ann Stickle, played by Cloris Leachman, came to Peekskill and took over for Mrs. Garrett supervising those wacky girls. After Charlotte Rae left *Facts*, the show got a much-needed makeover, giving it the edginess it always needed. As a kid I was inspired by the Cloris Leachman era of *The Facts of Life* and was eagerly anticipating my upcoming reinvention.

College was brand-new territory where you could change your whole identity in one moment, significantly altering the course of the rest of your life by way of the new you. That sounded great to me, and already I was planning on introducing myself to everyone at college as "Maggie." Because while "Margot" a.k.a. "Maggot" a.k.a. "Margot Fargo farts a lot" is a humongous freak who sits alone in the cafeteria, "Maggie" is a cute girl with freckles on her shoulders who attracts guys by fiddling with her guitar on the quad.

I had always hated my name. Correcting moronic people on a daily basis that the *t* on the end was silent was the bane of my existence. My mother always said to tell people who would mispronounce my name, "You don't say escar-GOT, and you don't say Brigitte Bar-DOT, so why would you say Mar-GOT?" While this seemed like an adequate comeback, it was a bit long-winded, and usually not worth repeating every time a pharmacist called out your name to come sign for your amoxicillin. Games of "Marco Polo" were especially unbearable. "Marco" sounded remarkably similar to my name, so whenever I walked past a game of "Marco Polo" at the pool club and heard someone calling out "Marco," I'd always stop and say, "Yes?" Thus I'd interrupt a game I was not invited to participate in and ruin everyone's fun. And when I actually would play Marco Polo, I could never fully get into it. I'd be so worried that someone was actually calling my name that I would always open my eyes to check. It made me anxious and I always ended up quitting, putting on my embarrassing bathing cap, and swimming in the lap lanes.

It made me especially annoyed to know that I was originally supposed to be named Carey, after the Joni Mitchell song. How inspiring it would have been to be named after a song that contained the lyrics, *And we'll laugh and toast to nothing and smash our empty glasses down.* Plus, Joni Mitchell was my dad's dream girl (my mother's dream guys being a tie between fellow tall person and actual Brit John Cleese and hunky president Bill Clinton). But a few days before I was born my mom became concerned about the cult-classic Sissy Spacek movie *Carrie.* My mother's fear was that the other babies my age would have seen the R-rated horror movie and then make fun of me for having the same name as its virginal, pig-blood-coated star. *Carrie* is a movie I did not see until I was about twenty-five, and by then another iconic "Carrie" had come front and center, Carrie Bradshaw, a woman whom half of all womankind wanted to be exactly like. So really? Would naming me Carey have been a horrible mistake? Because I went to school with a lot of Jasons during the *Friday the 13th* era, and they all seemed to be okay. And I went through middle and high school with a girl named Carrie, and she was never once teased for her name. I know this because I sat behind her in countless classes, and every day at roll call each teacher pronounced her name perfectly on the first try. Never once did I hear a snicker or whisper of "dirty pillows." I, on the other hand, was called MarGOT by virtually every teacher I ever had, resulting in a huge uproar of laughter from my classmates with phonetically spelled names like Rob.

It was obviously time to rebrand myself. If I never got to be Carey, I would settle for Maggie. I couldn't wait.

My parents and I arrived early afternoon at a dorm building in the middle of a scenic wonderland. There were waterfalls and flowers and birds chirping. There was a lake on the horizon and a smell of fresh air mixed with crisp fall. This was a far cry from the strip mall I called home. Here in Ithaca, I was smelling new smells! I was on my way out. I was going to be the new me. Maggie was about to make her life debut. My dad hadn't even cut the engine in the parking lot at school when I grabbed a bag and struggled to open the annoying sliding door of the backseat of my parents' minivan.

"It might help if you unlock it, Margot," said my father oh-so-helpfully, taking a swig of his now-hot seltzer that had been sitting next to him in the car for the last five hours.

With a huge sigh I flipped the manual lock, looking forward to soon traveling only in vehicles driven by cool artists with normal doors. I wouldn't have a car in college, and that was okay with me. I planned to make friends with people who had cars, learn the local public transportation system, and go on long walks where butterflies would land on my shoulders and I would have major breakthroughs about my life's calling.

My mom was silent for once, most likely because she didn't want me to know she was crying. I got my lanky frame out of the car and we all walked to the dorm to check in. Suddenly the same feeling of walking into Jessica Rosenstein's fashion intervention rushed over me. The dorm was filled with happy faces of late teens who were about to be free from parental supervision for the longest stretch of time they'd ever gone. Everyone seemed to have been there for hours and already made his or her best friends. I hadn't even started school yet and I already felt alone.

My parents came with me to the check-in table at the dorms, where I was to get my room number and key. Right away we discovered that there had been a glitch with my housing. A week before, I had gotten a letter informing me that I had been placed with a smoking roommate on the last remaining college "smokers' floor," and my mom called and complained.

"What is this, 1964?" my mother had screeched at the nineteen-year-old work/study student who answered the phone in the college housing department. Apparently, the nineteen-year-old work/study student did not take the initiative to resolve the situation and place me with a different roommate as promised. So a battle began to find me a place to live where I would not have to restart my childhood candy cigarette fetish in an attempt to trick my neighbors into thinking I was one of them. My mom served as war general for our side of the skirmish.

I was mortally embarrassed to watch my mom create a scene, but I actually agreed with her that I needed a new place to live. Despite my New York City grandmother's glamorous example of holding endless More 120 brown cigarettes between her perfectly manicured red nails, I had never taken up the habit. As chic as my grandmother made smoking look, my coworker at the bakery made it look equally revolting, really driving home that smoking just wasn't for me. I didn't belong on a "smokers' floor," and there was no "granddaughter of a smoker's floor," so I was going to have to go somewhere else. The college finally solved the problem by assuming that not only could I not live with a smoker, I couldn't live with anyone, and they assigned me to a single.

A single? Oh no. My mother's first college roommate was still her BFF. I had eavesdropped on countless phone calls between them where they laughed hysterically at endless private jokes. I wanted private jokes! My mom and her college roommate spent every New Year's Eve together drinking Bahama Mamas and dancing to sixties music. Who was I going to drink Bahama Mamas with?

"I'm so sorry, honey," said my mom, as she handed me the key we had just gotten from the RA. "Hmm . . . room 1310."

"Room 1310? I guess that's on the thirteenth floor . . ." I said, looking for the elevators and feeling lonely already.

"That can't be," my mom said. "Most buildings don't even have a thirteenth floor, too spooky. It's really bad luck. Have you ever heard of a thirteenth floor, Bob?"

My father shook his head.

My mom turned around again to plead with the RA. "There shouldn't be a thirteenth floor. It's unlucky. I don't want my daughter on an unlucky floor. My mother's high-rise had floor 12, then floor 14. Do you remember that, Margot? No 13!" she shrieked.

"Mom, it's fine," I interrupted. "I like being alone. I'm not superstitious, and I just want to move in. Let's do this. I've heard they put the people with really messed-up housing in student lounges and hallways."

"What? I don't want my daughter living in a hallway!" she shouted at the RA again.

"Mom. I'm not living in a hallway. I'm just living on the thirteenth floor," I said calmly, and watched my RA turn a little less pale.

We piled my bags of vintage jeans, psychedelic blouses, classic rock CDs, and posters of various ethereal women who all slightly resembled me into the elevator. On the dreaded thirteenth floor, we paraded down

the hall to room 1310, and I opened the door to the tiny space I would
be spending the next year in.

It was small but nice. The blinds were open to reveal a view onto
Lake Cayuga. If I looked far enough down, I could see students min-
gling on the lawn. It was isolated, picturesque, and calm. If I was going
to be all alone, this wasn't a bad way to do it.

My parents were more nervous than I was about the new development of my solo digs.

"Margot, who are you going to eat dinner with tonight?" asked
my mom.

"She'll be fine, Pam," said my dad, aware that I had spent my
junior year eating third-period lunch alone. I was no novice lone diner.
I could handle it.

Finally, with a tearful good-bye, they shut the door. I put on Bob
Dylan's *Blood on the Tracks* and began hanging up posters of flowy-
haired maidens as he sang through his nose with great passion. I wanted
to feel comfortable here. Ever since my growth spurt I had never felt
comfortable in my own skin. If I could have a fresh start here, where no
one knew who I had been back home, combined with a comfortable yet
possibly haunted living space, I could finally feel at ease. I lit two candles, unpacked a bag, switched the CD to Simon & Garfunkel, leaving
me alone with nothing but my "books and my poetry to protect me,"
and put up a poster of a butterfly and a fairy.

After I unpacked, I didn't really know what to do with myself,
so I sat on the bed and began writing in my journal. Soon after I
heard a sing-along beginning next door. First they sang "Tomorrow,"
from *Annie*. Then I heard "One" from *A Chorus Line*. *Theatre dorks,* I
thought to myself. I was sure the dorm room next door was filled with
Cats sweatshirt–wearing, piano scarf–donning Sondheim fans who
harmonized while singing "Happy Birthday" when the cake came out
in restaurants. I wasn't going to be that kind of theatre major. I was

going to be the kind who penned genius experimental plays and had bangs that grew over her eyes like Jackie Angel. Too bad my future bangs were sure to curl and frizz up like a bad Miss Piggy wig.

I opened my door a crack to make the Andrew Lloyd Webber–ites next door aware there was a lone person in this room. I sat down and began writing in my fairy journal with my purple fine-tipped pen just as the dork patrol began singing, "Life is a cabaret my friend, come to the cabaret," in perfect harmony. I was just turning up my Simon & Garfunkel when I heard a faint knock on my door.

"Hello?" said a nasal voice.

I opened the door to find a tall, skinny, perky, black-haired girl wearing head-to-toe Ithaca College attire combined with what seemed to be full stage makeup in comparison to the tinted Blistex I was wearing. There was no way I was going to find my niche here.

"Uh, yeah?" I asked suspiciously.

The perky girl walked in uninvited. "Cool room. Wow!" she said in a thick Buffalo accent. "You've decorated the place! Smells like lavender in here. Anyway, I was wondering, when you were done with your journal entry, of course, if you'd like to join us next door. We're having a sing-along."

"I know, I heard," I said, while quickly pondering if it was too late to accept the scholarship to Rutgers I was offered so I could stay as far away from this dork central station I had just agreed to spend the next four years in. When I visited Ithaca College it seemed like the college version of Camp Wallobee. I was excited to lie on a tapestry in the quad and bond with fellow artists who had also read *On the Road*. But after only a few hours in this place, it seemed less Sid and Nancy and more Donny and Marie.

"Okay then. Well, if you want to come by, you're more than welcome. You can even bring your guitar."

Shit. My guitar. I brought my guitar with me for more of a fashion accessory and room decoration than a musical instrument. Despite a year of guitar lessons, many coaching sessions from Jonah Hertzberg, and incessant listening to every classic rock album in my father's record collection, I still knew only four chords. I was more into having a guitar than playing a guitar. Well, who's kidding who, I was the most into wearing the guitar. But I didn't want this perky girl to find out that I was a fraud so instantly.

"Okay, thanks," I muttered. And then I gently shut the door, leaving it open just slightly enough to send the message *Don't bother me but don't ignore me either.*

I returned to my journal and tried to focus on my feelings but was incredibly distracted by the group rendition of "Everything's Coming Up Roses." I turned up Simon & Garfunkel a little louder. Still, I couldn't concentrate, and as Paul and Art belted "Sounds of Silence," I decided, *Fuck it.* I put down my fairy journal, blew out my lavender candles, turned off my music, grabbed my guitar and favorite songbook—*Great Songs from the Sixties*, which I had inherited from my grandmother's sheet-music collection she kept in the bench of her pink piano—and headed next door to see if I could possibly enjoy myself surrounded by perky people from upstate New York.

I opened the door, and the girl with the makeup stood up and said, "You came!! Everybody this is—"

"Margot." Shit! I forgot to be Maggie. Okay, next time remember to be the new you.

"Hi, Margot. I'm Adriana. And this is Eric and Lori and—" Adriana went on to rattle off about ten names of the various smiling faces in the room. I didn't realize that many people could fit in such a tiny space and still seem to enjoy themselves.

"So, you've got a guitar!" said Adriana. "Want to play us something?"

Shit. I knew I shouldn't have brought my stupid guitar. *From now on I will only accessorize with bracelets, barrettes, and scarves. No more guitars.*

"Uh, sure."

I took out my songbook and began aimlessly leafing through it to buffer the time before I confessed to the theatre dorks that I had no talent.

"Mind if I play something while you're looking through your book?" asked Eric, as I all too eagerly handed him the guitar and the book. "This is dedicated to you, Margot—I heard your music next door."

He began playing "Bridge over Troubled Water" and we all sang right along with him, including me. We then sang "Spinning Wheel" and "Do You Believe in Magic" and about a dozen other awesome songs from my book. The theatre dorks were very adaptable to my music and I felt bad for being so judgmental of them at first. They didn't judge me after all, so maybe I should be a little less closed-minded.

I hung out with the perky girl, Adriana, for the rest of the night. She told me about how at orientation she had participated in the sack races; I told her how I had sat on the sidelines and judged those who participated. She was looking forward to unlimited orange "pop" in the dining hall; I had brought my own herbal tea. Maybe Adriana would be my lifetime "college roommate BFF"—despite our apparent differences or the fact that we weren't actually roommates. I was excited I would have at least one friend to start off college with. I was also pretty stoked that she was already aware of my tendency to become reclusive and obsessed with my journal, and I respected that she had developed a coping mechanism of hosting a sixties sing-along to combat that. Adriana seemed to really embrace her inner dorky tall girl and didn't care if anyone thought she was lame. She wore her Ithaca tracksuit and red lipstick proudly, and I admired her for that. Not since Jackie Angel had I met another tall-girl misfit I related to so much. Except Jackie was whom I strived to be like one day, and Adriana was more like the present me. I imagined that being an artsy tall girl in Buffalo was just as trying as being one in Central Jersey. I went to sleep that first night on my own, feeling optimistic about my future here.

The next day while hanging up blue Christmas lights to give my room a calm, soothing feel, I heard a faint knock on my door. Before I could answer it, the door swung open.

"You're here!" said my new buddy Adriana, wearing both an Ithaca baseball hat and an Ithaca sweatshirt, as she let herself into my new sanctuary. "I had the most awful time finding you. I felt like real-life Nancy Drew. I forgot where you lived because I'm in a different dorm. Wow, thirteenth floor, huh? Ha! Bummer. Wow, nice blue lights. Anyway, I'm going exploring. Do you want to come? I mean if you're done decorating, I know how you're into that." I've never had someone pursue my friendship so aggressively, a far cry from Floyd Barstow snubbing me in the Puerto Rican rainforest. I much preferred Adriana's approach.

"Sure, I'll come," I said, half excited to see this new place and half needing to step away from my endless interior decorating. I got out of my smelly Eddie Vedder–esque clothes and put on a flowing sky-blue tank top, just in case I met any cute guys. Sky blue was my best color, while Ithaca College's school colors of navy and canary yellow made me look as if I belonged at a methadone clinic. Adriana and I walked around campus and eventually made our way to the theatre building, where we would be taking most of our classes.

"Ooh!" she said, excited at the mere sight of the building. "Let's go in there, find a room, and sing in the dark. That's the best way to really let yourself go." Adriana was majoring in music, which was really a competitive department to get into, so she must have been good.

I had never sung in the dark, or really sung in front of anyone since my horrific "Give Peace a Chance" cafeteria solo. But Adriana made me feel like everything was fun, so I was up for giving it a try. This time there would be no Chad Decker to make my life a living hell if I sang off-key.

As we walked towards the building, we passed a few people coming out, and Adriana called to them, "Hey, are you guys theatre majors?"

I was so embarrassed; that was something my award-winning "friendliest" mom would do. I was used to trying to be invisible and was uncomfortable drawing any sort of attention to myself. But the guys smiled and said yes. One of them had a slight resemblance to Rodreigo, which immediately made me want to talk to him, despite the fact that he was wearing overalls. A familiar face was just what I needed right now. I got a little closer and was instantly attracted to him.

"Hi," he said. "So, you're a freshman theatre major?"

"Yeah," I gulped, wondering why Adriana was awkwardly walking backward behind this guy making weird hand signals in this guy's general direction.

"I'm Jean Claude," said the Rodreigo-looking boy.

"Oh, cool," I said, realizing that Adriana was signaling some form of "Go for it! I'll leave you alone," though her gestures mostly looked as if she had been caught in a spiderweb. Regaining my composure, I asked, "Where are you from?"

"France," he said. Of course. Anyone named Jean Claude not born in France would be completely pretentious.

"France, cool! My name is French. It's Margot. But I'm not from France. I'm from New Jersey," I said, realizing once again I had forgotten my new identity as Maggie. Well, maybe I could fix this when classes started and the teachers called my name for roll call. I could simply say, "I go by 'Maggie,'" the way all Beckys had done throughout my youth when teachers called out "Rebecca."

Jean Claude laughed. "Well, I am from France, and Margot is one of my favorite French names."

After that, I watched Jean Claude walk away and fell instantly in love with him. He was foreign and witty and his overalls were covered in paint because he was an artist. And he pronounced my name "Maregeau," the proper French way. In that instant I decided I had no need to reclaim myself as Maggie. In college I was going to be "Mare-geau," accent on the second syllable. I wouldn't be Maggie, but I would be the new Margot; I would be Mare-geau. I stared at Jean Claude, hoping he would look back at me. Adriana grabbed my arm and pulled me into the theatre building, giggling the whole way about the cute guy I had just struck up a conversation with. I couldn't believe I almost wrote this place off last night.

✶ ✶ ✶ The next day classes started. I was given this useless thing called an "e-mail address," which everyone else had heard of before and was excited about. I thought, *Why would anyone e-mail when you can mail-mail?* Despite my near-death experience with Corey the stalker I still enjoyed the thrill of receiving a letter in the mail. My new e-mail address, along with my new complimentary rape whistle, were two things I hoped I would never have to use.

My schedule listed Acting, Modern Dance, Ancient Greek Theatre, and Writing for Theatre Majors—I was finally going to my dream *Fame*-like school. I got great feedback in acting, and even greater feedback in dance. After all these years, it turned out I was actually pretty good at modern dance, and not just because I wholeheartedly enjoyed wearing unitards with skirts over them as my daily attire. The weird thing was that unlike horseback riding, songwriting, poetry, babysitting, singing, fashion designing, volleyball, and playing the guitar, dancing was something I could do well. My ballet teacher explained to me that true dancers are notoriously clumsy because we are used to "gliding through an empty space." This wasn't like first grade when I played catcher on my town's girls' softball team "The Peacocks" just because I liked the catcher costume. Yes, I enjoyed wearing unitards on a daily basis and not being sent home for it, but I was also really moved by dance. Something about flowing movement taught by an artistically tormented teacher while a live drummer banged on bongos made me jump out of bed with excitement when my alarm clock went off.

★ ★ ★ Meanwhile, in Writing for Theatre Majors, I was assigned my first college paper: an analysis of a Shakespeare play. My teacher, a messy-haired guy way too relaxed not to be stoned, gave my class the following instructions:

"So, we're going to use this period as a group research time. You can look at any of the books on the shelf, or go to one of the computers and look information up on the Internet. Or whatever."

Right away everyone scattered to the computers to go use this so-called Internet they all seemed uberfamiliar with. What the hell was the Internet?

Confused, I raised my hand.

"Uh . . . what's the Internet?" I asked, while simultaneously a classroom of artsy kids jutted their heads around in shock.

"Have you never heard of the Internet?" asked my teacher incredulously. "Whoa!"

"No. Sorry."

"Seriously?" called out a hairy techie kid. "What have you been doing for the past few years?"

I don't know, I thought. *Dancing in a field with a scarf? Rereading* Go Ask Alice? *Playing the same four chords on my guitar in a poor attempt to get "discovered"?*

I said nothing.

"Margot, the Internet is a place to find facts. Just go over to one of those computers by the wall, call up a search engine like Lycos or Altavista.com, and then type in what you'd like to learn more about," explained my teacher, eager to be finished with me so he'd be one step closer to toking on his after-class joint.

I headed for a computer, intrigued to test out this cockamamie Internet thing. But what to type in as my very first search? Anything I needed to know about Shakespeare I could read in the hard copies of the plays my dad had given me from his college years. The yellowed pages and old-book smell were much more alluring than this boxy Intel computer shoved between a musical theatre dork and a male ballerina.

I stared at the computer screen and tried to think of something I wanted to know. I was currently reclaiming my name—perhaps this Internet could provide me some facts about the history of the name Margot. Being the self-indulgent narcissist that theatre school was encouraging me to become, I typed in my very first Internet search, *MARGOT.*

A few entries came up, all in French. I clicked on the first one. It appeared to be some sort of poem, but I wasn't sure. My French skills were truly horrific after dropping French in eleventh grade. My problems with that class began early. In the first week of high school, everyone was assigned cool French versions of their names like "Jacques" for John and "Andrée" for Andrea. I wanted a cool French name, too, like Delphine or Claudette. My French teacher (a Hungarian woman with pointy teeth and a bad perm) told me, "No! No French name for you!" Because Margot was already French, I wasn't allowed to play make-believe (my favorite game) with all the other half-baked Phish-loving twerps in my class. A few days into the school year, I stayed after class, talking her into calling me "Simone."

The next day my teacher, who sounded like an aging Miss Piggy with a Hungarian accent, reluctantly called on me.

"Simone, *quelle heure est-il?* . . . Simone? . . . Simone?"

I knew what time it was. I even knew what time it was in French. What I didn't remember was that my name was now Simone.

"That's it! I give you a chance, Simone. You're back to Margot!"

I slouched in my chair as "Genevieve" a.k.a. Teresa Carimonico, formerly known as the pregnant seventh grader, snickered at me.

Now was my time to really embody my unusual French name. Jean Claude said it was one of his favorites and any in I could get with him would be worth it. That gave me an idea. I decided to print one of the French poems that came up during my "Margot" search, figuring I could use it later as a conversation piece with Jean Claude. I waited patiently as the dot matrix took its time creaking out its last few drops of black ink to appease my curiosity. I tore off the printout and folded on the tear strips, careful not to attempt to separate the pages, knowing that being a lefty made simple things extra difficult and I would just end up ripping it down the middle.

And then, just like that, class was over. I had used the Internet for the first time and probably the last. It wasn't very fun. Why would anyone sit in front of a computer screen when they could find the answers using real-life experience? I waltzed out of the room with my poem in hand. The class filed out with me, and my teacher left with us, probably to find a deserted grassy knoll to roll a joint.

I headed off to lunch in the dining hall, where I was still getting over having unlimited access to Lucky Charms and chickpeas. After eighteen years of living in an exclusively Kellogg's All-Bran household, I couldn't believe that Ithaca College left out unsupervised Lucky Charms for our taking anytime we wanted. And the dining hall seemed incredibly encouraging of my vegetarianism, keeping a well-stocked salad bar complete with artificial bacon bits, my favorite. My mom was probably really happy right now; she wouldn't have to make special meals for me anymore—the dining hall would take care of me now. This was much better for me, too. I had always had suspicions that the chicken-free broths that she served me came from the same pot as the chicken broth. No longer would I have to be vigilant of foreign meat substances sneaking their way into my meals. No longer would my boss at the drug store call Vito and Vinnie at the pot/pizza parlor and ask them to slip some ham into my vegetarian calzone as his version of a hilarious joke. Now, I was in charge of my food intake. Chickpeas and Lucky Charms it would be.

I entered the dining hall and right away saw Jean Claude finishing his lunch at a table across the room. I thought about how this French poem would be a good way to strike up a conversation. I approached the table where he and his artist friends were finishing up their chicken fingers.

"Hi, Jean Claude," I said, making my best effort at being sexy without caring.

"Oh, hello, Mare-geau," he said, making me want to rip off my clothes.

"I'm sorry to bother you, but I was just in writing class and we used this thing called the Internet. Have you guys ever heard of it?"

"Yeah, we've heard of the Internet; we use it, like, every day," said one of Jean Claude's friends with paint on his artsy man hands, snickering as he said this.

"Yes. Is this the first time you're hearing of it, Mare-geau?" asked Jean Claude, confused by my ahead-of-its-time off-the-grid-ness.

"Well, yeah. Sorry. I think I get it now, though. My teacher said I could type in anything and facts would come up. So I typed in my name, but the first thing that came up was in French, and I was wondering if you could translate it for me? It's a poem."

"Uh, sure," said Jean Claude, as he wiped the fried grease from his hands with a crumpled used napkin, which was such an artist thing to do. He looked at my printout and paused. "Mare-geau, are you sure that you want me to translate this for you?"

"Totally, go for it!" I said, looking at his cool artist friends, wondering if they would accept me into this clique once I was Jean Claude's official girlfriend.

"Uh, okay," Jean Claude said with hesitation, looking sheepishly at me. "It says, 'Mare-geau, she is a dirty girl. Mare-geau she likes it really rough. Mare-geau she likes it all the time. Mare-geau she likes it from behind . . .' Shall I go on?"

I snatched back my pornographic poem and tried to remain calm. "That's okay. I get the gist. Thanks for translating." I walked away hearing his friends erupt in laughter as soon as I was gone. My poor attempt to connect with the hot French guy had completely backfired. Why did I decide to be Mare-geau? Why couldn't I have stuck with the original plan to be cute Maggie? I was going to be the same gigantic dork I was back home. I was still good old Maggot.

I grabbed a salad with extra chickpeas, canned beets, and Bac-Os and sat down with Adriana, trying not to cry. It was all that stupid Internet's fault. Was this what the Internet was? People's names with dirty things written next to them? I thought everything on there was supposed to be facts! That poem was not factual. I had never taken it from behind; how could someone write such a thing, albeit in French? I had really blown it with Jean Claude. I had humiliated myself in front of all his friends and now I was never going to get the guy. Why did I even think I would? Just because I was slightly cooler in my first week of college than I'd been in high school didn't mean shit. It was impossible for me to have been less cool here than in high school. I had nowhere to go but up. But this poetry incident was ranking up there with my Gulf War protest. Maybe not that much had changed for me after all. I wanted to fake sick for a few days just as I had after no one joined me in my cafeteria sing-along.

Why were my most humiliating moments all set in cafeterias?

* * * That night, I sat alone in my thirteenth-floor single with my blue Christmas lights, replaying the humiliating-poem moment

over and over again as I listened to the Indigo Girls harmonize about lesbian heartache. I tried to do research for my Shakespeare paper, but I couldn't focus. I smelled and resmelled my father's old books to get inspired, but nothing seemed to work. I knew I'd blown it with Jean Claude and that slowly but surely everyone here would learn what a huge dork I was. This wasn't my Cloris Leachman–jumpstarting-boring-old-*Facts of Life* moment. This wasn't my *Laverne & Shirley* Hollywood moment. This was just another stale season of *Maggot, the Story of a Hulking Loser.*

As I wallowed in my self-pity, clutching the smoothest rocks of my collection to calm my anxiety, there was a knock on my door. I opened it, thinking it would be Adriana stopping by to show me her new Ithaca College sports socks and Maybelline eye shadow. It was Jean Claude. *Crap!* There was no time to turn off my embarrassingly indulgent music. No time to check my teeth for remnants of canned beets. No time to fix my blonde half–Jew fro. No time to put down my piece of rose quartz. I stood in the doorway trying my best to look as though I was the type of girl whom boys wanted to spontaneously visit.

"Jean Claude, hi! What are you doing here?"

"Well, I wanted to . . . Can I come in?"

"Sure," I said, secretly beaming that a full week of interior designing my concrete sanctuary was not all in vain. Jean Claude entered my world of mood lighting and fairies, shutting the door behind him.

"Well, I wanted to . . ." Jean Claude stopped midsentence, grabbed me passionately, and kissed me. This was my first post–high school kiss. And I couldn't believe it was a kiss from a man with a foreign passport and a penchant for Matisse. The chemistry was on. I was game.

Finally we stopped, although I could have kissed him forever.

"What was that for?" I asked, quickly regretting it, realizing that was something only dorky girls not used to being kissed would say. *Seriously, Margot? "What was that for"?* I might as well have puffed out the neck of my shirt while saying "Hot enough for ya?" God, I couldn't stop myself sometimes. Then I got it together and assumed that by now he had noticed my prominently displayed rock collection and known exactly the level of uncoolness he was dealing with here. I'd never in my life heard someone say, "That college freshman's got a totally rad rock collection." Well, at least my mood lighting was on.

"Mare-geau. Ever since I met you that night outside the theatre building I've been so intrigued by you. But I was so confused as to whether or not you liked me. I couldn't tell. But then you came to my table with that dirty, dirty poem and I thought, *She's definitely flirting with me. This is a girl who knows how to get what she wants.*"

This was too cool. He was right—somewhere buried beneath years of bullying and teasing was a girl who knew how to get what she wanted. He channeled something in me that had been waiting for years to come out. I kissed him again, this time to prevent myself from saying something embarrassing like, "Wow! Jeepers, thanks!" and also to prove I was the girl he said I was. Jean Claude stayed for a long while that night, making out with me while the Indigo Girls sang with every ounce of power behind those flannel shirts.

CHAPTER 19:

Losing My Relevé

I loved my new life. I was actually going to get the guy!

That being evident, I knew that all ties left hanging behind must be severed. Even though Adam and I ended things before we left for school, I wanted to make sure he understood that I really just wanted to start over. We talked on the phone after Jean Claude's visit and it erupted into an argument.

"Look, Adam, I'm really sorry. What we had was fun, but after what I've experienced here, I just don't think there's a connection anymore."

"What do you mean? Of course there's a connection," he whined.

"Well, for one, I'm a dancer now. How can you possibly understand that?"

"I don't understand it, but that doesn't mean—what do you mean you're a dancer now?"

"I make art with my body, Adam."

Silence.

"Maybe you're right," he finally declared, after an undeniably long and awkward pause. "I make art with my body" was just pretentious enough to enable Adam to cut the cord a little earlier than he had hoped. My last-minute high-school-boyfriend experience was left in high school. I was almost free of home. I tried to break the awkward silence.

"It's amazing," I said, using a chipper tone, "there are so many vegetarian options for me to eat in the dining hall. Soy meats and a salad bar. You can't beat it!"

"I gotta go study," he replied. "See you over Thanksgiving."

And with that, Adam hung up the phone, making it clear he had no interest in making small talk about soy meat with the girl who just ditched him, again.

*   *   *   My schedule at school was jam-packed and I became incredibly busy with schoolwork, memorizing lines for acting class and going to late-night choreography sessions in the studio with my new dancer friends.

After the poem misunderstanding, Jean Claude and I began what I believed to be dating. We saw each other here and there, and when we hung out, we kissed. That's dating, right? I wanted to go on romantic picnics backdropped by the Cayuga Lake, but I settled for an occasional group lunch in the dining hall. I had memorized his schedule to the minute and would show up in strategically chosen spots not too near his classrooms, and I'd pretend we were accidentally running into each other, using quips like "What, are you stalking me?" We were nowhere near walking hand in hand across campus or attending "Free Tibet" rallies in the commons as I had hoped we'd be by this point. I figured things were pretty vague in the college world, unlike back home. In high school there was "hooking up" (a onetime thing), "going with" (a multiple-time hookup with no commitment), "seeing each other" (pretty sure you want to be exclusive but keeping your options open just in case Jon Bon Jovi gets divorced), and "going out with" (a committed relationship that is most likely consummated).

I was pretty sure that if I initiated the dreaded relationship talk, I would seem cooler to Jean Claude if I added the caveat, "But you know me, I'm totally laid-back. I mean it's not like I need a label."

The truth was, every journal entry I wrote was about Jean Claude; every time I came home to my answering machine blinking I hoped it was Jean Claude. When I succeeded at "accidentally" running into him, I would feel a rush of adrenaline in the same way my heart had raced after narrowly avoiding a car accident. I tried to remain cool in his presence. I ignored him in front of his friends in the dining hall and waited for him to say hi first. I wanted it to seem like I was "fine with whatever," and when I'd find myself getting too worked up about how much more serious I wanted things to be with him, I refocused my attention on my studies. This happened a lot, and I ended up writing A+ papers, doing kick-ass script analyses, and reading way ahead in the Twyla Tharp biography required for Modern Dance I. So even when Jean Claude slept over one night and half asleep said, "Good night, Diane," I let it go. I didn't know who Diane was, but who was I to ask? Jean Claude was an artist and could not be tamed. And I was an artist dating an artist—an older, worldly, French one no less. I looked in my bedroom mirror and recited my new artsy mantra inspired by Twyla: *I have not chosen this lifestyle, it has chosen me.* If I'd wanted stability, I would have stayed with Adam. Not every young girl from Jersey gets to be schooled by a wise, experienced Frenchman. Who cared about Diane?

Classes were a dream. While doing a *rond de jambe* one day in ballet, my teacher called me a "long-stemmed beauty." I liked that, and it made me wonder if I could now lead a "long-stemmed life," filled with perfect posture, self-acceptance, and unlimited vegetarian menu options. No one here knew anything about my awkward and humiliating teen years.

I was a new woman. For the first time ever I felt grateful to be tall. And I thought I had possibly even found my true calling—as a dancer. That made sense. The only thing I had stuck with all through my awkward phase was modern dance. No one made me do it, the way I was forced to sign up for church volleyball. It was a hobby that I enjoyed, and it seemed as if some of what I had learned stuck with me. My turnout was positioned properly, I already knew the first through fifth positions, and I had taken just enough French in high school to understand that *pas de chat* meant "step of the cat." My ballet teacher even had me demonstrate the moves a few times—and moved me from the back line to the front! (Although, as I headed to my new spot, she said, "You are not a noodle. Stop walking like one." Had I been walking like a noodle? How exactly does a noodle walk? A cooked or raw one? Because walking like raw spaghetti would be a positive thing, I think.)

I felt great passion for my art. I took time to plan out fun dance ensembles each night and got to class early every day to warm up. I even bought a *Flashdance* sweatshirt downtown and wore it over my unitard on cold days. I looked cooler in that unitard than I ever did in my lesbian shoes.

Life was so good, so right, that I basically forgot that I ever had a life before this. Chad Decker? Who's he? Until, one late September night, when I came home from set painting for *The Pirates of Penzance* to find my AT&T answering machine with the ladybug stickers flashing its little red light.

"Hi, Margot, it's Mom. Sorry to bother you. I know you're busy with whatever it is you're always so busy with there. What is it you do there? You don't tell me anything. Anyway, I wanted to remind you to start asking around for a ride home for Thanksgiving. Call me back. Love you."

Ah yes, home. I would have to go back there soon and revisit the past. Maybe this wasn't a clean break after all.

A few days later it was my birthday, which always made me feel lonely, especially because it comes at the beginning of the school year. It was only October. My friendship with Adriana was great but still establishing itself, and my relationship with Jean Claude was confusing. I didn't have a defined group of friends to celebrate with, and I was worried I would spend my special day alone. On my way to modern dance, walking all alone in my wraparound dance sweater, I thought about my big-boobed neighbor Alyssa. I missed her. Even if my new friend Adriana tried to throw me a surprise party like Alyssa had, there would be barely anyone to invite. I was feeling sad and lost in my thoughts as I walked into the theatre building and bumped into Jean Claude.

"Hello, Margot," he said, perfectly accenting the *geau*, as always.

"Hi," I said, as I nervously tried to walk into the building without embarrassing myself by choosing the door that always remained permanently locked. Why couldn't I ever remember which door that was? Every day I'd yank at the wrong door like an idiot, almost falling over when it wouldn't budge.

"How's it going?" he asked.

"Good, I guess . . ." There was an awkward silence. We hadn't hung out in at least a week, and I was starting to think he had ditched me for "Diane." As we shifted our feet in uncomfortable silence, I had extra time to become increasingly aware of my makeshift dance ensemble, my unitard with a skirt over it, which seemed like a fabulous idea in my dorm room, but less fabulous in front of the guy I was obsessed with. I waited for him to say something, anything.

Finally, I couldn't stand it anymore. I blurted, "Today's my birthday."

Well, it was. I had never been one of those people who were indifferent to their own birthdays. Once my paternal grandmother was visiting and my dad casually asked, "Mom, isn't it your birthday?"

My grandmother looked at her watch with the tiny calendar feature and replied, "Oh yeah. That old thing?"

How laid-back to think of your own birthday as "that old thing." I was more a walk-through-the-hallways-with-a-clump-of-balloons-I-had-bought-for-myself-in-the-school-store type of birthday celebrator. But to Jean Claude, I wanted to give the impression that I was relaxed and care-free. I also didn't want to scare him off, acting as if I expected to spend it together. I had heard acting too needy was an easy way to die alone.

"Wow, really? Well, maybe I'll stop by tonight and say hi in honor of your birthday."

"Sure, that would be fun," I said nervously. "Thirteenth floor."

"Thirteenth floor? Is that really where you live? Wow, all these times I never noticed that. I've always just walked up the stairs a few flights. We have a thirteenth floor? That's unlucky. Most buildings don't—"

"I know, it's fine. I like it. Good views."

"Okay, cool, I'll try to stop by around nine or ten. See you then."

Jean Claude walked away, and I ran down the stairs to my modern dance class feeling as high as I did when I first smoked pot with Jackie Angel. Jean Claude was coming over tonight for my birthday! Maybe he would bring me flowers or, even better, a bouquet of handmade paper flowers he had slaved over tediously because he was an artist.

* * *   When I got home to my room later that evening, I walked in the door just as my multicolored Conairphone was ringing. Finally I had achieved my lifelong dream, to have a phone in my room and to have my own line. My teal-and-pink model was exactly the mechanism I needed to celebrate my tiny victory of independence.

"Hello?" I said, out of breath, hoping it was Jean Claude.

"Happy birthday, Maaaargot!" said my mother. "Do you have someone to celebrate it with? Don't stay in that spooky cave of a room alone all night. You're nineteen now. Can you believe it? You know, nineteen's the age I met your father. No pressure!"

"Actually, Mom, I am not spending it alone."

"Good, well, if it's a date, no lesbian shoes. No man likes a girl in combat boots. No man. And eat a piece of meat if he offers it to you, don't be rude like I know you will be at this year's Thanksgiving. I'm done making special meals for you, Margot. You can eat the side dishes or cave in and eat the turkey. Would it really be that big a deal for you to eat a piece of turkey? What would happen? Really, Margot. I'm sure you would survive. You used to love the dark meat. Your father would never say this, but it hurts him every year when you refuse to eat the turkey after he's spent so much time carving it. Do you want to hurt your father again, Margot? Did you find a ride home yet?"

"Actually, Mom, I have to get ready, but I'll see you very soon for Thanksgiving. I'll consider the dark meat. Okay? And I'll find a ride. I have to go, love you."

I hung up the Conairphone and began setting the mood for Jean Claude's visit. I lit all my lavender candles, put on Joni Mitchell's *Blue*, and plugged in my blue Christmas lights. I swapped my leotard and tights out for some jeans and a '70s men's button-down shirt so I would look my hottest, unlocked my door, and experimented with various "sexy/mature/French girl" poses I could be in when I called for Jean Claude to "come in."

Nine came and went, then ten . . . Maybe he was stuck in a place with no clocks and didn't realize how late it was. Or perhaps he liked me so much he was just trying not to seem too desperate. But when ten-thirty came I started to believe he was blowing me off. Even though he was probably swept away in the depths of an elaborate oil painting he was working on, it was still rude. I waited for almost all my candles to burn out and for Joni Mitchell to sing her entire album, including an extra play of "Carey" in honor of what I was supposed to be named, before finally giving up. I blew out the last of the candles, and they bellowed black smoke. With less than two hours left to my birthday, blowing out lavender candles alone on the thirteenth floor was not the traditional make-a-wish moment I had hoped for. I should have swiped a piece of cake from the dining hall and allowed those theater dorks to sing *Happy Birthday* to me in perfect harmony.

Just then, I heard a faint knock on the door. I ran to my bed, laid down on my side, making sure my long blonde hair was tousled all to one side and called out, very casually, "Come in!"

Jean Claude entered and seemed oblivious to the remnants of the mood I had so carefully set and dismantled. The smell of lavender was now replaced by the smell of sulphur.

"Hi! Happy birthday! Want to go for a walk?"

A walk? What kind of a birthday seduction is that? Whatever, it was still my birthday, and a walk was better than being here by myself. I got up and grabbed my combat boots, then remembered my mother's advice and reached for a sexier shoe choice. I put on my purple Converse All-Stars and we headed out the door.

Outside the dorm, we walked and talked about his latest art project and my extracurricular late-night choreography until it started to rain. It came down fast, and we hadn't brought umbrellas, so Jean Claude pulled me under a blue campus safety light to keep me dry. I remembered from orientation that if you were being attacked you were supposed to blow your rape whistle, fight off your assailant, run under a blue light, and pick up the phone. Not exactly a sexy spot. But I couldn't help but feel that standing under the rape light with Jean Claude was incredibly romantic, which made me feel guilty, like the time I first discovered I was mildly attracted to Lee Harvey Oswald. The blue light in the rain made me feel like I was Molly Ringwald at the end of a John Hughes movie, and when Jean Claude kissed me under its glow, I tried to stay focused on the kiss instead of thinking about how, unlike other women who had stood beneath this light before, I didn't want this moment to end. Eventually it did end, though, and Jean Claude went back to his room for the night, claiming he still had a lot of work to do. As disappointed as I was to be falling asleep alone, replaying the blue-light kiss over and over in my head was a pretty superb image to fall asleep to. Overall, it was a good birthday.

   ✳ ✳ ✳ November came, and I was really frustrated to leave Ithaca, Adriana, Jean Claude, and my dance classes to go back to Jersey for Thanksgiving. At college I was regal and graceful, but at home I would still be the only tall half-Jewish person to ever warm a bench at a church volleyball game. Also, I had let my mother down by not finding rides home and back to school for Thanksgiving break, despite her incessant reminders. I had been too busy working on that *Pirates of Penzance* set to think about finding a ride. And also, I didn't know that many people yet. In the end I boarded a crowded, smelly Short Line Bus filled with strangers from my college and New Jersey–native Cornell students. The trip dragged on and on despite the ample supply of Beat poetry books I'd packed to pass the time.

"No complaining. You're the one who just had to go to school five hours away, despite your scholarship to Rutgers," my mother said when she picked me up at the station inconveniently located over an hour away from our house.

Back home, my old bedroom seemed incredibly spacious compared to my thirteenth-floor sanctuary. My former domain was about the size of a double-occupancy room at school. I had never noticed the extra floor space before. The clothes left in my near-empty closet seemed so out of style to me now, and not in a cool vintage way, but in a wearing-a-banana-clip-in-1991 kind of way. I sat there taking it all in before heading out for my big homecoming plans.

Adam and I hadn't spoken since I'd blown him off with my puffed-up artsy proclamation, but I was hoping that enough time had passed and that Adam would want to be friends. I didn't really know how that kind of stuff worked but I had admired Jerry Seinfeld and Elaine's hilarious postcoital friendship and figured Adam and I would ease right into witty banter and private jokes and catchphrases like their classic "Hel-looooo." Besides, I had needed something fun to look forward to at home to take my mind off my mother's imminent force-feeding of dark meat, so I'd organized a group of high school friends to hang out with the night I got home, and included Adam. That way there would be other people there in case it got awkward, and he wouldn't have to talk to me unless he wanted to. For all I knew, he was over it, but he might not be. Maybe I'd given him a lifetime aversion to soy meat as it now would forever remind him of getting redumped.

Truthfully, though, I really didn't know what to expect. And it's not like there was a big plan for how to spend the evening, which didn't help. We gathered at my house, stood around a little, and decided we should drive about town and see where the night took us. We all piled into Adam's car, the mood loosened, and everyone began rattling off about their awesome new lives away at school.

"Have you guys ever tried Jägermeister?" asked Derek, excited beyond belief to share his love for the black licorice–flavored shot. Everyone mumbled in agreement at Jäger's awesomeness. I did not agree, as I had already had an overdose of black licorice every Christmas morning when I opened my stocking to discover a large pack of the British candy Bassetts Liquorice Allsorts, given to me by "Santa."

"All environmental studies majors are required to spend a week tracking an animal of their choice. Everyone's doing deer but I'm gonna try and do rabbits to shake things up," said Eli, really excited to be in his element.

I couldn't wait to tell all my former classmates back home about my new life and how I was going to be a dancer.

"My teacher, a former prima ballerina, thinks I have star potential," I said. I chatted on about ballet, not noticing no one was listening, until Derek asked the far more important question, "Guys, how are we getting beer tonight?"

I didn't care. I was a long-stemmed beauty, and finally, being tall made sense to me. But as we drove aimlessly around the hometown we didn't really live in anymore but hadn't quite left, the carefree feeling of those last few months of high school was missing. Everyone was now too cool to engage in a buttercream fight or late-night Fudge Factory dance party. Plus, as we chatted about beer pong, keg-party hookups, and roommate drama, I thought I sensed tension between Adam and me. He didn't say much, so it was hard to tell what he was thinking. And I was banished to the backseat, a major step down from the permanent shotgun I used to enjoy in his Toyota Corolla. As everyone suggested different places we could go to spice up the night, Adam barely acknowledged my presence.

With no real plans for the evening, we decided to do the nerdiest thing possible and stop by the high school homecoming dance. I didn't really want to go to a high school dance (actually I didn't want to go to a high school dance during high school either, for that matter). The last high school dance I had gone to was prom, and a teacher almost got beat up over my fashion choices, and I'd long ago figured school dances just weren't for me. Besides, dancers didn't go to dances. We lived a dancer's lifestyle every day; why did we need to go to an organized function? I was sure that real singers never went to karaoke for the exact same reason. I didn't want to make the situation tenser by being disagreeable, though, so I just sat in the back left seat and waited while everyone argued as to whether or not this would be cool or totally lame. In order to move things along, I opened the door, hoping everyone would follow suit and get out. And just as I had one foot in and one foot out of the car, Adam made a rash decision that this dance was "gonna suck" and attempted to drive off, running over my left foot in the process. I screamed, and Adam reacted by stopping the car directly on my foot, which was now at an excruciating angle.

As that ton of car sat on top of my left foot, I couldn't help but think, *I don't think this guy wants to remain friends.*

I screamed in pain, and the passengers in the overfilled Corolla yelled at Adam to "get the fuck off her foot." I hoped this was all a dream. For years, my mother had told me my feet were too small for a girl my height and that was why I fell down so much.

"You tip over on those little hooves. They just aren't big enough to hold your frame. Did you bind them?"

I had always loved that one part of me was below-average size (aside from my boobs and my pinhead), but it appeared that they weren't small enough to avoid the treads of Adam's Corolla. As Adam finally moved the car off my foot, after what felt like an hour but was probably about twenty seconds, I looked down at my once-dainty body part and knew it was about to swell to the size of a ham hock.

I cried in pain as a carload of late teens panicked and yelled at each other, making everything worse. Adam was speechless. He had just damaged the most essential body part of an aspiring dancer. He had accidentally screwed with what enabled me to do the thing I had dumped him for.

Despite my screams for him to take me to the hospital, Adam thought it would be a better choice to drive me to our friend Samantha's house because her mom was a nurse. As if in her house she had an X-ray machine and Vicodin. He screeched into her driveway, made hasty and incomprehensible explanations to Samantha's mom, and sped away with the others, wiping off his proverbial prints in the process.

While Samantha's mom examined my foot, I felt obligated to explain the entire situation with a little more clarity. I told her that he had run over my foot but also that we had dated a few months at the end of high school and that maybe Adam would have been a little more sympathetic if I hadn't once used the phrase "I make art with my body now," and I suggested that while this was certainly not an act done on purpose, it was an excellent fuck-you. Samantha's mom seemed to care less about the failed high school romance and more about my foot, which would now fit snugly into a clown shoe.

Eventually Samantha's mom did the sane thing and drove me to the emergency room. Somewhere along the way my father was called. The doctor told us my foot was sprained very badly, my tissue was all swollen, and there might be permanent bone damage. She also said I would have to sit out of dance class for a while, and when I got the cast off I could do moderate dancing but "absolutely no relevé."

No relevé? How could I dance without ever rising up on my feet? How could I be a "long-stemmed beauty" if I only had one working foot?

A few hours later, my dad pushed me out the door of the hospital in a wheelchair, angrily clenching his teeth and muttering something about auto insurance. I cried silently, worrying that Adam's accident had ruined my chances of being a dancer, and on top of that caused my father's insurance premiums to go up.

If there was a shred of doubt about how Adam now felt about me, he made it even clearer the next day, which he spent not calling to see if I was okay. I ate my Thanksgiving vegetable side dishes (my mother still holding her ground on not making me a 'special meal for a rude meatless diet') with my foot elevated and iced.

A few days later, I boarded the Short Line Bus on crutches, well stocked with unmalleable cold packs left over from my brown-bag school lunches. I wrote in my journal during the five-hour ride, trying my best to distract myself from the fact that I really had to pee. Using the world's smallest and smelliest bathroom was not appealing to me on two legs, let alone one.

I had left college for Thanksgiving break really thinking I was hot shit. Maybe I deserved to be taken down a notch. Gawky girls like me didn't have French boyfriends and aspiring careers as dancers. Girls like me date nerds with an edge and hobble around on crutches. Who was I to think that I could go from a disgraced weirdo wearing an orange unitard to a graceful artist who's heard of the Internet?

Jean Claude visited me the night I got back and was very kind to me as I wept about the bone-crushing incident. Well aware that no man is attracted to a blubbering cripple, I tried repeatedly to hold it together, but nothing seemed to work. Turned off by my histrionics and possibly also by the giant plaster sock I was ordered to wear, he headed back to his room for the night without even bothering to sign my cast.

I returned to dance class the next day on crutches, making a grand entrance. The doors clanged as I swung them open and hobbled into the studio. I considered wearing dance attire anyway, but realized that would just make me more depressed. Besides, I didn't want to stretch out the spandex by forcing my dance attire over my plaster boot. Instead I opted for my newest chic look, a skirt over pants, over crutches. I know most women wear either a skirt or pants, not both at once, but I felt the double garment was a cool college thing to do. I had seen many other girls around campus rocking this look and I wanted in.

All the dancers stared at me as I clunked into the studio. Girls with neat buns and perfect posture stopped bending gracefully over bars to take a look at my megafall from grace.

"Margot, my dear! What happened?" my teacher asked, gliding over to me with such grace I wanted to applaud.

"Well," I began, positioning myself at the center of the studio, looking out at the twenty or so taut-bodied girls in pink and black. "I used to date this guy in high school, briefly, and he was a nerd. But then he got into Brown and went totally wild and didn't care about school anymore, and so I found myself strangely attracted to him. No guys liked me in high school before because I was weird and artsy and really, really too tall too soon."

The ballerinas all chuckled in solidarity. If I had been delivering this speech at the world-famous Apollo Theater, they would have been shouting things like "You said it, gurl," and "Ummm-hmmmm," but this was ballet, so they all nodded politely while practicing their turn-out. I shifted my weight a bit to ease the pain and continued.

"So the thing is, this nerdy guy actually liked me back. Before him, my only option was a guy who stalked me after a They Might Be Giants concert."

The ballerinas laughed. This time harder. I was killing it!

"Oh, and also the Puerto Rican camp counselor I lost my virginity to."

Silence. Too much. I needed to get back on track.

"So before I came here, we parted ways, the nerd and I, and I thought we were on good terms, ya know? I was going to theatre school, he was going into politics at Brown, not exactly a lifelong match but we had our memories. We spoke a little after I got here, and I told him how much I was into dance, how I was finding my niche, how we were going in different directions . . ."

My audience was rapt. Rapt. I continued.

"Then, I go home, and we're hanging out, and I'm thinking all is cool between me and this nerd gone wild, and then he ran over my foot with his car."

Silence. Did my audience think I was making it up? Did I lose them?

"Seriously, ladies, he ran. Over. My. Foot. With. His. Car. Conveniently just a few months after I told him I wanted to be a dancer. So, maybe we're not on such good terms, right?"

Laughter! There we go.

"I mean, there's no chance we can remain 'just friends,' am I right?"

The dancers all agreed.

"But now I'm wondering, how can I be a long-stemmed beauty with only one working foot? I guess my only choice is to take up flamingo dancing."

Awkward pause. Silence.

"You know, because flamingos stand on one foot. Ladies, come on, stay with me here."

One by one the dancers began to laugh, which eventually all came together as one giant laugh, which was the most pleasing sound I had heard since I'd snuck into that awesome Tom Petty concert. When the laughter subsided they made sympathetic faces at my horrendous luck. Throwing in the inside joke of "long-stemmed beauty" really sealed the deal. Then I brought it home.

"I guess my mom's childhood warnings of 'Be careful walking' don't seem so ridiculous now. I apologize if I'm more of an angry limper than a 'long-stemmed beauty' now"—the class laughed even harder.

I paused for effect, then clunked away feeling the noise of the crutches echo with every hobble I took.

I nailed it. It seemed so natural to stand in front of a crowd, recounting an unfortunate story and making people laugh. Although the experience was painful, literally, to endure, when I shared it with a crowd I felt better. I liked hearing the girls laugh and commiserate over my misfortune. I never wanted this moment to end.

The laughs finally subsided. It was time to start class. I hobbled over to the chairs on the side to observe class with my leg elevated.

I smiled as I took my seat, and took out a notebook to take careful notes on what I observed in class that day. Well, that was my intention. What I really did was spend the class writing down the funny speech I had just improvised in front of the class. I wasn't sure of when or how or why, but I had a feeling that one day, remembering the details of unfortunate situations from my youth just might come in handy.

Epilogue

And that's how it all began for me. Sometimes life's events lead you to a very clear decision, and sometimes they don't. I can't tell you that when I fell off that stationary horse at horse camp that I was thinking, *Someday this will lead me to a career in comedic performance.* But I can say that recounting to a group of much thinner, much more talented ballerinas the events that led to me getting my foot run over by a nerd gone wild did make me think for the very first time that I might want to pursue comedy. So sometimes the pain is worth it for the final result.

One of my all-time favorite quotes is "Comedy is tragedy plus time." I've always wrongfully accredited it to Woody Allen, but I just looked it up, and you know who is actually credited with saying it? Carol Burnett! My hero! And I couldn't agree more. No, these stories are not tragic. But when they were happening, it felt as if the world was going to end. And now, because of time, they make me laugh.

Carol, once again, you are my queen. You said it best.

I'd love to tell you that after all this I love being tall, I always feel beautiful, and I am no longer a dork but a totally cool person. But that would be a lie. I still slouch, I am still annoyed when trying on short dresses only to discover they don't even cover my crotch. I still get even more annoyed when at the dry cleaners they try to charge me the dress rate when I give them a blouse, arguing "This is dress!" while I retort "Well, it's a shirt on me!" And yes, perhaps it would have been easier to have had a more gradual rise in height. But it all led me here, and for that I am grateful for the experience.

Whenever I meet a really tall girl, I always ask about her experience growing up. The emotions are almost always uncannily similar—feeling supremely awkward, being treated too old too fast, wanting attention for the wrong reasons. Almost every tall girl I have met felt pigeon-holed into the tall-girl triumvirate: volleyball, basketball, and modeling. I hope my story helps a few tall girls out there feel better about their awkward stages and encourages them to pursue their own ideas of what's interesting and exciting.

★   ★   ★   My favorite part of "based on a true story" movies is always the "where are they now?" part—the "what happened, did he go to jail or not?" big reveal at the end before the credits roll. You know, where white letters appear on the screen while motivational music plays, and it says something like "Thomas went off to invent seven other computing devices, eventually leading him to be the youngest self-made millionaire to graduate from Brigham Young University." So I thought I'd do that for you now.

Things did not work out with Jean Claude. After a tumultuous on-and-off two-year-plus relationship and many dramatic getting-back-togethers, we called it quits. However, we managed to have enough over-the-top dramatic moments that have bred hilarious comedy. For that alone, I think it was worth it.

Adam and I have not been in touch since the foot incident. I mean, that makes sense, right? I wish him the best and heard he lives in New York City, which is good for him because he won't ever have to get behind a wheel again. You can survive on subways and cabs alone in that city. I think he made a good life decision in that particular respect.

Rodreigo and I actually saw each other recently. We are on very good terms and are still in touch. He is very successful and rich and kind. He actually gets paid a lot of money to teach big companies how to help save the earth. And ladies, if he sounds too good to be true, he is. He prefers men. So keep searching for a handsome rich Puerto Rican guy who is saving the earth. Rodreigo is not your man.

Jackie Angel married her high school sweetheart, had a son, and moved to Tennessee, where she has led a free-spirited yet much more conventional life than I had expected her to lead when I met her and immediately wanted to become her in a *Single White Female* kind of way. I imagined she would have some sort of career that would require her to live on a tour bus and have a P.O. box, so I am pleasantly surprised at her attainability. She's doing great and we are also still connected.

I lost touch after high school with the childhood friends featured in this book—Amanda, Alyssa, and Jonah Hertzberg—although thanks to Mark Zuekerberg, Amanda and I are back in touch online. I do hope they find this and read it and realize how much their kindness and friendship during my formative, most physically awkward years really made an impact.

My family is all still in New Jersey. My mom now has a "tea cabinet," which has overflowed onto the counter. My father now works out of the house and after I finally sat him down and asked, "When realistically are you ever going to use all these tiny soaps?" he finally stopped swiping them from business hotels. My brother is a writer as well and, despite my pleas, will not give me the videotapes of his childhood movie reenactments. I imagine he has something much bigger planned for them in the future. And after ten years of living in New York City myself, I now live in Los Angeles with my husband, a very *undersize* dog (he, ironically, is the runt of his litter—he was supposed to be twelve pounds and barely made it to five), and my son, who was 9 pounds 10 ounces at birth (although I still refuse ever to use a super tampon) and already in the 95th percentile for height. In case you had a shred of doubt, no, I am not a dancer. But thanks for humoring me. I perform live comedy, tour nationally, write, and teach people the art of storytelling. It's a pretty fun way to make a living.

My adorable friend Adriana from Ithaca College is still one of my best friends and I am so proud of her that she managed to become a professional singer, which is no small feat. And I have a very clear memory of returning to school after the foot-running-over incident and sitting with her on the floor of my dorm room, listening to Bob Dylan and talking about how we couldn't wait for the rest of the year to unfold. I recall being extremely excited about the play I was about to start directing. It was Sam Shepard's *Action*, and the opening line is "I'm looking forward to my life. I'm looking forward to, uh, me. The way I picture me."

Acknowledgements

Special thanks to my tiger of an agent, Brandi Bowles, who believed in this project from the very start, even when it was a scattered mess. Your fierce business sense really kept me in line in order to make this a reality, and I thank you. Thanks to my editor, Laura Mazer, who saw the humor in this book despite our vast height difference. Also thanks to my ferocious managers, Ava Greenfield and Sarah Klegman, who not only understood and took to this material immediately, but also saw what else we could do with it.

Thanks to my original writing teachers in New York City, Nancy Davidoff Kelton at the New School and Glenn Michael Gordon at Media Bistro, whose class assignments forced me to write very early versions of many of these stories, eventually leading me here. A very special thanks to my teacher and friend Kimberlee Auerbach Berlin, whose instruction, guidance, cheerleading, and friendship helped me figure out how to make these stories into a book. You calmed me down so many times and never lost faith in this project. I've never met anyone so giving in my life.

Thanks to the people who looked at an early version of this book and helped me figure out problem areas. Those include the way smarter than me Jim "Iceland" O'Grady, my dear friend and cheerleader Adriana Lomysh, the talented and tall Brandy Barber, my twin brother from another mother Darren Belitsky, and the hardest-working gal in New York, Rachael Mason. Thanks to Theo Greenly for being a pinch hitter in the end and helping me with the last few additions to this book. And thank you to Marcelle Kerp, the coolest lady I've ever met, for your help on the final tweaking of the manuscript. And the biggest thanks of all goes to my husband, Dan Curry. Thanks for listening to me bitch, watching me work countless hours, letting me vent my frustrations, helping me with problem areas of the book, and telling me repeatedly that everything will be okay. I love you. Is it weird to thank my dog? Because I'm going to. Even though you can't read, thank you, Scoops, for sitting with me and keeping me company for the endless hours I have put in over the years on this project. Writing is a little less lonely with a tiny black dog curled up next to you. Thanks to my family, Pam, Bob, and Greg Leitman, for their humor and eccentricities and willingness to forgive me for the comedic portrayals of them in this book (at least I hope you forgive me). Also thanks for the height gene . . . I've really cashed in on that one. And Greg, I am beyond impressed that you managed to outdo me by getting back surgery in your midthirties, causing you to "grow" an inch taller afterward. Well played, sir. Thanks also to Kristy and Natasha for being such supporters over the years, and to all my students, who continue to inspire me.

Thanks to Karolyn Gehrig for brainstorming titles with me, finally getting us here. Thanks to Anthony King, John Frusciante, Neil Campbell, and Nate Dern at the UCB Theatre for being way too generous in terms of stage time for me to work out these stories live. Thanks to the hilarious and kindhearted Giulia Rozzi for letting me work through the kinks of many of these pieces live onstage with you in "Stripped

Stories" and for letting me cry and threaten to abandon this project many times in your presence. You wouldn't let me give up, and I needed that more than you could ever know. Thanks to Jenifer Hixson and the rest of the staff at the Moth for helping me figure out which stories were the strongest by your very democratic scoring system. And thanks also to the Moth for playing my stories on your podcast and NPR and helping me build a name for myself.

Additionally, thanks to all the people who booked me on your live shows, which really helped the process of compiling stories to tell in this book. There are so many of you, but to name a few: the hilarious Tom Shillue, my partner in crime Adam Wade, the insufferable Peter Aguero, the gregarious Nikki Levy, and all the various bookers over the years at Asssscat—including Justin Purnell, Susan Hale, and Amanda Sitko. I feel like I wrote half this book on the fly improvising monologues in that show, and that stage time has truly been a gift. Also, thanks to the very tiny Jenna Brister for the L.A. stage time. Okay, also everyone else who ever booked me on a show. Thank you!

Also, I was tremendously influenced by a number of writers who inspired me to try my hand at the first-person genre. Thanks to Spalding Gray for having the guts to put it all out there in a way that revolutionized live theatre. I know we never had a chance to meet, but your style of writing and performing helped shape me as an artist. Your work will live on forever. Thanks to Jonathan Ames, whose books made me want to stop telling setup/punch lines onstage and start telling stories from the heart. Your work greatly inspired me to try writing out my own stories, and your bravery and voice have influenced me tremendously even though we don't know each other. Thanks also to David Sedaris, who is the undeniable master of this genre. Without you, I wouldn't have a living hero, and I hope to have the pleasure of meeting and working with you one day.

And most of all, thanks to everyone who was cool and accepting during my horrendous youth. Sarah, Melissa, Aaron, Devin, Ken, Tara N., Gretchen . . . your kindness is not present in this book, as the wretched moments make for much better comedy. But I appreciate all of you who stuck up for my bell-bottoms and me. And to the girl who waited at my locker every day of high school to threaten me to varying degrees based on how much of a freak you thought I looked like, well, what's the use? You're not reading this anyway. I forgive you. I hope you are a nicer person now, because it would be impossible for you to have gotten much worse.

About the Author

© ANYA GARRETT

New Jersey native Margot Leitman is a four-time winner of The Moth Storyslam and was the Moth Grandslam winner in New York City. Her stories have been featured on the Moth podcast, NPR's Good Food, and in print in *Playgirl* magazine and the *NY Press*, among others. Along with her husband, she is the co-writer of the Hallmark movie *Cupid's Bed & Breakfast*, how romantic! She is the co-creator/co-host of "Stripped Stories," a comedic storytelling show, running since 2007 and performing monthly at the Upright Citizen's Brigade Theatre. She can be seen regularly at the UCB Theatre, where she also teaches and is a frequent monologist in "Asssscat," their longest running improv show.

On camera, Margot has appeared regularly as various characters on *Late Night With Conan O' Brien*, and has made appearances on VH1's *Best Week Ever*, AMC, E!, Comedy Central, MTV, and more. Most importantly, she competed on both *The Price is Right* (where she won $1664) and *Let's Make a Deal* (where she won a Toyota Prius). Margot currently lives in Los Angeles with her husband, Dan, her very small dog, Scoops, and her very tall son, Levon.

Selected Titles from Seal Press

We Hope You Like This Song: An Overly Honest Story about Friendship, Death, and Mix Tapes, by Bree Housley. $16.00, 978-1-58005-431-7. Bree Housley's sweet, quirky, and hilarious tribute to her lifelong friend, and her chronicle of how she honored her after her premature death.

Body Outlaws: Rewriting the Rules of Beauty and Body Image, edited by Ophira Edut, foreword by Rebecca Walker. $15.95, 978-1-58005-108-8. Filled with honesty and humor, this groundbreaking anthology offers stories by women who have chosen to ignore, subvert, or redefine the dominant beauty standard in order to feel at home in their bodies.

Beautiful You: A Daily Guide to Radical Self-Acceptance, by Rosie Molinary. $16.95, 978-1-58005-331-0. A practical, accessible, day-by-day guide to redefining beauty and building lasting self-esteem from body expert Rosie Molinary.

Airbrushed Nation: The Lure and Loathing of Women's Magazines, by Jennifer Nelson. $17.00, 978-1-58005-413-3. Jennifer Nelson—a longtime industry insider—exposes the naked truth behind the glossy pages of women's magazines, both good and bad.

Found: A Memoir, by Jennifer Lauck. $17.00, 978-1-58005-395-2. Picking up where her *New York Times* best-selling memoir, *Blackbird,* left off, Jennifer Lauck shares the powerful story of her search for her birth mother, and lays bare the experience of a woman searching for her identity.

Dancing at the Shame Prom: Sharing the Stories That Kept Us Small, edited by Amy Ferris and Hollye Dexter. $15.00, 978-1-58005-416-4. A collection of funny, sad, poignant, miraculous, life-changing, and jaw-dropping secrets for readers to gawk at, empathize with, and laugh about—in the hopes that they will be inspired to share their secret burdens as well.

Find Seal Press Online
www.SealPress.com
www.Facebook.com/SealPress
Twitter: @SealPress